LEE KUAN YEW

BLAZING THE FREEDOM TRAIL

QUOTES BY LEE KUAN YEW

The verdict of the people is a terrifying thing.

Life should be more than just existence, the business of making a living. This is the new way of life.

To have a better life, all must play good music.

I know in 10, 15 years, I can breed a generation that can man missiles.

Your child has a brain bigger than the biggest computer man has ever built.

They would never know what they did to a whole generation like me. But they made me and a whole generation like me determined to fight for freedom—freedom from servitude and foreign domination. I did not enter politics. They brought politics upon me.

How long will it take before we become all Singaporeans? I have no idea. It will improve with another generation.

I am on parade all the time. Why need I be a dictator? They come to violent ends.

No, no. I have a pretty scarred hide. I am accustomed to arrows and bolts of lightning.

To build a country, you need passion. You will trample over us, over our dead bodies. We dug our toes in, we built a nation.

And even from my sick bed, even if you are going to lower me into the grave and I feel that something is going wrong, I'll get up.

Your future really depends on how you make of it.
The government can give you the framework, and give expression to the will of the people, but the people must have the will. If you do not have it, there is nothing a government can do.

I shall now play goalkeeper...But the goalkeeper should not wait till the ball gets into the penalty area.
That's dangerous. Keep it outside the penalty area.

Eat less than you want to. Work more than you need to. Sleep well.

I used to believe that you can learn two languages at the same time, whatever your IQ. I was wrong.

I think we made a mistake in not building a Formula One course... I think I was dim-witted then.

All I can say is, I did my best.

LEE KUAN YEW

BLAZING THE FREEDOM TRAIL

Exploring the leadership of Singapore's first Prime Minister from 1959 to 1990

Anthony Oei

Marshall Cavendish
Editions

Cover and layout design by Adithi Khandadai Shankar
Cover photo of Lee Kuan Yew: Larry Burrows/The LIFE Picture Collection/Getty Images

First published 1992 by Heinemann Asia as *What If There Had Been No Leee Kuan Yew?* and revised 1998
Revised and updated 2005 by Times Editions as *Days of Thunder: How Lee Kuan Yew Blazed the Freedom Trail*

This 2015 edition published by
Marshall Cavendish Editions
An imprint of Marshall Cavendish International
1 New Industrial Road, Singapore 536196

Other Marshall Cavendish Offices
Marshall Cavendish Corporation. 99 White Plains Road, Tarrytown NY 10591-9001, USA • Marshall Cavendish International (Thailand) Co Ltd. 253 Asoke, 12th Flr, Sukhumvit 21 Road, Klongtoey Nua, Wattana, Bangkok 10110, Thailand • Marshall Cavendish (Malaysia) Sdn Bhd, Times Subang, Lot 46, Subang Hi-Tech Industrial Park, Batu Tiga, 40000 Shah Alam, Selangor Darul Ehsan, Malaysia

National Library Board, Singapore Cataloguing in Publication Data
Oei, Anthony, author.
Lee Kuan Yew : blazing the freedom trail / Anthony Oei. – 3rd revised edition – Singapore : Marshall Cavendish Editions, 2015.
pages cm
Revised edition of: Days of thunder : how Lee Kuan Yew blazed the freedom trail, published in 2005.
ISBN : 978-981-4677-77-6 (paperback)

1. Lee, Kuan Yew, 1923-2015. 2. Singapore – History – 1963-1965. 3. Singapore – History – 1965-1990.
4. Singapore – Politics and government. I. Title.

DS610.7
959.57051 -- dc23 OCN909838747

Printed in Singapore by Fabulous Printers Pte Ltd

To my daughters,
Charmaine Tsu Min, Michelle Yu Min and
Dawn Li Min, members of the younger generation
in whose hands lies the future of Singapore.

CONTENTS

PROLOGUE

Among the former colonies, Singapore is one of the most successful in nation-building after gaining full self-government from the British in 1959 and independence in 1965. The recipe is, to put it simply, a government that delivered and continues to deliver.

In the first 31 years of nationhood, the government was led by an indomitable Cambridge-educated lawyer, Lee Kuan Yew. Lee was the nation's first Prime Minister. When he stepped down in 1990, he left behind a system of a clean and efficient government, world-class infrastructure and a business-friendly economy, which he termed "gold standards".

His successor, Goh Chok Tong, a former senior civil servant and managing director of a shipping company, continued to build Singapore up in the next 14 years, with Lee serving as his Senior Minister. Singapore's future now lies in the hands of Goh's former deputy, Lee Hsien Loong, who assumed office on 12 August 2004. He is a top Cambridge graduate in mathematics. Goh was Number 2 as Senior Minister, while Lee Kuan Yew was adviser with the title of Minister Mentor.

Lee Hsien Loong's appointment in this second leadership change is historic for Singapore for he is Lee Kuan Yew's son. What had been widely expected has come true. He had been Deputy Prime Minister and Finance Minister, discharging his responsibilities creditably. How has he been performing as Prime Minister? Naturally, one would compare him with his father. But comparisons are misguided because the missions and the circumstances are totally different.

His father lived in the days of thunder, the most turbulent and dangerous period in Singapore's history. His mission was to demolish British colonial rule, communism and communalism, and deliver Singapore from want, servitude and danger. He was the founding father and the master craftsman of modern Singapore. The social revolution he led successfully and his prodigious achievements in nation-building remain an open book for it is an unforgettable story.

In stark contrast, today's Singapore is relatively peaceful and prosperous. Lee Hsien Loong inherited the "gold standards" set by his father and fine-tuned by Goh Chok Tong. Thus, his task is to propel the nation to higher levels of growth and ensure its security. He should be judged by what he can achieve to satisfy present needs under present conditions. So far, he has shown he has steel in him.

Following the death of Lee Kuan Yew, it is timely to recount the full story of the social revolution—the basis of modern Singapore—and the resulting socio-economic development that has taken place.

The anti-colonial battle began after World War II. Lee Kuan Yew and his team vied with other freedom fighters who included the communists directed by Chin Peng of the Malayan Communist Party, later renamed Communist Party of Malaya (CPM). The campaign convulsed the nation and exploded into the blackest days in Singapore history, with frequent industrial strikes, violent street demonstrations, riots and racial conflicts which left many dead and injured, and properties damaged.

As the dust settled, it was Lee Kuan Yew who emerged triumphant. Lee was Secretary-General of the People's Action Party (PAP). The party won the historic general election for a fully elected self-government in 1959 and formed the government that ended 140 years of British rule.

As Prime Minister, Lee orchestrated the movement to build a prosperous and peaceful Singapore. In one generation, he and his team elevated the nation from the Third World to the First World league. They also moulded a new Singaporean as an essential part of the nation-building process, an identity that Singaporeans are proud to own.

The road to independence was long, arduous, traumatic and dangerous. The most traumatic was the issue of merger with Malaya. Reunion was the PAP's greatest political ambition as it sought a democratic, socialist and non-communist Singapore. The most dangerous enemy was the CPM because its goal was a communist Malaya that would include Singapore, and it opposed reunification. At one stage, the CPM even tried to control the PAP to use it as a front. The clash of ideologies turned into a cloak-and-dagger battle. Displaying their calibre and political acumen, Lee and his men overcame these adversities.

Lee had confessed that fighting the communists was the most perilous task in his life and that of his fellow freedom-fighters. They faced personal risks for the communists were not "to be trifled with". They did not fully realise the frightening extent of the hazards until they were in the heat of battle. He recalled that "we were young and naïve" and that he would not want to run through the fire again as "it is too dangerous". If his team had lost, "they would have pulled our fingernails out".

What made them go into battle then? It was the unquenchable desire to live as a free people. They felt duty-bound to realise that dream and they pursued it with passion and a tenacity of purpose. Like Lee, his comrades were dedicated, committed, trustworthy, gallant and fearless. They were stalwarts like Dr Toh Chin Chye, Dr Goh Keng Swee, S Rajaratnam, Ong Pang Boon and Othman Wok. They comprised the Old Guard who laid the foundation that built a nation of international repute.

Lee was a formidable and combative politician, and "the stainless steel of frightening competence", as he was once described. However, not everyone in Singapore or elsewhere likes him. There are bouquets and brickbats. His detractors, while acknowledging his leadership qualities and accomplishments, regard him as arrogant, domineering, autocratic and dictatorial when he was captain of the ship. Cynics even say he built a Lee Kuan Yew cult, that Lee Kuan Yew is Singapore and Singapore is Lee Kuan Yew, that he created a climate of fear and a nanny state, and that he should have retired after stepping down instead of remaining in the government.

In some ways his critics are not off-beam. The late Minister Mentor is still very much in the picture and is as controversial as ever. During his premiership, he governed with a firm hand and formulated many unpopular policies, causing much unhappiness among Singaporeans. There are also some Western journalists who have a penchant for aiming pot shots at him, even to this day. They would poke and probe, trying to find the skeletons in the cupboard that would embarrass him and put him in a bad light. Certain books that have been written about him can only be described as a demolition exercise.

But Lee made no apologies for the tough stand he adopted during his long stewardship. His political philosophy was epitomised in the following statements he made during the Global Brand Forum in Singapore in December 2003:

> I belong to the old school. I believe that it is better to be feared than to be loved. My younger colleagues sometimes want to be both. I decided a long time ago that popularity is something volatile. They feel good, they get their bonuses, you're popular. They're squeezed, there's a recession, you're blamed for it; your stocks go down. And the key is not to hold an election when people are not feeling good.
>
> I do not believe that popular government means you have to be popular when you govern. I think the best thing to do is to do all the unpopular things when you are governing so that at the end of your term, you have the choice of a date when you feel that they will

> be most grateful that you've done all these unpopular things and they vote for you.
>
> I don't know about branding. I do know that you need a good reputation, not just outside Singapore but within Singapore, with your own people. This is a place that works, that must work and continue to work, because it is based on principles. And the first principle is nobody owes us a living.

Whatever one's opinion of him, Lee Kuan Yew stood alone in Singapore's political theatre. He was a legend in his time and a symbol of Singapore's success. Of course, he had his successes and failures. Arguably, Lee could be compared with other giants of men, like Dr Sun Yat Sen and Mao Zedong of China, Tunku Abdul Rahman of Malaysia, Mahatma Gandhi of India, Sukarno of Indonesia and Nelson Mandela of South Africa, whose names still ring a bell across the globe for their great deeds. They are a special breed of leaders who appear but once in a blue moon.

An interesting fact is that Lee and many in the PAP leadership, such as Dr Toh Chin Chye, Dr Goh Keng Swee and S Rajaratnam, were English-educated and Straits-born, "Straits-born" being a common definition given to those born either in Singapore or Malaya. They were descendants of the early immigrants and were considered sons of the soil, deserving the term "nationalists". As events have shown, they proved their strength and capability against the British.

Turning back the pages of history, it is also interesting to find that the anti-colonial movement was not of post-World War II origin.

The script was first written in the early 20th century by Chinese business and community leaders. Coincidentally, they were likewise English-educated Straits-born.

In his book *Chinese Political Leadership and Power in Colonial Singapore*, Dr C F Yong says these Straits-born Chinese were the dominant socio-economic force in those days. They initiated the demands for better living conditions, better education, more employment opportunities and improvements in other domestic matters for their community.

These pioneers included physician Dr Lim Boon Keng, lawyers Sir Song Ong Siang, Wee Swee Teow, S Q Wong and T W Ong, and merchants Tan Jiak Kim, Seah Liang Seah and Lee Choon Guan. In 1900, they formed the Straits Chinese British Association (SCBA), the forerunner of today's Peranakan Association, to strengthen their position. Dr Yong notes that the British often nominated them as unofficial members of the Straits Settlements Legislative Council, Municipal Commission and other government bodies to allow them to participate in local affairs.

One of their greatest breakthroughs, after years of agitation in the Legislative Council, was opening the door for Singaporeans to work in the Straits Settlements Civil Service, hitherto shut to non-Europeans. In the 1920s and 1930s, some of the SCBA leaders were even bold enough as to talk about a self-governing Malaya. They wanted the people to play a greater role in running their country.

Dr Yong adds that in the 1930s also, other SCBA leaders such as merchant Tay Lian Teck and physician Dr Lim Han Hoe, fought to adopt English as the *lingua franca*, establish a university, build a technical and agricultural institute, start the teaching of science in grants-in-aid schools, and open an engineering faculty at Raffles College. As one can see, many of these proposals have materialised into reality.

The Chinese immigrants of yesteryear played little or no part because they were only sojourners, treating Singapore as their second home. They were more preoccupied with the revolutionary movement in their fatherland led by Dr Sun Yat Sen, the Father of the Chinese Republic. Therefore, as Dr Yong says in his book, they kept their Chinese nationalist fervour alive in Singapore. In any case, "the British paternal rule offered little opportunity for the creation and emergence of a Singaporean nationalism with a Singapore loyalty as its objective". That gave these sojourners little or no prospect for their socio-economic advancement in the country.

However, while both the SCBA and the PAP had the same objective, that is, improving the people's lives, there were two distinct differences between them. First, the former held the British in high esteem and pledged its loyalty to the Crown. Secondly, the association worked for its own people, since it was an exclusive ethnic body and not a multi-racial organisation, although the results of its programmes indirectly benefitted the other communities.

On the other hand, the PAP pledges its loyalty to Singapore and is multi-racial. It seeks to create a just, fair and equal society for all. Its members comprise Chinese, Malays, Indians, Eurasians and others. During the social revolution, they pulled together to demolish British rule, the communists and the communalists.

Dr Yong does not mention whether the pre-war Straits-born "revolutionaries" pursued their aspiration for a self-governing Malaya. Presumably they made no further headway, even if they had wanted to, because of the war erupting in Asia in 1937 when Japan attacked China, followed by the war in Europe in 1939 that culminated in World War II.

Nonetheless, it can be said that the post-war freedom fighters picked up the thread left behind by their pre-war predecessors, whether or not they were aware of the political consciousness brewing in those days. Certainly, the pioneering Straits-born Chinese leaders of the 19th century and the early half of the 20th century merit a prominent place in the history books for planting the political seeds.

Travelling farther back in time, one makes yet another interesting discovery. Singapore civilisation began at least 700 years ago, and not after Stamford Raffles' arrival in 1819, as people had been led to believe. Archaeological excavations underway for some time have unearthed ancient artefacts that provide concrete evidence of that. These include Chinese coins from the Tang and Sung dynasties, shards of exquisite porcelain from the Yuan and Ming dynasties, even beads from India.

Their existence suggests that Singapore was a vibrant ancient city, teeming with life and trade as early as the 14th century, transacting business with these regional countries. Little is yet known about what happened in the ensuing centuries. The Singapore History Museum, which is spearheading the archaeological research, is continuing to support the diggings to get to the bottom of it.

There is some indication, though, that life and trade had continued after the 14th century. For when Raffles set foot on 29 January 1819, he was reported to have been impressed with what he saw and with the potential. This would seem to suggest that the island was more than a fishing village or mud flats then. Furthermore, it has been reported that Singapore was earning revenue by 1820. Can anyone transform an island of mud flats into a trading settlement and make it revenue-generating all in one year?

The assumption that a settlement existed when Raffles landed is reinforced by the fact that the Lieutenant-Governor of Bencoolen and an agent of the East India Company, concluded a preliminary treaty the day after his arrival with Temenggong Abdu'r Rahman, the *de facto* ruler of Singapore, to set up a trading post for the British and open a new trade route to China. About a month later, a formal treaty was concluded with the Temenggong and Sultan Hussein of Johor, the *de jure* ruler of Singapore.

Subsequent treaties made Singapore a British possession and eventually a Crown colony under the jurisdiction of the Colonial Office in London, along with Malacca and Penang, the two British settlements in Malaya.

Raffles is held up as the icon of Singapore, perhaps overly done. His name is all over the place—on land, sea and air. A local real estate company has even named one of its projects in Shanghai after him. The gospel is that without him, there would have been no Singapore. Those who subscribe to this belief ignore or minimise the solid contributions of the pioneering Chinese, Indian and other immigrants. They deserve more recognition than they are getting.

Singapore, indeed, is a nation rich in history with enormous potential. The battle for independence had been worth the pains and sacrifices. Singaporeans of all races are now in sole possession of it, a nation with the prospects of more accomplishments as it entrenches itself deeper in the global grid under its own power.

The story of Singapore's social revolution is a typical story of oppressed people whose innate desire for their inalienable right to self-determination cannot be extinguished once the fire is lit, and of outstanding leaders appearing at the most critical moments to guide them to victory. It is a story of what a free people can achieve with good governance. Indisputably, Lee Kuan Yew and the Old Guard accomplished immeasurably more for Singapore in one generation than the British did in 140 years. Singapore civilisation, which began at least 700 years ago, is all the richer for it.

It is a saga worth telling and preserving for posterity. The point at issue is whether Singapore could have achieved as much without Lee Kuan Yew, the founding father and master craftsman of modern Singapore. He was the right man at the right place and time. So totally dedicated was he that he served Singapore to his last breath. When he died from severe pneumonia in the early hours of Monday, 23 March 2015, at the age of 91, he left behind a shining Singapore as his legacy.

August 9, 2015 marks a momentous milestone in Singapore's modern history as the day it celebrates its 50th National Day. It was a cruel twist of fate that the founding father who proclaimed the nation's birth at City Hall 50 years ago died before the celebrations of this golden day.

Anthony Oei
June 2015

Power is of two kinds. One is obtained by the fear of punishment and the other by acts of love. Power based on love is a thousand times more effective and permanent than the one derived from fear of punishment.

– *Mahatma Gandhi*

01

WHEN A HAKKA CAME TO TOWN

Singapore owes much of its early economic development to Chinese and other immigrants who came here centuries ago for greener pastures. Those with capital and enterprise set up businesses and many of them succeeded and became wealthy. Those without money sought work in firms, some of whom later charted their own destiny. Others were indentured to toil in menial tasks. Many of these immigrants married local women, producing descendants who are now part of the local community. Whether it was talent, entrepreneurship, capital or sweat, their contributions were welcome.

But one 19th century Chinese immigrant by the name of Lee Bok Boon contributed more than that. He was to become the progenitor of two prime ministers—Lee Kuan Yew and his son,

Lee Hsien Loong. Of Hakka stock, a tough tribe originating in northern and central China, he arrived in Singapore in 1863 and married Seow Huan Neo, a local-born with Hakka ancestry. From there, the family tree goes down to Lee Hoon Leong, Lee Chin Koon and Lee Kuan Yew. Lee Bok Boon later returned to China and became a mandarin.

Born in 1871 and educated at Raffles Institution, Lee Kuan Yew's paternal grandfather, Lee Hoon Leong, started work as a pharmacist. Then he joined Heap Eng Moh SS Co Ltd, a leading shipping line operating between Singapore and Indonesia. The reputable and successful company was majority-owned by Indonesian Sugar King Oei Tiong Ham, one-time Chinese Mayor of the central Java city of Semarang. Lee was a shrewd businessman and earned Oei's trust, so much so that he was given power of attorney over his boss' affairs. In Semarang, he met and married local-born Ko Liem Nio. Their son—Lee Kuan Yew's father—Lee Chin Koon, was born in 1903 in that city. His parents brought him back to Singapore when he was a baby. An old boy of St Joseph's Institution and a former Shell Company depot superintendent, Lee Chin Koon married Chua Jim Neo, eldest child of Singaporean Chua Kim Teng and Indonesian-born Hakka Neo Ah Soon.

Like Lee Hoon Leong, Chua Kim Teng was a successful businessman, making his fortune from rubber and property. He was vice president of Cheng Kee Bean Association, a Chinese society founded in 1893. Both Lee and Chua shot to prominence in business and community circles, to the extent that they merited a place in the pages of Sir Song Ong Siang's monumental *One Hundred Years' History of the Chinese in Singapore*. They shared the honour with other eminent personalities of the day such as physician Dr Lim Boon Keng and businessmen Tan Jiak Kim, Tan Tock Seng, Tan Kah Kee, Eu Tong Sen, Choo Kim Kiat and Lim Nee Soon.

The marriage of Lee Kuan Yew's parents was match-made following the common custom in those days. As it happened, the arranged union was a propitious one and their son's birth on 16 September 1923 was, in retrospect, a historic moment for Singapore. The Lee and Chua families were not to know this, of course. They only knew the birth was heaven-sent as he was the first-born and he was a boy, a most precious gift in the eyes of traditional Chinese families. Swelling with pride and joy, paternal grandfather Lee Boon Leong decided the child should be educated to become the equal of any Englishman, that is, the model of perfection.

Grandfather Lee was very much Westernised, with a great admiration for English conduct and dress code, like most of the English-educated in Singapore. Nevertheless, he upheld his ethnic roots and values. So he asked a good friend who was a specialist in auspicious Chinese names to select the most felicitous one for his grandson. The friend, an intellectual, chose "Kuan Yew", meaning "the light that shines far and wide". Being pro-English, grandfather Lee added the English name of Harry. Then a soothsayer friend predicted that the boy would one day cross a big ocean and become famous on his return.

Whether or not any human being has powers to foretell and determine the future by gazing into the crystal ball, or whether some things are pre-ordained, the light did shine far and wide. Unfortunately, grandfather Lee did not live to see his grandson become Prime Minister of Singapore, as he died during the Japanese military occupation. He would have been the proudest patriarch in the land.

Certainly, Mr and Mrs Lee Chin Koon were proud to have earned the rare distinction of being the parents of a prime minister. But relatives say Mr Lee, who had four siblings in Siok Neo, Chin Tong, Wee Neo and Kim Neo, was not one to strut around with his nose in the air. Outwardly, he remained humble and unobtrusive, and lived his normal life. He was reticent about himself and his renowned offspring, once telling a nephew: "I don't like publicity."

Lee Chin Koon, despite his seemingly reserved nature, was friendly, jovial and got on well with relatives and friends, although his son revealed that he was a tough disciplinarian in the family. He loved music—one of his favourite songs was *Hello, Dolly*. Younger sister Wee Neo to whom he was particularly close, offered her own favourite, *Ramona*. Whenever they met at family gatherings, for example, the two would link arms and burst into this haunting ballad. He also relished his sister's *poh piah*, a Chinese-style spring roll common in Singapore.

In contrast, wife Chua Jim Neo was the loquacious, outspoken, aggressive, determined and resourceful type. She was a model mother. She devoted her life to her children's education and welfare, and was the driving force behind them. An intelligent woman, she always strove for excellence and perfection. One incident epitomised this quality. Once when a relative fell seriously ill, she advised her: "Get the best medical attention. Never settle for anything less. If the best fails, you get satisfaction." As Lee Kuan Yew later told a writer, his mother had a great influence on him and that "she was a tower of strength, she encouraged me".

Lee Kuan Yew was born at 92 Kampong Java Road, a rambling, imposing bungalow belonging to maternal grandfather Chua Kim Teng situated near Newton Circus. The premises later became the Singapore headquarters of the Convent of the Good Shepherd. The building disappeared long ago under the hammer of urban redevelopment. When he was very young, Lee and his family lived with paternal grandfather Lee Hoon Leong at 147 Neil Road. The pre-war two-storey terrace house still stands today. Then they moved to Chua's house again which by then was located at 11 Still Lane. The Great Depression, which shrank the fortunes of the Chua and Lee families, had a bearing on the changes of residence.

Lee had four siblings—Dennis Kim Yew (lawyer), Freddy Thiam Yew (stockbroker), Monica Kim Mon, and Suan Yew (medical doctor). They were closely knit, a bonding cemented while growing up, and would help one another in a crisis. Relatives say that like all good big brothers, Lee took on the responsibility of protecting his younger siblings. It would pain him when any of them faced difficulties and he would do everything possible to help and console them. It was therefore a tragic loss to him when Dennis and Freddy died on 14 December 2003 and 28 June 2012 respectively.

There are other descriptions of Lee Kuan Yew's character as a boy circulating among relatives. One remembers him as a bright boy and strong in English, and lively and rather mischievous, given to practical pranks. Another says his leadership qualities were already apparent even at an early age. He was always at the head of his group of friends. Yet another relative paints him as a chubby, quiet and well-behaved boy, always keeping to himself. A late aunt who used to look after him loved to tell the tale that whenever paternal grandfather Lee Hoon Leong gave him pocket money, usually five cents, he would promise to save it so that when his grandfather grew old, he would have the money to care for him.

In the book, *Lee Kuan Yew: The Man And His Ideas*, Lee gave another side of his boyhood personality. He said:

> I didn't do any work. I was too keen on running around, catching fighting fish in the drains along Changi Road, Joo Chiat Road. There was great fun also flying kites and putting thread on two poles, pounding the glue and the glass, fixing the line so you can cut the other fellow's line.

Nevertheless, Lee was an outstanding student. At the age of six, he attended a Chinese-language school, Choon Guan School at Joo Chiat, which he did not like. He then entered Telok Kurau English School where he distinguished himself and won a coveted place at Raffles Institution, the top school in the country, for his secondary education leading at that time to the Senior Cambridge certificate. He continued to excel at Raffles Institution, winning many prizes for his excellent academic results. In the Senior Cambridge final examinations in 1939, he not only topped his class but also all the students in Singapore and Malaya. Scholastic achievements aside, Lee was an excellent orator, taking part in many debates. He was also the sporting type, indulging in swimming and games such as cricket and tennis.

His ambition was to be a lawyer and he had planned to pursue this field of study in London. But the war erupting in Europe in 1939 caused him to postpone that aspiration. As the next best thing, he accepted a scholarship to study at Raffles College, which offered the arts and the sciences. He read English, mathematics and economics. He thought he had a monopoly on these subjects, until he met his match in the form of fellow student Kwa Geok Choo. She topped the class in several term examinations, especially in English and economics, much to Lee's chagrin.

Kwa, daughter of a prominent banker with Oversea-Chinese Banking Corporation, Kwa Siew Tee, had been a top student at her *alma mater*, Methodist Girls' School. In the Senior Cambridge final examinations in 1936, she had come first in the whole of Singapore and Malaya. At Raffles College, she was contending for a Queen's scholarship for further studies in Britain. Lee, who was also vying for it, saw her as a threat to his ambition. But their college rivalry was interrupted in 1942 when Japan invaded and occupied Singapore, Malaya and several other Southeast Asian countries. Later on, this rivalry was to tum into a love match as their friendship blossomed. They were suited to each other from the beginning, although she was three years his senior.

When Japan's surrender in August 1945 ended World War II, Lee opted to start on his postponed law studies in Britain immediately, instead of wasting time by returning to Raffles College to finish his interrupted education. He applied to Middle Temple and got a place at the London School of Economics. But unhappy with student life in London, he looked around and decided on Cambridge where he got a place at Fitzwilliam College. He started his term in January 1947. He had already missed a term. Still, although he did eight terms instead of nine, he got a double first in law and a star for distinction.

But the best news he received while in Cambridge was that girlfriend Kwa Geok Choo had won the Queen's scholarship she had competed for. She entered Girton College in Cambridge in October 1947 and also got a first in law. She was the first woman from Singapore and Malaya to achieve the scholastic feat, and in six terms instead of nine. In his memoirs, Lee Kuan Yew said that they were so much in love that they got married secretly during their student days. The wedding took place at Stratford-on-Avon, Shakespeare's birthplace. They were called to the Bar in the Middle Temple in June 1950 and returned to Singapore on 1 August. They held an official nuptial ceremony on 30 September. Working life for them began with a pupilage at Laycock & Ong, before they formed their own law firm of Lee & Lee, and before Lee Kuan Yew entered politics full-time.

Lee was a formidable politician—bold, firm, fearless and combative. He got things done. He was a hard taskmaster, expecting only the best from everyone. He was endowed with a sharp intellect, relishing intellectual discussions and debates but disliking insincerity. His grasp of events, foresight and analytical ability were legendary. A great visionary and a long-term planner, he had a satellite view of things and long-range vision, like a chess player who thinks steps ahead of his opponent. As he had said, he played chess, not draughts.

World leaders from Asia to Africa to Europe to the United States sat up and took notice of his ideas and commentaries on international events, whether or not they agreed with him. If need be, they were not abashed to seek the benefit of his advice and political experience.

One useful lesson he learnt about leadership was the necessity to surround himself with "good, strong men". He explained in an interview with *Newsweek* in September 1989:

> The stronger the men around me, the abler they are and the more expertise they bring along with them, the more likely I am to resolve the problems that confront me. To be able to use other people's strength-that's the heart of the leadership.

Although English-educated, he was fluent in Mandarin, Hokkien and Malay, tongues he had taken great pains to master to reach out in Singapore's multi-racial society. He vigorously upheld Asian values, imparting these values to his three children when they were young: Hsien Loong, now the Prime Minister; Wei Ling, Director of the National Neuroscience Institute; and Hsien Yang, Chairman of the Civil Aviation Authority of Singapore.

During his stewardship as Prime Minister, Lee Kuan Yew highlighted the importance of Asian values to Singaporeans constantly, stressing that these were a vital shield against the insidious onslaught of undesirable Western fads and fancies. As he had once said during a BBC interview in 1971, if he had allowed hippie and drug cults in Singapore, "we would be crawling on all fours".

Lee had no religion. He said that he did not know whether there is God or no God. All the same, his moral values were the equal of those of God-fearing religious people, and Singaporeans are free to practice their respective religious faiths in the nation's secular society. He is on record as having said that he greatly admired the Roman Catholic Church because of its organisation and administration efficiency, and consistency in policies, some of the qualities that have held the religious establishment strong and cohesive for over 2,000 years. The PAP learnt something from the administrative efficiency, he said.

Another sterling quality of Lee was that he was absolutely incorruptible, a key factor which has made Singapore such a success. He inculcated this virtue in everyone in his government after becoming Prime Minister in 1959 and made it perfectly clear that he meant business. He had no hesitation in exposing and punishing corrupt officials. He even drove home the point to his own family, telling them they should not expect favours from him.

But while he was a lion in the political theatre, he was a typical family man at home who loved his family and lived a simple life with simple tastes. He once boasted: "I can live on soya beans." His home at 38 Oxley Road, which is a stone's throw away from the Istana and the famous Orchard Road shopping belt, was his haven from the rough-and-tumble of politics. He found solace in his family. He valued family life dearly, deeming it the pillar of society. His wife whom he addressed as Choo, children and grandchildren meant the world to him. In fact, Choo was his "tower of strength, giving me constant emotional and intellectual support", as he once said.

S Rajaratnam, a former Deputy Prime Minister who had held several key ministerial portfolios, once revealed: "He is completely disoriented without his wife. In his position, she is the only one he can lean on."

Here is another insight into Lee's private life given by Rajaratnam, who had known and worked with him since 1951:

> He doesn't go to parties, even get-togethers with MPs. He is not that kind. If he has a dinner, it's with two or three close friends, so he doesn't mix a lot, unless it is something very official. My guess is that his close friends may not be more than a dozen. He reads a lot, but really more practical stuff because it helps him to make decisions, to understand change. He doesn't read novels. He doesn't like to read things which are not of practical value. He likes statistics. I think he enjoys them. He's a man who reads a lot about health matters. I think he even instructs doctors how to diagnose him. That's true. He carries lots of medicines for colds, coughs and so on. And I'm quite sure he's got big encyclopaedias around the place to do with health. He's not the kind of man who goes in for music. He is completely tone deaf, I think.

Lee did an excellent job in demolishing British colonial rule and delivering the people from want, servitude and danger. It had been his abiding obsession. What had lit the fire of his nationalist spirit?

02

FIRE IN HIS BELLY

"Look, Ma, another strike," the small boy shouted excitedly, pointing to the colourful banners strung at the gates and fencing of St Andrew's Cathedral.

His mother looked at the child's object of interest, smiled and said: "No, those are fun fair banners, not strike banners, silly boy."

Indeed, a fête was to take place in the grounds of the Church of England the following weekend, and the banners were proudly announcing the forthcoming event and inviting one and all to attend. Mother and son, who was about six or seven years old, were among the evening strollers on the Padang across the Church and City Hall, enjoying the sea breeze. I had chanced to walk past them after work that day and overheard the conversation. My family, colleagues and friends found it amusing when they heard the story.

However, it was not a laughing matter. This was the tumultuous mid-1950s, the blackest days in Singapore's history. The fight against British colonialism was gathering momentum. Singapore was in the midst of a historic political transition. The situation was grave. Everyone in Singapore could sense the tension, the uncertainty, the fears and the foreboding. Industrial strikes riddled the country as workers downed tools in demand for higher wages and better working conditions. Angry banners proclaiming their grievances and denouncing the injustices of management became part of the scenery. The bewildered boy on the Padang had come to associate all banners with industrial action, so his mistake was understandable.

The striking workers put the public at their mercy. During the days without public transport, the public had to resort to their wits to get to their venues—by walking, getting a lift from sympathetic motorists, or hiring the "pirate taxis" or unlicensed taxis plying throughout the island. Worsening the plight of the people were the frequent electricity outages caused by insufficient power-generating capacity. At night, residents burned candles or lit kerosene lamps. Whenever a blackout occurred, Singapore resembled a nation under attack in wartime. Life was a misery, to say the least.

Statistics painted a grim picture. Between 1955 and 1959, considered the most explosive years, there were 393 work stoppages, an average of six a month. The total cost to Singapore was a staggering 1.6 million man-days lost. The worst year was 1955 with 275 strikes and over 946,000 man-days lost. The industrial strife often exploded into rioting, bringing death and injuries and destruction to property. It was a crippling blow to an economy still struggling to recover from the ravages of World War II. The frequent labour unrest was the last thing the people needed as they struggled to make a decent living.

However, there was more to the labour disputes than met the eye. Most of them were communist-instigated. The communists were trying to overthrow the British and build a communist Singapore and Malaya. Their *modus operandi* was violent revolution. Their tactic was using front organisations like trade unions as cover. The communists infiltrated these labour bodies and exploited the workers' grievances, inciting them to strike, hold demonstrations and to riot to serve their own ends. That was why the strikes often led to civil commotion. Directing them behind the scenes was the Malayan Communist Party, later renamed Communist Party of Malaya (CPM), led by top communist Chin Peng working in the jungles of Malaya. The CPM operated an efficient underground network.

It was frightening to see angry mobs, aroused to a frenzy and blinded by fury, screaming and rampaging through the streets in several parts of Singapore. They indiscriminately attacked those standing in the way, even the police, and damaged property with sticks, broken bottles, stones and other deadly missiles. The streets where the skirmishes took place looked like war zones in a war-torn country. Island-wide curfews were imposed.

I was a reporter with *The Straits Times* then situated at Cecil Street. As a junior reporter, my first "beat" or assignment was to report the failings of human nature, unfolding every working day in the Subordinate Courts at South Bridge Road. I covered several trials of those arrested and charged for rioting and unlawful assembly. One of the most interesting cases concerned four male youths. In evidence, six detectives told First District Judge J W D Ambrose that they mingled with an unruly crowd at a bus depot at Alexandra Road where the workers were on strike and saw the four accused shouting and flinging stones and broken bottles at the police. All four pleaded not guilty.

How the detectives nabbed the young men was bizarre. It took place at the Singapore General Hospital in the early morning of 13 May 1955 as the four of them brought in a Chinese middle school student killed in the rioting which took place the previous day. The rumours made the round that the boy had been shot by the police. The police denied it. Eventually, the detectives recognised the accused as the ones they had seen attacking the police at the bus depot. They later officially identified the alleged offenders in separate identification parades.

My newspaper published the story the next day: *Memories of One Night and a Mob*. The four youths were found guilty at the conclusion of the trial. One of them was jailed for 18 months and the other three one year each. Judge Ambrose told them "Your offences struck at the very foundation of law and order in Singapore. The punishment must fit the crime you have committed."

It was a tense and dangerous period. But reporters like me and those in other essential services had to perform our duties, regardless of the perils, and during the curfew we were given curfew passes allowing us freedom of movement. I had no trouble going about town except one night when I got the fright of my life. I was returning home in the office car to my house at Thomson Road. At the roadblock at the Red Bridge, a soldier thrust his loaded rifle through the open car window and pointed it very close to my chest as another soldier checked our passes. I just sat there, frigid with fear. With orders to shoot on sight, he would probably have pulled the trigger had I made the slightest suspicious movement.

Around this time of social revolution, as politicians rose to demolish colonial rule, a new name was being increasingly heard above the din. It was a young lawyer called Lee Kuan Yew. Lee had returned from Cambridge in 1950 after completing his law studies and was practicing at his office at Malacca Street. He and a group of like-minded freedom fighters had formed a left-wing political party, the People's Action Party. Lee held the seat of Secretary-General.

Although a relative newcomer on the local political scene, Lee was making a great impact as a revolutionary firebrand. He was vocal and held radical views and he uttered them forcefully and fearlessly. He appeared tough and firm, matched by his stern face. He positioned the PAP as the champion of the underdogs. Fiercely fanning the fires of nationalism, he pledged to change the system to make Singapore an equal, just and fair society for all. These promises appealed to the working class because they were the most disadvantaged in Singapore, and his fiery delivery and strong conviction impressed them. They regarded him as their saviour from poverty and slavery. They saw the big difference between him and the existing politicians from the other parties. The proletariat threw their weight behind him.

Lee made it known to everybody that he was a non-communist and was fighting the communists to prevent them from taking over the country. He described them as Singapore's most dangerous enemy. But he caused some confusion among the people when he said the PAP was prepared to work with them. Radical statements like this made headlines in the media, and brought disquiet among the British rulers and the Special Branch which took charge of national security. Doing their level best to discredit Lee and the PAP, the British labelled them extremists and wild men, and watched them with a hawk's eye. The rich, the English-educated and business circles, too, were nervous. These groups of people were accustomed to their sheltered life under the colonial power. They were making a relatively good living, and did not relish the prospect of change. They feared Lee and the PAP, believing they were communists.

Such were the fears and suspicions generated that Lee was to admit years later that he had friends in the early days of the social revolution "whose wives literally chased me away and made it known that I was unwelcome". He said: "In those days, even before the PAP was formed, to be associated with me was to invite Special Branch attention." He was that kind of a revolutionary.

Undeniably, Lee and the PAP were a big threat to their political opponents. So they launched ferocious attacks on Lee and his team. They branded them leftist rabble-rousers and trouble-makers who had no capability of getting rid of the British and improving the lives of the people. Some accused them of being communists. Singling out Lee, they charged that he was a newcomer, with no political experience. He was just making a lot of noise to gain a seat in government. They pointed to the PAP logo, a bolt of lightning, and warned the people: "There you see, the symbol is a bad omen. Watch out, they want to break your rice bowl."

This was the picture the British and Lee's political opponents painted. But I discovered another side of Lee when I first saw him in the flesh. The venue was one of the subordinate courts I was covering for my newspaper. One afternoon, sitting at the Press table waiting for the court to begin its session, Chua Kim Yew, my rival reporter-friend from *The Singapore Standard*, nudged me and whispered: "Look who's here." There, striding in with a purposeful gait, was one of Singapore's leading anti-colonialists who was creating big waves in the sea of local politics. In his arm was a pile of legal documents. In tow was an assistant carrying more legal papers. Obviously, he had come to defend a client in trouble with the law.

With his reputation having preceded him, everyone in the courtroom recognised him instantly. My first impression of him was that he had an overpowering personality and that he looked more handsome than in his photos in the newspapers, in a rugged sort of way. He was tall and broad-shouldered, had a bright face, glinting, intelligent slit eyes, and a prominent forehead under thick, black wavy hair. He appeared to be a self-assured man. Certainly, he looked distinctly different from the other learned members of the legal profession who stood before the Bench daily to lock horns with the prosecution on points of law.

Another of his attributes impressed me and remains imprinted in my mind to this day. Lee showed civility towards the Press table. As he sat down at the Bar table nearby and waited for the judge to appear, Lee turned his gaze towards us, nodded and smiled. I thought to myself what a decent chap he was. In my years of covering court stories, no other lawyer in my memory had acknowledged the existence of reporters in that manner. Most treated us as though we were part of the furniture. Or they were quick to show their displeasure if they found the stories we wrote about their clients in the newspapers the next day were not to their liking. Even the court officials had more respect for us.

This was the other side of Lee Kuan Yew I saw that day, a rising young politician who was galvanising the nation but displaying exemplary courtesy in the judicial room. Were all revolutionaries like him? Perhaps he was one of those strong men who could also be a gentleman. Perhaps he had a friendly disposition and was uncompromising only towards his foes, in this case the British, his political opponents and the communists. Anyway, I looked forward eagerly to seeing him in action in court, hearing his legal arguments for his client, and writing the story. It would have been the experience of a lifetime.

Unfortunately, just then my team leader Peter D'Cruz breezed in and told me breathlessly: "Anthony, let me cover this one. Go to the next court. There's a murder case there." Obviously, Lee's case must have been a very important one, too "hot" for a junior reporter to handle. But not having covered it, I cannot remember what it was. And there had been no other chance because soon after that, I was transferred to the Business Desk to write economic news.

Outside the courtroom, Lee Kuan Yew stepped up his anti-colonial campaign. Could he succeed in his political ambition? There were other politicians fighting the same cause, not to mention the underground communists. The British were not easy to dislodge. In fact, they had no intention of leaving. But by all appearances, Lee was proving to be a committed anti-colonial fighter determined to achieve his goal, not the run-of-the-mill type who came and went in the tumultuous stream of politics.

Day by day, he was demonstrating his political will and the fire in his belly.

03

BIRTH OF AN ASIAN NATIONALIST

In his youth, politics was far from Lee Kuan Yew's mind. He was more concerned with getting a good education, whether or not he aspired "to be the equal of any Englishman", as paternal grandfather Lee Hoon Leong had dreamed about. Law was his chosen profession as he was not inclined towards engineering or the sciences. But people can change. There are certain compulsions that drive professionals to switch horses in midstream, like doctors becoming writers or engineers becoming businessmen. For Lee Kuan Yew, the compulsion came during the horrendous Japanese military occupation. That was the key factor that drove him into politics. This is not to say that life under British colonialism was idyllic.

When Singapore became a British colony after Stamford Raffles' arrival on 29 January 1819, the people lost their inalienable right to determine their own future. The Colonial Office in London controlled the administration, economy, defence, education and other vital sectors. Only those who have experienced being treated as the lower order of the human race in their own land, would know the depth of the humiliation and deprivation they suffered. Colonialism was an abhorrent system of government. Its sole purpose was the exploitation of the riches of the conquered for the sole benefit of the conquerors, leaving most locals to struggle with bare living standards.

The people's resentment was understandable. Picture the scenario in Singapore during the British colonial regime. They used Singapore's strategic geographical position and exploited the cheap local labour to increase the flow of trade between Britain and Asia. The goal was to enrich the Crown's coffers. They occupied all the top posts in the civil service and in the firms they set up. The highest position Singaporeans could aspire to was that of chief clerk. The locals were their subjects (not citizens) and were generally derogatorily dismissed as "these lesser mortals".

Some British bosses even practised the humiliating habit of shouting "hey, hey" to draw your attention and crooking their forefingers as a signal for you to approach them. They were condescending, patronising and sarcastic. They were fond of issuing threats of punishment. Their contempt showed in their faces. The locals had no choice but to grin and bear it as they had to make a living. The genuinely kind Britons in Singapore who wore no superior air were few and far between in numbers.

Education opportunities were dismally inadequate. Primary and secondary schools were in dire shortage. In the turbulent mid-1950s, according to statistics, the primary schools had vacancies for just 80 percent of the school-going children, while the secondary schools could take in only 23 percent. Parents who could afford the fees placed their children in private night schools as an alternative. The less fortunate children, numbering in the thousands, went without education. The highest education local students could attain was college level until the University of Malaya, the precursor of today's National University of Singapore, was established in 1949.

The British developed exclusive residential districts for European staff and their families, while the majority of the local people lived in lower-class, run-down dirty housing districts, a large number even living in cramped, squalid quarters. In the early days, certain restaurants, hotels, clubs and swimming pools were out of bounds to locals. Tales of flagrant racial discrimination in some supermarkets and shops abounded. They reserved their best products and smiles for their European customers. One incident should suffice as an illustration. A friend of mine related the time when his mother went to the Cold Storage supermarket at Orchard Road for a loaf of bread. The salesgirl (under strict orders no doubt) gave her a stale one. My friend's mother promptly threw it back at her and stormed off.

At one time, there was segregation in public buses. The buses were built with two compartments. The front compartment with soft cushioned seats and backrests was reserved for European passengers, the rear compartment with hard wooden benches and backrests for locals. Cinemas and theatres offered reserved sections in the best vantage points in the hall for their European patrons. The rest had to scramble for the wooden seats.

Municipal services left much to be desired. Running water was a luxury. Most had to depend on public standpipes. Blackouts were common occurrences because of below-capacity power generators. Sanitation was the bucket system, with night-soil workers collecting human waste from homes each morning, loading it into trucks, and the trucks trundling through the streets presented an unsightly scene. The roads were dirty and drains smelly and choked with leavings. The Singapore River was one mass of polluted water.

Needless to say, Singapore was overwhelmed by all things British; Made-in-Great Britain products (which enjoyed preferential tariff treatment over those from elsewhere), literature, music, culture, customs, and traditions. These predominated over Asian goods and services, cultures and values. English education was the norm as it was the passport to a relatively better standard of living, with jobs in the civil service and in British firms. Most of the English-educated became so obsessed with English culture and lifestyle that they abandoned even their own mother tongues. Parents gave their children English names. Some of the English-educated even went to the extent of behaving like the English and fawning for their friendship, for to be seen with them was a status symbol. They became known as Westernised Oriental Gentlemen (WOGs) and Westernised Oriental Women (WOWs).

To this day, much of Singapore remains immersed in English and other Western cultures, with American values increasingly predominating. To be fair, however, Singaporeans did derive some benefits from British colonialism. They became more world-wise, enriching their knowledge and lives. They inherited the English language, a most useful language which is now the *lingua franca* of government and business, a time-tested parliamentary system of government, an efficient civil service, an established rule of law and new insights into the management of business, finance, legal, medical and other professional services. They also enjoyed national security. In fact, it was the British who initiated the Internal Security Act. If only there had been political and socio-economic equality, colonialism would not have been so objectionable.

On Sunday, 15 February 1942, Japan ended 123 years of British colonialism when it conquered Singapore and many other Southeast Asian countries like Malaya and Indonesia. War had erupted in Asia in 1937 when part of Japan's expansionist policy purportedly launched to ensure its own economic survival. Unfortunately, the end of British rule plunged Singapore into an even more horrifying era. Japanese reign was inhuman. It was the goriest chapter in Singapore's history.

At the time of the invasion, Lee Kuan Yew was 18 and a student at Raffles College. Like the rest of the population, Lee was taken aback as the first bombs fell from the sky in the early hours of 8 December 1941, targeting the city and the airfields. The dawn air raid killed more than 60 people, injured over 700 others, and destroyed several buildings. The day before, the Japanese had blown the American fleet at Pearl Harbour into the sky, invaded Hong Kong and the Philippines, and deployed forces in southern Thailand and Kota Baru, northern Malaya. More bombs rained down on Singapore in the next two months, killing and injuring hundreds more and destroying more buildings. At sea, they sank the pride of Britain's navy, Prince of Wales and Repulse. On the ground, their troops, supported by heavy armoury, were also unstoppable.

Patriotic Singapore Chinese had formed the Anti-Japanese Volunteer Battalion, code-named Dalforce, and other battle units to fight alongside British and Allied troops and the Malay Regiment. Although they inflicted heavy casualties on the invaders, they failed to repel and defeat them. They themselves suffered heavy losses. The surviving members of Dalforce fled to the Malayan jungles to join a guerrilla unit called the Malayan People's Anti-Japanese Army (MPAJA). The MPAJA was a special underground force formed by the Communist Party of Malaya (CPM) then known as the Malayan Communist Party. The British had banned them, but with the enemy at their doorstep, had allowed them to help in the war effort. The British even supplied them with arms and military advisers. But it was a lost cause.

That fateful day, 15 February 1942, when Britain surrendered, was the first day of the Lunar New Year. It had taken Japan months to bring the mighty Britain to its knees. The triumphant Japanese Commander, Lt-Gen Tomoyuki Yamashita, accepted the terms of the surrender from Lt-Gen Arthur Percival, General-Officer-Commanding Malaya. The flag of the Rising Sun replaced the Union Jack. Singapore was renamed Syonan To (Light of the South). *The Straits Times became Syonan Shimbun*, while *Nanyang Siang Pau* and *Sin Chew Jit Poh* were published as *Syonan Jit Poh*. The Japanese had destroyed the so-called "impregnable fortress".

Lee Kuan Yew and other Singaporeans were incredulous and stunned by the relative ease with which the Japanese military had conquered their country. The British had promised that they would defend Singapore to the last man. Even during the height of the assault, British Prime Minister Winston Churchill had bragged that

Singapore would never fall because it was an impregnable force. But when the crunch came, they wilted and disappointed the people. The public began to form the conclusion that the British were neither superior nor invincible after all.

Lt-Gen Percival and his troops were imprisoned in Changi. They were forced to do manual labour and some were tortured. Many were carted away to work in the infamous Burma-Siam railway project. Few lived to tell the tale. The entire European population, including Governor of Singapore Shenton Thomas, was also imprisoned. Thomas, Percival and a large number of military and civilian prisoners were later transferred to Taiwan.

For the locals, the Japanese military meted out their brand of justice and punishment. One of their first acts of brutality was to round up Singapore Chinese males whom they suspected of having supported China's war effort against Japan and of being members of the anti-Japanese forces. The conquerors did not forget that. The unfortunate men were taken to concentration centres and then to the beaches and other places for summary execution. The number massacred ran in the thousands. No one knows the exact figure to this day. The gruesome operation was called *sook ching* (to purge). One is reminded of the Nanjing massacre and of the holocaust during Nazi Germany.

Then followed three-and-a-half years of oppression, fear, humiliation, tortures, beheadings and deprivation of a decent living. Stories of their unbelievable atrocities are already well-documented and bear no repetition here. Suffice to say that the most dreaded organisation was the Kempeitai (Japanese military police). Woe betide those who fell into their clutches for one reason or another.

Food and other essential supplies were in acute shortage. Inflation shot through the roof. Japanese currency was called the "banana note" and its value fell day by day. At that time, I lived in Indonesia where I was born and the situation was equally grim. I remember my father, who worked at the British Embassy in Jakarta, coming home on each pay day with his salary in a large sack. In fairness, however, it must be said that their savagery against civilians grew less frequent and less harsh with the passage of time, although the deprivation and degradation continued.

Lt-Gen Yamashita, dubbed the "Tiger of Malaya", had closed down Raffles College to use as his military headquarters soon after his forces had overrun Singapore. With no college, the teenage Lee Kuan Yew took up several jobs to earn a living, including working as a clerk in a Japanese firm called Shimoda and as an English-language cable editor of *Hodobu*, a Japanese propaganda agency. He even studied Japanese.

Meanwhile, the surviving members of Dalforce continued their fight in the Malayan jungles along with the MPAJA. Several war heroes emerged from the guerrilla warfare. One prominent Singaporean war hero was Lim Bo Seng, a wealthy trader who had migrated from China at the age of 16. To support the resistance groups, Lim went underground to infiltrate behind enemy lines. Tragically, the Japanese caught him and tortured him to death. He was only 34. His memorial at the Esplanade stands as a permanent tribute to his bravery and heroism, as does a road named after him.

Like everyone else, Lee Kuan Yew was horrified by the brutalities committed on civilians, causing him to fume: "Have the Japanese a right to do this? This is our country. We will govern it ourselves."

To aggravate his outrage, he himself literally felt the sting of their cruelty. He was slapped in the face on a number of occasions, one of which occurred while he was passing by a bridge known as the Red Bridge, not far from the Kampong Java Road house where he was born. A Japanese sentry stopped him for no apparent reason and slapped him. Unprovoked and wanton bullying acts like these remain a bad memory for him. He even had a brush with death. Only his wits saved him, as we shall see later.

The nightmare of the occupation ended on 15 August 1945 when Japan surrendered after the United States had dropped two atomic bombs, one on Hiroshima on 6 August and the other on Nagasaki on 9 August, killing and maiming for life thousands upon thousands of innocent men, women and children. In Singapore, Admiral Lord Louis Mountbatten, Supreme Allied Commander, Southeast Asian Command, accepted the terms of the surrender on 12 September from Lt-Gen Seishiro Itagaki, who signed the instrument of surrender on behalf of Field Marshall Count Hisaichi Terauchi, Commander-in-Chief of the Southern Army, who was ill in Saigon (now known as Ho Chi Minh City) in Vietnam.

The Japanese war criminals against civilians were tried in a special court set up by the British military administration. Due to lack of conclusive evidence of individual responsibility however, not all were found guilty, and only two of those convicted were hanged. The others convicted received life sentences. Families, relatives, and friends of the victims were utterly dissatisfied that the punishment did not fit the crime. Lt-Gen Yamashita, who had moved to the Philippines in 1944 to resist American invasion there, was tried in Manila, found guilty and hanged by the Americans. The physical abuse committed on thousands of innocent Singaporeans brought into stark reality the evils of foreign domination. These excesses opened the eyes of Lee Kuan Yew and ignited the fire of his nationalist spirit. After the British had returned and re-governed Singapore, Lee decided that they, too, had no right to remain as colonial masters.

And so an Asian nationalist freedom-fighter was born. Lee dramatically described in public his entry into politics on 25 August 1963, after he had become Prime Minister. It was a Sunday and the occasion was a mass rally at the Padang opposite City Hall. This was the event organised to pacify angry Singapore Chinese who had been vociferously clamouring for appropriate compensation from the Japanese Government for the deaths of their family members, relatives and friends during the grisly *sook ching* slaughter. The painful memories still lingered in their minds. Their demand was known as the "blood debt" issue. Some 100,000 people packed themselves into the Padang.

The mood was ugly. This was also the time when Singapore was about to merge with Malaya and the communists, who were against the proposed merger, tried to exploit this issue as an excuse to create trouble. There were also Chinese chauvinists in the throng bent on blowing the case out of proportion. Fortunately, save for a few scuffles here and there, the police managed to keep the situation under control.

Lee calmed the restless crowd and proposed ways of resolving the prickly "blood debt" issue. (Eventually, the Japanese gave Singapore $50 million as atonement, half of it as soft loans. It was small beer, but it was accepted.) He assured the gathering that he knew how cruel the Japanese military had been and that he himself had personally experienced a share of their cruelty. He said:

> They would never know what they did to a whole generation like me. But they made me and a whole generation like me determined to fight for freedom—freedom from servitude and foreign domination. I did not enter politics. They brought politics upon me. From that time onwards, I decided that our lives should be ours to decide. That we should not be pawns and the playthings of foreign powers. Humiliation and degradation by foreign European powers is bad enough. It was worse at the hands of a conquering Asian nation like Japan.

Then he related his escape from the jaws of death:

> As I was queuing up at the Weld Road, Jalan Besar Concentration Centre in February 1942, the scrutineers at the gate looked at my physical size and asked me to join some people on a lorry, presumably to do some work for the Japanese. Somehow, I felt that lorry was not going take people to work. I asked them to let me go back to get my belongings which I said were left behind with my gardener whose *kongsi* [office] was in Upper Weld Road and with whom I had put up for several days when we were kept in that Concentration Centre. I never returned to the exit point until they changed sentries and scrutineers. When they did, I walked out and they allowed me to

> go home. Those who were sent into the lorry never came back. Such was the blindness of their brutality.

He declared:

> We shall be our own masters in our own country. If anybody tries to dominate us, we are not without friends. And rather than have a new master, death would be preferable. We have a will of our own, and a right to live in peace on our own. So let us unite in Malaysia and prevent it ever from happening again.

There was another occasion when he escaped death. The incident took place in 1951 at Thomson Road. It was a rainy day and he was going to play golf at the Singapore Island Country Club when the car with his wife aboard "just skidded and then rolled over two times" at a bad turn. Fortunately, the car landed on soft grass and they had absolutely no injuries. There was a large water pipe at the roadside further up. If he had hit the pipe, he and his wife, who was expecting their first child, would have met their end. "So I think it was deliverance," Lee said.

It appeared that Lee was correct in saying it was deliverance. Lee was destined to lead Singapore to freedom and prosperity. The religious would say it was God's will. Ironically, it was in Britain that he plotted his moves to bring down the Union Jack.

04

LEE PLOTTED HIS MOVES

Lee sailed to England on a troopship, *Britannic*, on 16 September 1946, his 23rd birthday, to pursue his law studies. The ship docked at Liverpool. From there, he took a train to London where he enrolled in the London School of Economics. But after three miserable months in the British capital city, he packed his bags for Cambridge.

At Cambridge, Lee applied himself to his studies and, as stated earlier, he passed his exams with flying colours although he had missed a term. In between cracking law books, he indulged himself in politics with many Singaporean and Malayan students studying at London universities. Among his Singaporean friends were Toh Chin Chye and Goh Keng Swee. Those from Malaya included Tunku Abdul Rahman and Abdul Razak. Goh, in fact, had been

Lee's economics tutor at Raffles College. Goh and Toh were to play big roles in Singapore politics. The Tunku was to become Malaya's first Prime Minister.

They were all politically active and had formed themselves into a group called the Malayan Forum in London. They had one common denominator: they were anti-colonialists. Their objective was a non-communist, democratic Singapore and Malaya and their *modus operandi* would be peaceful revolution. They made great efforts to dissociate themselves from the communists whose aim was a communist Singapore and Malaya achieved through violent revolution. The nascent freedom-fighters huddled regularly to plot their moves. They discussed ideas on the best way of gaining freedom and dealing with the communist threat.

A great source of inspiration and encouragement was the knowledge that the anti-colonial movement was gaining momentum in other colonised Asian countries. Indeed, colonies, such as India, Pakistan and Indonesia, had gained their independence. Eventually, the British would have to bow to pressure and grant freedom to the colonies they still ruled. They would be unable to stem the rising tide. These developments strengthened the resolve of the Malayan Forum members. Rubbing shoulders with them kindled Lee Kuan Yew's nationalist spirit first lit during the terrifying Japanese military occupation.

The student revolutionaries also talked of Malaya as it was then recognised that Singapore and Malaya should be one entity sharing a common background. The issue was brought up because the British had constitutionally severed the two countries in 1946 and reconstituted Singapore as a separate colony, leaving it on a limb to write its own history. Malacca and Penang were left intact in the peninsula and incorporated into what later became the Federation of Malaya.

The British explained that these constitutional changes were necessary as Singapore was still an important military base to them. They also feared that the overwhelming Chinese population in Singapore would upset the racial balance in Malaya if they had left the island in the peninsula. They qualified their explanation by promising that the arrangement would not "preclude or prejudice in any way the fusion of Singapore and Malaya into a wider union at a later date".

But political observers saw the separation as a British attempt to remain in power, and it followed their well-known policy of divide-and-rule. Opposition to separation came not only from genuine nationalists but also the communists, both of whom believed that fighting for Malaya as one entity would make the struggle easier, although their eventual goals differed. In fact, reunification became one of the major items on Lee's agenda for independence, and one of the most contentious issues. He was convinced that merger would benefit both countries.

Reunion was a logical proposition. After all, the two countries had been one entity historically, geographically and economically before the British drove in the wedge in 1946. Biologically, the people were the same and looked alike. They had relatives and friends on either side of the causeway. Whether they were Malays, Chinese or Indians, they spoke the same languages and dialects, ate the same kinds of food and dressed in the same types of clothes. Those who spoke English had the same quaint accent. The only difference was their ethnicity. The separation made by the British was therefore unnatural.

For Singapore, the economic and political reasons were also compelling. Reunification would create a larger domestic market for its factories, commercial and financial establishments, thereby enabling the country to realise its economic potential. A prosperous Singapore would benefit Malaya. Politically, merger with staunchly anti-communist Malaya would provide the security that Singapore needed, particularly from the communists who were ready to pounce when the British left. This merited serious consideration since Malaya did not relish the prospect of a communist state at its doorstep.

Singapore recognised that the matter was a complex one. In Malaya, the two major population groups were the Malays and the Chinese. At that time, the former outnumbered the latter by just 54 percent to 45 percent. In Singapore, there were one million Chinese to about 150,000 Malays. Obviously, if the two countries became one entity again, the Chinese would overwhelm the Malays numerically and thus upset the racial balance. The vital question was how to create an atmosphere where they could work and live in harmony and peace. There was also the fear that the communists, who were mostly Chinese, could exploit the situation for their own ends, with disastrous consequences.

The Malayans were anxious on another score. They believed that Singapore had too many leftists who could become a menace to rightist Malaya. At that time, they regarded any force that was leftist to be communist or potentially communist. They could not discern the distinction between democratic socialism and communism. To the Malayans, they were the same. Singapore had to convince them that their impression was wrong.

These were knotty problems which the Malayan Forum decided to leave for discussion another day. It would have been less problematic if the British had left Singapore intact in Malaya, although no one can say with certainty how the political histories of the two would have developed. The point was that now Singapore had the difficult task of re-tying the severed bond.

In between the Malayan Forum talks, Lee also seized the opportunity to learn about the machinery of British politics and how the people lived. For example, he sometimes attended the House of Commons sessions to listen to the speeches and see the art of parliamentary debate. He made contact with several Labour Party MPs for their views on politics. He even learned to campaign in an election. This was for a Labour Party candidate, an old Cambridge friend. Lee joined the Cambridge University Labour Club where he gave speeches and heard the views of the members. He was the richer from all these experiences.

Meanwhile in Singapore, the post-war evolution of local politics was beginning to take shape. A brief background will give readers the complete picture. After resuming control of Singapore in September 1945, the British formed a 17-member Advisory Council in November to help govern the country in lieu of a civil administration. Headed by Governor Franklin Gimson, the Council was dominated by British officials, naturally. The few indigenous members included prominent personalities of the day, such as businessman Lee Kong Chian and banker Tan Chin Tuan, as well as communist and former guerrilla leader Wu Tien Wang.

However, these political developments were as yet meaningless to the ordinary Singaporean. He was more concerned with getting a job and a good living for him and his family. The economic situation was dreary. Living standards were low. Tens of thousands were unemployed, and thousands of school-leavers entered the job market each year. Jobs were not being created fast enough. The salaries of those fortunate enough to have work were measly. Food and other essential items were in short supply, resulting in high inflation. The poor and the destitute, seen with their patched clothes, worn-out footwear or even their bare feet, were common sights on the streets of Singapore at that time.

Public housing was inadequate, forcing thousands to sleep in crowded cubicles. The government organisation in charge, the Singapore Improvement Trust (SIT), was inefficient, unlike today's Housing and Development Board (HDB). Health, municipal and other essential services, such as electricity, water and transport, were appalling. Crime and gangsterism were rampant. This was Singapore during the colonial era—poor, illiterate and ignorant.

Making the socio-economic burdens even heavier, the population had doubled to more than one million over the pre-war numbers. The rapid population explosion was fuelled by the unusually high birth rates on the island, a unique phenomenon of the war years. Adding to the numbers was the growing influx of Malayans pouring down across the causeway to vie for the scarce jobs and services in the southern island city. The poor remained poor. The British failed to improve the sorry state of affairs adequately and quickly enough. Feelings of discontent, resentment and disillusion rose.

The Communist Party of Malaya (CPM), with its Singapore headquarters at Queen Street, was the first to exploit the people's unhappiness and to launch the attack against the colonial power. The communists had been in Singapore since 1923, when they sent their first group of agents from Shanghai. They had helped the British fight the Japanese through the Malayan People's Anti-Japanese Army (MPAJA). After the war, the CPM was the only organised and the strongest fighting force in Singapore and Malaya, apart from the British colonial rulers. The CPM was led by Secretary-General Chin Peng. He was an ardent anti-colonialist.

In December 1945, the CPM founded a front organisation named the Malayan Democratic Union (MDU) to fight for the cause. The CPM was allowed to operate, on condition that it refrained from violence Indeed, the British decorated Chin Peng with two campaign medals and an Order of the British Empire for services rendered during the Japanese Occupation. But the awards did not detract Chin Peng from pursuing his communist mission.

The MDU, the first political party in Singapore after the war, proclaimed itself to be a force dedicated to peaceful struggle. The Chairman was Philip Hoalim, Sr, a British-trained Singapore lawyer and a non-communist. But the other leadership posts were filled with well-known communists of the day like Eu Chooi Yip and Wu Tien Wang, and pro-communist such as Lim Kean Chye, Lim Hong Bee, John Eber and Gerald de Cruz.

The communists placed themselves as the champion of the people, the solution to their dire economic problems. The British cared little about their livelihood, they cried. The people should therefore rise up against the colonialists and free themselves from their shameful shackles if they wanted a better future for them and their children. Needless to say, their "sales pitch" drew a large following from the proletariat.

Aware of the changed political mood and realising that nothing could stop the anti-colonial movement, the British announced in 1947 their decision to create a representative government in the form of a Legislative Council to replace the Advisory Council which they had set up in 1945. A date, 20 March 1948, was set for the first election to the new Legislative Council.

At first sight, the election appeared to be a step forward in the process of decolonisation. Actually, it was merely a red herring as the British had no intention of handing over power. This was evident from the fact that only six of the 22 seats were open to local representation. The other seats were held by British officials and some appointed local nominees. And the only party contesting was the pro-British Singapore Progressive Party. Independent candidates made up the rest of the contestants. The MDU boycotted the polls, for obvious reasons.

Established on 25 August 1947, the Progressive Party was the brainchild of three British-trained lawyers, C C Tan, John Laycock and N A Mallal. They toed the British line that self-government should take place in stages. The three party leaders won their seats in the Legislative Council election, with the independent candidates taking the remaining three. Only about 14,000 of some 200,000 eligible voters, all British subjects of course, cast their ballots.

In September 1948, a group of leading trade unionists formed a new political party, Singapore Labour Party (SLP), to throw their weight behind the process of decolonisation. The founders included

M A Majid, President of the Singapore Seamen's Union, and M P D Nair and Peter Williams of the Army Civil Service Union. The President was school-teacher Francis Thomas. Their objective was self-government by 1954 and merger with Malaya.

As the political events developed, the CPM decided to resort to violent means by infiltrating trade unions and fomenting industrial strikes, student unrest and other civil disorder for its political ends through the MDU. The British arrested a large number of communists and deported many of them. In June 1948, the CPM launched an armed insurrection in Malaya. The British enforced the Emergency Regulations and promptly banned the party. Chin Peng and his men went underground to continue their fight. With the ban and the Emergency, the MDU was left to its own devices. Unable to survive by itself, the party decided to disband.

The CPM's targets were the British, not the local population, according to Chin Peng in his book, *My Side of History*. He said British planters "had histories of exploiting workers and hiring thugs to break up strikes on their plantations". Many of the thugs were ex-servicemen, de-mobbed from British World War II units. He maintained that "the British colonials used terror tactics to retain their hold on Malaya", that "they shot innocent, unarmed civilians demonstrating in the countryside for food and jobs", and that they "burned villages, cut rations and shot civilians". He denied British claims that his men attacked innocent civilians, insisting that this was never a CPM policy.

This was the political scenario in Singapore when Lee Kuan Yew returned from Cambridge on 1 August 1950 with wife Kwa Geok Choo. The ship was the Dutch liner, *Willem Ruys*. He was happy to be back. Decolonisation was still in its infancy and he had not missed much. The field remained wide open. Lee had benefitted greatly from his Malayan Forum discussions and the meetings with British politicians which would be useful in his political career. He had become "highly politicised and anti-colonial", as he reflected later in his memoirs.

But his happy homecoming was marred by an unpleasant encounter with the European immigration officer who kept Lee and Choo to the very last. When he finally checked their passports, he said: "I suppose we will hear more about you, Mr Lee." The officer tried to intimidate Lee, but he "was not going to be intimidated".

Lee later discovered that "among the black marks against me" was British suspicion of his attendance at the World Festival of Youth in Budapest in August 1949, a communist rally organised by the Soviet Union. Lee was not in the group of Singaporean and Malayan students who attended the event. The Singaporeans who went included Goh Keng Swee, Maurice Baker and Lee's brother, Dennis Lee Kim Yew. As it happened, the Special Branch had mistaken Dennis for him because their Chinese names had the same initials, K Y Lee. Lee Kuan Yew was also to learn that the Special Branch had in fact wanted to detain him and Choo on their return. But the commissioner of police had vetoed the proposal.

It was apparent that British Intelligence had been aware of the Malayan Forum and its activities, and had sent the names of suspects to Singapore Special Branch and the police. Their close attention on Lee Kuan Yew must say a great deal about him as an anti-colonial fighter and of their natural concern, even before he had begun to sink his teeth into Singapore politics.

05

THE COMING OF THE PAP

The days of 11 to 13 December 1950 were black blots on Singapore's multi-racial fabric when Malays attacked Europeans and Eurasians in the streets. The bone of contention in this first post-war racial incident was a 13-year-old Dutch girl named Maria Bertha Hertogh. A Catholic, Maria had been left in the care of a Malay couple when her parents were interned in Indonesia by the Japanese during the occupation. The couple brought up the girl as a Muslim. After the war, the parents returned to claim her. When the couple refused, they brought the case to court and won. That incensed the Malay community and the rioting that followed left 18 people dead and 173 others injured. I witnessed some of these attacks, one of them in front of my house at Thomson Road. The victim was a Eurasian on a motorbike. A group of Malays pelted him with stones as he passed by. He fell and lucky for him, they left him alone. He was not badly hurt and managed to ride away. Even then, it was a frightening sight.

The police arrested 13 Malays. They were tried in court for the murder of a Royal Air Force non-commissioned officer, his wife and child about a year later. The jury system was in force then. Lee Kuan Yew, who had become a lawyer with Laycock & Ong, was assigned to defend four of the accused. The jury found nine of them guilty of grievous hurt, one of whom was Lee's client. His three other clients were acquitted. This was his first big court tussle. But he also saw the weaknesses of the jury system where the fate of the accused was determined by lay people. (He abolished it later when he became the Prime Minister.)

However, it was in the labour movement that Lee made his name and earned a reputation as a champion and friend of the working class that paid huge dividends in his political career. Lee became legal adviser to a staggering number of about 40 trade unions. He handled workers' grievances about poor pay and bad working conditions, providing them with the necessary legal brain and negotiating skills in their wage disputes with their employers, including the government. Significantly, his work with the unions brought him into contact with the communists and pro-communists who controlled many of the trade unions. That was the start of his association with them.

The labour dispute that first propelled Lee into the limelight was the one involving the Postal and Telecommunications Uniformed Staff Union in 1952. The postmen had downed tools for three weeks to press their demands. Denied their daily mail, the public fumed and fretted. As the letter-less days dragged on, they turned their ire towards the government, accusing them of being unreasonable. Lee deftly negotiated the case on behalf of the mailmen and won. They never forgot it.

As workers' confidence and trust in him grew, it dawned on Lee and his political comrades that the labour movement was the source of the mass base they had been seeking to support their political objectives. It would be the political muscle they needed to mobilise mass support, the vital ingredient for the plan of action first discussed at the Malayan Forum in London. Indeed, in any revolution anywhere, workers are a potent force. In Singapore, the workers, who were suffering from dismally low wages, abnormally high inflation, acute food shortage and social indignity, had good reasons to rise up.

The realities of the political situation at that time also made it necessary for Lee and his fellow freedom-fighters to woo the Chinese-educated and the communist-controlled trade unions, as well as to work with the communists in an anti-colonial front. So when they decided it was time to form their own political party and draw up their anti-colonial campaign during their regular meetings in the basement of Lee's house at Oxley Road, they would take this line of action to enjoy popular support. They agreed that the party should be a left-wing, mass-based, multi-racial, democratic and socialist organisation.

They believed their chances in the political arena were good as the political parties in existence then lacked clout and mass support. The main ones were the right-wing pro-British Singapore Progressive Party and the moderate left wing Labour Front. They were unlikely to cause any problems. The Malayan Democratic Union (MDU) formed in December 1945 by the Communist Party of Malaya (CPM), had gone into oblivion after the declaration of the Emergency in 1948. Only the underground CPM posed the biggest threat.

After deliberations, "the basement anti-colonial plotters" named their party People's Action Party (PAP). For the symbol, they chose a red flash of lightning over a blue circle on a white background to reflect what the party stood for. The red flash represented action; the blue circle, unity of all races; and the white background, purity and integrity.

The party positioned itself as non-communist rather than anti-communist. Its leaders included old Malayan Forum comrades like Lee Kuan Yew, Dr Toh Chin Chye and Dr Goh Keng Swee, as well as S Rajaratnam and Ong Pang Boon. Rajaratnam, a veteran journalist, drafted the manifesto. It was a difficult task because as he put it, "individuals in the group had different views and interpretations of terms such as democracy and socialism".

The PAP's inauguration took place on Sunday morning, 21 November 1954, at the Victoria Memorial Hall. The Hall and the adjoining Victoria Theatre, built by the colonial government, were the favourite entertainment grounds of the colonial masters, families and friends for their concerts, dances and other social functions. In front, on a tall concrete pedestal, stood the statue of Stamford Raffles with arms folded on chest, feet placed apart and eyes glowering over the local populace as if to say: "I am master of all I survey." The spot is said to be Raffles' landing site. No place could have been symbolically more appropriate for the birth of the anti-colonial PAP. Although a quiet, low-profile affair, it was the largest political event yet, with more than 1,500 supporters and guests witnessing the historic occasion. The meeting elected Dr Toh Chin Chye as Chairman of the First Central Executive Committee and Lee Kuan Yew as Secretary. The designation was subsequently renamed Secretary-General. The other committee members included some communists and pro-communists, in line with Lee's policy of working with them to achieve the ultimate goal: independence through merger with Malaya.

From across the causeway came leading nationalists such as Tunku Abdul Rahman, President of the United Malay National Organisation (UMNO), and Tan Cheng Lock, President of the Malayan Chinese Association (MCA). The Tunku had been one of the Malayan Forum members in London.

The manifesto spelt out the PAP's purpose and its plan of action. Colonialism was evil as it served only the commercial fortunes of the British and therefore must be removed as soon as possible. Those who believed that colonialism would go away by itself failed to understand its nature and workings. They were fooling themselves and the people, because the British had no intention of leaving.

But the PAP had no illusions about the British scheme of things. The party knew full well the primary purpose of the constitutional changes the British had made in 1946 when they hived off Singapore from Malaya. The struggle was a serious matter to be tackled with purpose and vigour. The party wanted genuine independence through merger with Malaya and was not afraid of it. Independence meant complete control of the administration, economy, defence and other spheres of endeavour. The party would oppose any constitution that merely gave lip service to the cause. The PAP believed that unity of the economic, political and cultural interests of the Malayan people was vital. It debunked the argument that linguistic differences were a barrier to political unity and independence. Given the multi-racial composition of Malaya, official recognition should be accorded to Chinese, Tamil, English and Malay languages. The party was prepared to work with others who were genuinely interested in attaining real, not spurious, independence for the country. Independence was a viable proposition. The party had a genuine interest in the problems of the people on both sides of the causeway.

Every true Malayan with any self-respect wanted freedom, as millions of other Asians did. Everywhere in Asia, its people who had won independence were marching forward. They had pride in their worth as human beings with the confidence and ability to direct their own destiny as they wished. Singapore should do the same. What the country needed was a popularly elected government which really believed in the need for and the urgency of self-government. The PAP was the answer to the people's dreams of a free and better life. It would lead the way.

The manifesto also called, among other things, for the abolition of the Emergency Regulations which the British had enacted in June 1948 to stamp out the communists' armed insurrection in Malaya. The PAP considered the regulations serious restrictions on the activities of progressive anti-colonial forces and on the work of trade unions.

In his maiden speech, Chairman Toh Chin Chye, then a lecturer in physiology at the University of Malaya, laid down the foundation for the arduous task ahead. He declared: "A country, big or small, can only be great if the spirit of the people is great. That spirit must be devoted to the service of the country and of the people. The People's Action Party will foster this spirit. We have every confidence that the people are with us and that the Malayan people can shape their own destiny."

The coming of the PAP drew mixed reactions. The pro-British *The Straits Times* dismissed the party with derision, inferences and sarcasm. The newspaper's editorial on 24 November 1954 said the PAP policy was nicely calculated to attract the unthinking and that it was a feast of promise with little regard to facts. The paper expressed surprise that Tunku Abdul Rahman and Tan Cheng Lock had attended the inauguration ceremony because their own policies would be completely opposed to the new economic order for which the PAP stood.

Said the editorial: "The founders of the PAP could not be expected to be keen on the campaign against communism, but it was remarkable that they should ask for the abolition of the Emergency Regulations, when it was the communists who were the deadly enemy of Malayan nationalism and democracy. The birth of the new party promises at any rate to enliven the political scene in Singapore, and among 230,000 people who had never voted before, there will no doubt be recruits for redistribution."

The English-educated and the business community were suspicious and fearful of the PAP. They regarded it as ultra-left, anti-capitalist and communist. Their misgivings were understandable. During the colonial era, the English-educated, whether they were Chinese, Indian or Malay, were a privileged class, second only to the

Europeans. They had better education, better homes and enjoyed more comforts of life than the non-English-educated people. They held better jobs in the civil service and commercial establishments. As a matter of fact, the then University of Malaya admitted only English-educated students into its faculties. All of the professionals were English-educated and they were happy, contented and apolitical. Now the PAP was vowing to change the comfortable life they were accustomed to. Given the choice, they would rather the British remained.

The English-educated became prophets of doom. As they knew it, socialism meant the end of their privileged position and personal fortunes. This had happened in other countries like China and Russia where everybody was equal and where the state reigned supreme. There was no incentive to work hard and make money. They did not want to live in communes and be contemptuously treated as mere mindless cogs in the wheel, slogging for the greater glory of the country with no fitting rewards for their efforts. A classless, regimented society was not for them. The PAP's symbol alarmed them. It looked menacing and ominous. It aptly exemplified the party's revolutionary intentions. To the English-educated, it was hardly reassuring and comforting.

The apprehension of the English-educated was clearly evident in the letters to the newspapers. In one series of correspondence in *The Straits Times* in August 1958, a Singapore reader calling himself "Anti-Petir" (*Petir* is the PAP's official organ) wrote: "The object he [Lee Kuan Yew] has in mind is admirable but what would it ultimately lead to with the Malay, Indian and other foreign-educated people claiming a share, all of whom have the right to participate in the fruits of *merdeka* [freedom]?"

From across the causeway, a critical Singapore-watcher from Kota Bahru in northern Malaya, Wong Yeow Wye, wrote in August 1958: "Communism professes to fight for social justice. This is very tempting to simple-minded students and the illiterate workers who are not satisfied with the existing social order."

Lee, as Secretary-General of the PAP, rebutted these criticisms and allayed their anxieties. In one of his letters published in *The Straits Times* on 8 August 1958, he said: "It is the misfortune of the English-educated that they were never educated to understand the social revolution which has swept across the Asian continent. Democracy does not mean the preservation of the present privileges of the English-educated. If we are going to make the democratic system a living and integral part of the lives of our people, the English-educated must understand that they have to compete on equal terms with the others."

The English-educated were also puzzled by the intentions of the PAP's leaders such as Lee, Dr Toh Chin Chye, Dr Goh Keng Swee and S Rajaratnam. These men were themselves English-educated and of middle-class stock. So why were they trying to build a communist-like state in Singapore? What did they mean by socialism and equality? Were they anti-capitalist? The PAP was also consorting with the communists and even had some of them as office-bearers. Adding to the fears and suspicions of the English-educated, the PAP's huge following comprised the Chinese-educated and Chinese middle school students. At that time, it was widely believed that all Chinese school students were either communists or pro-communists.

Dispelling the belief that all Chinese-educated are communists, Lee said: "This assumption is not only fallacious but dangerous. For a policy based on this assumption could well make the assumption ultimately true."

In another letter published on 28 August 1958 in reply to more critiques, Lee said: "The dominant attitude among your correspondents is fear for their personal fortunes, and resentment against those who appear to symbolise social revolution. The English-educated must discard the sterile mental habits of the past and regard the revolutionary era we all live in today as a unique challenge. They have a vital role to perform in this country and if they fail in this, the country will be the poorer for it."

On the other hand, the non-English-educated hailed the new PAP as their saviour from the social injustices to which they were being subjected. They had the worst of the economic bargains. For most, life was a hand-to-mouth existence. Unable to speak or write English, they became shop assistants, hawkers, taxi-drivers, trishaw-riders, delivery boys, postmen, labourers, maids and the like. They lived in *kampungs* and other humble dwellings, many even in crowded cubicles. Even teachers in Chinese, Malay and Tamil schools were paid less than their counterparts in English-stream schools. They were the ones who had much to fight for.

Of course, not all the non-English-educated were destitute or illiterate. Their main drawback was they knew little or no English, a great disadvantage in a country where the English-speaking dominated. Yet, there were many enterprising non-English-educated who were wealthy, even millionaires. They went into business as provision shop owners, importers, exporters, textile merchants, commodity traders, stockbrokers, contractors or public transport operators. But here was the paradox. They were the non-English-educated who did not relish the prospect of a PAP rule. Their fears can be summed up in one line: "What would become of our business?"

Being English-educated myself, I was anti-PAP in those uncertain, hazy days of the social revolution. One day at the Novena Church at Thomson Road where I used to worship, I met a member of the church choir, Teresa Tan, who said she was a first cousin of Lee Kuan Yew, her mother Lee Wee Neo being the younger sister of Lee Chin Koon, Lee Kuan Yew's father. I asked Teresa whether her cousin was a communist. She replied that she was not sure, but she and the rest of her family members (and her father was a civil servant, too) would not vote for the PAP. All her neighbours were also afraid of them and would do the same. But there was a girl from an English-educated family living a few doors away who attended a Chinese middle school. While the rest of her family members were against the PAP, she was forever shouting: "PAP! ...PAP!"

There was no doubt that Lee and the PAP were having great success in amassing a large following among Chinese-school students as well as the working class and the illiterate. With their inequitable social status and/or low subsistence level in the stream of Singapore's economic life, they all believed they had nothing to lose but much to gain from supporting the party. It was clear whom they trusted. The groundswell rose as the anti-colonial campaign gathered speed. Could they win the day? A climate of fear descended on the English-educated. Did they have a fighting chance? The ballot box would soon provide the answers.

06

LEE VS MARSHALL

In 1955, Lee Kuan Yew began his political career when he participated in the general election for the Legislative Assembly on 2 April. The election followed Britain's decision to grant Singapore limited internal self-government under what was called the Rendel Constitution. This was a momentous development in the decolonisation process for it marked the first breakthrough on the road to independence. The Legislative Assembly comprised 32 seats with 25 of them reserved for local representation who would serve a four-year term headed by a chief minister. The new body replaced the Legislative Council, which held its second and last election in 1951, where the pro-British Progressive Party had once again dominated.

The grant of limited self-government to Singapore came in the wake of the British decision to accord Malaya its national independence. Although the move was a boon to Singapore politics, the real reason was to stamp out the communist insurgency which was attacking British planters. It was calculated that with independence in Malaya, the communists would no longer have any more excuse to continue with their anti-colonial fight. The British had full confidence in staunch anti-communist Tunku Abdul Rahman and his moderate, broad-based UMNO-MCA-MIC (Malayan Indian Congress) Alliance. The right-wing Alliance also had a solid base of support.

The April election was the defining moment for the *dramatis personae* in the political drama, the time for testing their popularity or unpopularity. For the first time, the people were able to discern their strengths and weaknesses, to separate the men from the boys, so to speak. The players who stood out, other than Lee of the PAP, were David Marshall and Lim Yew Hock of the Labour Front, and C C Tan and John Laycock of the Progressive Party. The Labour Front was a new political party which Marshall and Lim had formed in 1954 to replace the Labour Party founded in 1948. Marshall was a famous criminal lawyer. Lim was a leading trade unionist, an ex-member of the Progressive Party and the former Labour Party, as well as a nominated member of the now defunct Legislative Council.

The PAP was unimpressed with the Rendel Constitution, dismissing it as inadequate and below expectations. Among the shortcomings, the chief minister would hold the internal affairs portfolio only, with the British controlling internal security, foreign affairs and defence, and a British governor as head. Thus, the PAP decided on a token participation and fielded only four candidates, one of whom was Lee. The party took the opportunity to publicise its policies and aspirations and enhance its profile. Participation would also demonstrate its sincerity that it was pursuing the independence fight through constitutional means.

The historic election drew 69 candidates from six political parties and 10 independent candidates contesting for 25 constituencies. Lee deliberately chose Tanjong Pagar. As he described it, the constituency was a working-class area. No other division had such a high proportion of workers, like wage earners and small traders, or such a low proportion of wealthy merchants and landlords. A large number of the residents were members of the trade unions he had helped, including the Postal and Telecommunications Uniformed Staff Union. Lee knew their hardships and problems. He wanted to represent them. His three PAP candidate-colleagues were Goh Chew Chua (Punggol-Tampines), Lim Chin Siong (Bukit Timah) and C V Devan Nair (Farrer Park). These were also relatively poor residential districts.

Marshall of the Labour Front stood at Cairnhill, a classy rich man's enclave, while colleague Lim opted for Havelock in Chinatown, home of the proletariat. In all, the party offered 17 candidates. The other contestants, besides C C Tan and John Laycock of the Progressive Party, were lesser-known politicians from the Democratic Party which was regarded as a rich man's club, the UMNO-MCA-SMU (Singapore Malay Union) Alliance and the Liberal Socialists. The electorate numbered about 300,000.

The month-long election campaign served as a wake-up call for those who were still apolitical. Certainly, the hustings generated greater interest than the two previous ones for the old

Legislative Council. The people were witnessing a real election for local representation, not bogus sideshows serving the interests of the British. Huge numbers attended the over 40 rallies. But it was the PAP which drew the largest gathering, particularly Lee's rallies. They had heard of this radical freedom-fighter and of his reputation in the trade unions. They surged around to hear him denounce colonialism and pronounce his promises for the future. The enormous, throbbing crowds were unnerving to the English-educated, not to mention the Special Branch.

As this was his first election campaign, Lee battled hard to establish his public profile to win the ground. His speeches were electrifying as he rallied the people in a booming, compelling voice to vote for the PAP for an equal, just and fair society for all. He emphasised his points with gritted teeth, clenched fists, wild gesticulations of arms and shouts of *Merdeka*! (the Malay word for freedom). Lusty cheers reverberated as his points struck home. The PAP's election platform was all-encompassing. It covered political, social, civil administration and economic matters. No other party contesting the polls offered such a comprehensive package.

Among the political issues the PAP championed were a fully elected Legislative Assembly with complete sovereignty, merger with Malaya, abolition of the Emergency Regulations and amendment of the Labour Ordinance. The social matters included a minimum wage, equal pay for men and women, free education for all children under 16 years old and slum clearance. In civil administration, the PAP promised the same pay and condition of service for employees in the British military bases as for those in the civil service. On the economic front, the party would impose tariffs to protect local industry and to have complete control of the Malayan trade. The audience was impressed.

Lee also strove to prove he was a Chinese. At that time, his proficiency in this tongue was low. Still he tried. It was at the Bandar Street square where the crowd was estimated at 60,000, the largest ever seen, that he made his first speech in Mandarin. He was fortunate to have a friend and supporter, Jek Yeun Thong, with him. Jek wrote a simple speech in Mandarin for him. As Lee was to say later, the speech was crucial and a life-saver when he could not speak Chinese. He never forgot Jek's help.

When polling day came, 53 percent of the electorate cast their votes. Although voting was not compulsory, the good response confirmed the new political mood in the country.

An interesting fact at that time was that voters chose the candidates they liked, not so much the party they represented per se. As yet, ideologies meant very little to them. Their first priority was filling their stomachs. They knew who represented the poor and could help, and who represented the rich. So it was that the residents of Tanjong Pagar gave Lee a thumping majority of more than 5,000 votes over his opponents from the Progressive Party and Democratic Party. The other two PAP candidates were also successful. Only Devan Nair lost, to Labour Front's A R Lazarous and that by a slim margin of 366 votes. Lee and the PAP had passed their first baptism of fire. The electorate rejected the pro-British Progressive Party and the rich man's Democratic Party.

Marshall and Lim won as the Labour Front carried the day by capturing 10 of the 17 seats it had contested. Although it failed to gain a majority in the Legislative Assembly, the party formed

Singapore's first elected government. The government was set up in coalition with the UMNO-MCA-SMU Alliance which won three seats, and with the Chief Secretary, Financial Secretary and the Attorney-General on the British side. The three, in their ex-officio capacities, had the legal duty to support the government. Marshall became Singapore's first Chief Minister.

Marshall and Lim were popular among the English-educated and business circles. This section of the population perceived them as moderates and sensible men, never proclaiming radical views that threatened to upset their settled order of life. They were their answer to the radical Lee and the PAP. One of Marshall's favourite methods of reaching out to the people was holding court under a so-called apple tree at Empress Place with the lunchtime crowd, lambasting the British and vowing to gain immediate independence and merger with Malaya. He was a familiar sight with his trademark dress code, a white bush jacket, which earned him the picturesque nickname of "the man in the bush jacket under the old apple tree".

Marshall got his chance to show his mettle as a politician when he became Chief Minister. But alas for him, the communists found this was the time to show their teeth in their grand design for a communist Malaya. Presumably, they were trying to gauge his strengths and weaknesses.

On 24 April, before Marshall had a chance to warm his seat, workers of the Hock Lee Bus Company went on strike. They were members of the communist-dominated Singapore Bus Workers' Union. As they picketed at the bus depot at Alexandra Road, their counterparts in seven other bus companies, and employees of about 50 business firms, staged sympathy strikes. A group of

Chinese middle school students went out to support them.

Before the industrial strife ended three weeks later, rioting had erupted on 12 May. This was one of the most explosive civil unrests of the mid-1950s. Rampaging mobs swarmed through the streets, shouting, yelling, attacking those in the way, burning cars, damaging property and battling the police with sticks, broken bottles, stones and other missiles. Soldiers in full battle gear helped the police quell the disturbances, using tear gas, water cannons and warning gunshots. Roadblocks were erected at strategic points. When they failed to get through, the rioters turned and surged in other directions, still screaming and wreaking havoc. Dozens were arrested. Frightened Singaporeans huddled indoors. The street violence left four people dead and 31 others injured. The dead were Detective Corporal Yuen Yan Peng, Volunteer Special Constable Andrew Yeo Bok Lan, United Press correspondent Gene Symonds, and 16-year-old Chinese middle school student Chong Lon Chong.

During the height of the civil unrest, an island-wide curfew was imposed, allowing people to go out only for a few hours each day for their shopping, banking and other necessities. Civilian life came to a standstill. The police periodically warned over the radio: "Stay indoors, or you are liable to be shot." At *The Straits Times* where I was a reporter, the European staff cowered in fear in the canteen during the mayhem.

Marshall blamed Lee and the PAP for the street violence. He accused them of being a communist base. Lee retorted that his party was committed to a peaceful political process. He said the PAP could not be held accountable for the actions of every member acting in his individual capacity. It was the duty of the government to keep law and order and detain the rabble-rousers.

Lee and Marshall were always at loggerheads on many national issues. In the Legislative Assembly, Lee was an able opposition Assemblyman, a thorn in Marshall's flesh. They tore at each other hammer and tongs. Lee performed his duties creditably. He was firm, consistent and forceful. He had an excellent knowledge of the ground. He supported or criticised the Chief Minister as the case may be. In contrast, Marshall was inconsistent and seemed to be out of his wits on certain matters. Examples were his poor handling of the violence besetting the country and his wavering stance on the question of self-government which was to prove costly to his political career.

Marshall did take some action about the civil commotion. He detained several trade union and student leaders involved in the Hock Lee Bus riots. He ordered Chinese High School, Nanyang Girls' High School and Chung Cheng High School, hotbeds of communist activities, either to expel their rebellious students or he would close the schools. But he failed to carry out his threats. His reasons were that shutting the schools would tar his party image and that in any case, the students had genuine complaints about the colonial education policy. He promised to study their problems and to register the Singapore Chinese Middle School Students' Union. This was a triumph for the students.

Marshall also had an acrimonious relationship with the British. He was particularly irked by the overriding power of the governor. The British components in the administration, comprising the Chief Secretary, Financial Secretary, Attorney-General and Commissioner of Police, reported to the colonial authorities, not to him. He loathed being just a figurehead. He demanded immediate full internal self-government to give him wider powers than the Rendel Constitution did. He also pushed for, among other proposals, Malayanisation (localisation) of the civil service, repeal of the Emergency Regulations and citizenship for those born in Singapore and those who had lived here long.

After some reluctance, and realising that they could not stop the decolonisation process, the British agreed to discuss the proposals and set London as the venue. The first Merdeka Talks, as they became popularly known, opened in London on 23 April 1956. Marshall led a 13-member all-party delegation, including six Assemblymen from his government and six from the opposition. The opposition members included Assemblyman Lee Kuan Yew.

At first, the talks yielded some results. The British agreed to grant Singapore full internal self-government, Malayanisation and its own citizenship laws. However, they insisted on controlling internal security besides foreign affairs and defence. They told Marshall that he was soft since he had failed to contain the civil disorder in Singapore. They did not believe he could control internal security and were not prepared to leave it to chance. Marshall was unhappy about the British having the last say on internal security. On this score, the talks reached an impasse and broke down after three weeks of hard negotiations.

Marshall had promised to resign as Chief Minister if the talks failed. The beleaguered man kept his word on 6 June after his return to Singapore. He had led the nation for only 14 months. Labour Front colleague Lim Yew Hock succeeded him on 8 June. Marshall became an ordinary Assemblyman. The English-educated were deeply disappointed with his poor performance. They had held high hopes for him and now concluded that he lacked political acumen, political will and staying power. Where was the fire he spewed under the old apple tree at Empress Place? The English-educated now placed their trust on his successor, Lim Yew Hock.

Lim proved to be a different kettle of fish. Between September and October 1956, he de-registered two communist front organisations, banished the president and six members of the Singapore Factory and Shop Workers' Union, and banned the Singapore Chinese Middle School Students' Union which Marshall had allowed to be registered. The students protested vehemently and several of the leaders were arrested.

However, the drastic measures only sparked more civil unrests. Communists and pro-communists made inflammatory speeches, accusing the Lim Yew Hock government of suppressing Chinese student activities. They incited the people to rise and save the students. Rioting broke out on 25 October 1956 and in five bloody days, 13 people died, more than 100 others injured and over 100 vehicles burnt or damaged. One of those killed was a reporter friend of mine. He was cleaved on the skull when he went too close to the angry rabble while covering the rioting. Another island-wide curfew was imposed and the Preservation of Public Security Ordinance was invoked to end the bedlam and bloodshed.

In all, about 900 people deemed responsible for the havoc were arrested. The detained included 15 Middle Road trade union leaders (so-called because Middle Road was their headquarters). It was a prize catch as among those nabbed were known communists or pro-communists such as Lim Chin Siong, Fong Swee Suan, C V

Devan Nair, James Puthucheary and S Woodhull. As a follow-up action, the government de-registered the Farmers' Association and the Singapore Factory and Shop Workers' Union.

I had met Puthucheary, Fong and a few other Middle Road unionists previously regarding a labour story I was assigned to write. To my great surprise, they were all courtesy and politeness. "Come in, come in. Please sit down. Have a drink. What can we do for you?" They did not strike me as wild extremists determined to overthrow the government by violent means.

I also once attended a bus workers' meeting where Lim Chin Siong was one of the speakers and where I saw the raw side of these revolutionaries. Lim was a mild-faced man, but he was fiery and eloquent. Speaking in Hokkien, he kept the workers cheering as he attacked the establishment, the exploitation by employers and other contentious issues of the day.

Needless to say, Lim Yew Yock was labelled a British stooge for his strong arm tactics. Indeed, the British were pleased with him. So was Tunku Abdul Rahman who was now Chief Minister of the Federation of Malaya and who had been watching the situation with growing anxiety. He declared: "That's the stuff. They should have done it long ago." The British found Lim to be stronger and more capable of keeping law and order than Marshall. They were therefore more accommodating when the Merdeka Talks resumed in London on 11 March 1957. Lim led an all-party delegation which again included Lee Kuan Yew.

In the month-long negotiations, the two sides resolved the thorny issue of internal security. The British now agreed to equal representation in the Internal Security Council. The Council would be filled by three British, three Singaporeans and one representative from the Federation of Malaya who would have the casting vote. Singapore was promised a new constitution, its own head of state to replace the British governor, as well as its own citizenship laws. Britain would look after defence and foreign affairs only. Lim Yew Hock returned to Singapore on a triumphant note.

The PAP accepted the new Singapore Constitution, declaring it a vast improvement over the Rendel Constitution. The Legislative Assembly sat on 26 April1957 to debate the issue and recommended that the agreement be finalised. During the debate, David Marshall voiced his opposition in the strongest terms. His main objection was the clause on subversion. Fireworks then flew between him and Lee, as such recriminations often did. But this was the most heated. Briefly, Marshall accused Lee of "double-crossing" the people at the London talks. He shouted across the floor: "I will go to his constituency and challenge him there."

It was a grave error of judgement. The challenge proved to be his downfall when Lee stood up at once and replied: "Accepted." Marshall had thrown the gauntlet at the wrong man.

At a news conference afterwards, Lee explained:

> This will be a clash between individual criticism and collective steadfastness. I will take Mr Marshall on in any constituency, Tanjong Pagar or Cairnhill. It is a clear-cut issue of whether the people are prepared to accept the new constitution and reject the clause on subversion or would prefer to accept the clause and reject the constitution. We support the constitution which we agreed to and we oppose the clause on

> subversion which we did not accept. On the contrary, Mr Marshall termed the constitution a sell-out and agreed to the principle of the clause banning subversive elements from the next elections. The people of Singapore will have to decide between the two stands.

Marshall retorted:

> Good, good. Certainly I will fight him. I will fight him in any ward he chooses. Do the people of Singapore want the constitution or not? It's up to the people to decide whether they want his monkey business or my integrity.

Lee and Marshall resigned from the Legislative Assembly to go back to the people, leaving the Tanjong Pagar and Cairnhill seats vacant. The by-election took place on 29 June 1957. In the end, Marshall stood neither at Tanjong Pagar nor at his own constituency of Cairnhill. Lee retained his Tanjong Pagar seat, defeating two unknown opponents by a majority of 3,392 votes. With Marshall not contesting, his Cairnhill seat went to the Liberal Socialists. He announced that he was "leaving politics permanently". The sworn anti-colonialist had been in politics for just over two years.

But the Lee-Marshall collision at the Legislative Assembly was more than the usual heated exchange of words between hard-headed Assemblymen. There was apparently a sinister motive behind Marshall's challenge, according to Fong Sip Chee's *The PAP Story* quoting from an article, *An Open Conspiracy*, written by a "Founder Member" and published in the PAP's 6th Anniversary

Souvenir publication of 31 December 1960. Basically, Marshall was the victim of the manipulation of "left-wing adventurers". They used him to attack the new constitution and discredit Lee and the PAP. In return, they promised to help him regain his declining political fortunes. Whether or not Marshall realised the implications and consequences of the conspiracy, he agreed. But the PAP knew of their machinations and when Lee accepted Marshall's dare to resign, their scheme backfired, leaving the former Chief Minister out on a limb.

A senior PAP member who had been a school classmate told me ominously after the 1955 general election: "We will show you what politics is all about. You have not seen anything yet. We will change your thinking." Unfortunately for David Marshall, he did not learn the finer points of politics quickly enough.

However, the communist united front continued with their bid to usurp the PAP. They launched their boldest attempt yet during the election for the fourth Central Executive Committee (CEC) on 4 August 1957. The brazen move was typical of their standard tactics of using proxies, in this case the PAP, in their grand design for a communist Malaya. It must be remembered that the first CEC had four communist officials. Although there was none in the second CEC, there were four in the third.

Before the voting for the 12-member CEC began, Lee told the gathering of over 3,000 that eight of the 12 officials were prepared to hold office again. But when the votes were counted, only five of the eight he had proposed were returned. They included Chairman Dr Toh Chin Chye and Lee himself. Among those rejected was Treasurer Ong Eng Guan. The communist faction filled six of the other seven seats with their own people. Quick to discern their intentions, Lee and his other elected colleagues declined to take office. They refused to be used as a communist front, arguing that this would destroy the PAP's reputation as a democratic, socialist, non-communist party. The counter-move was a masterful stroke which, to use chess game jargon, checkmated them. The *coup d'état* failed. All the six communists elected shunned the job as well. Lee and his team stood their ground, despite appeals for their leadership. For more than a week, the PAP was leaderless. Finally, on 13 August, the communist side was forced to assume office. T T Rajah, a teacher-turned-lawyer, became Secretary-General, replacing Lee. But their reign was short.

The end came when the Lim Yew Hock government conducted a mass arrest on 21 and 22 August, detaining 35 communists and pro-communists. They included five of the six communist PAP CEC officials. The purge left Rajah holding the baby. Unwilling to carry out his responsibilities, he resigned on 25 August. Lee concluded that Rajah simply had no leadership qualities. The episode again demonstrated the calibre of Lee and his team. Had they fallen into the trap, the course of Singapore's history would have been different.

Was Lim Yew Hock's crackdown coincidental? Whatever the reasons, the clean-up paved the way for Lee and his group to resume control of the PAP. The party immediately took steps to safeguard itself from similar manipulations in the future. In previous CEC elections, voting had been thrown to the floor. The party amended its constitution permitting only cadres to vote.

A new political process was developing. This was the City Council election held on 21 December 1957 under the Rendel

Constitution. With its internal crisis resolved, the PAP was fully geared up to contest the polls. The City Council was actually the local government charged with municipal tasks. Eighty-one candidates from five political parties, plus several independents, contested the 32 divisions. The PAP fielded 14 candidates, while the Liberal Socialists went for all 32 seats. Oddly enough, the ruling Labour Front fought in only 16 wards. Absent was the Progressive Party. A newcomer was the Workers' Party which fielded five candidates. The big surprise was the party founder—David Marshall. He had announced his retirement after the debacle in the Legislative Assembly. Now he was back on the scene. However, he did not take part but supported his five colleagues.

The PAP won, capturing 13 seats. The victory further consolidated the party's standing among the people. The Labour Front performed dismally, winning only four seats, the Liberal Socialists seven, and the Workers Party four. The remaining four seats were split equally between the UMNO Alliance and Independents. The Labour Front had lost a great deal of ground. Realising the realities after a post mortem, Lim Yew Hock later founded a new party, Singapore People's Alliance, to try to strengthen his position and regain the people's confidence.

With the victory, the PAP Treasurer Ong Eng Guan became Singapore's first and only mayor. Ong acquitted himself well in his job. He introduced drastic reforms such as revamping Singapore's municipal services from water supply to healthcare to bus shelters. The improvements brought into sharp focus the utter neglect of the colonial government. The people began to see the fruits of the PAP's promises. Even the English-educated could not but be impressed with the party's good track record. (The City Council was later abolished as Singapore's small size had no need for such a body.)

Flushed with the rapid progress the PAP was making, Lee Kuan Yew prepared himself to take part in the third and final round of the Merdeka Talks convened in April and May 1958 to finalise the new Singapore Constitution. Chief Minister Lim Yew Hock again led an all-party delegation. The negotiations went well, with all the relevant points resolved. The agreement was signed on 28 May. The pact gave Singapore full powers of internal self-government and the status of a state. The nation would no longer be a colony. The old shameful stigma was gone forever. The next stage was the first general election under the new constitution. The date was set for 30 May 1959. Voting was made compulsory this time.

Returning to Singapore on 2 June after the successful Merdeka Talks, Lee was brimming with excitement and anticipation. He announced at a news conference at the airport that the PAP was ready to assume power if elected. Singapore was about to witness the dawn of a new era, as it moved closer to independence, a plan that Lee first plotted at the Malayan Forum in London in the 1940s.

07

A NEW ERA FOR SINGAPORE

During the tumultuous 1950s, I lived in a quaint pre-war terrace houses at Thomson Road, each with a wall-enclosed garage in front and a flat cement roof served by a spiral stone staircase. On an evening, one could sit atop the open-air roof and gaze at the stars. About 200 metres to the right was the Red Bridge near Kampong Java Road, where Lee Kuan Yew was born and where a senseless Japanese sentry had manhandled him during the early days of the occupation and where, as I have mentioned, an armed soldier had pointed his loaded rifle at my chest as I stopped at the road-block there during one of the riots in the mid-1950s.

The houses have since been ploughed under to make way for the United Square complex. While they stood, however, the humble middle-class neighbourhood boasted a piece of Singapore's history. We had in our midst one of the PAP's leaders—Ong Pang Boon. Ong, educated in both Chinese and English, lived just a few doors away from me. As most of us were English-educated and yes, anti-PAP, his presence seemed rather ironic. It was like having the enemy within. We felt a bit embarrassed, probably the same way that residents of Oxley Road must have felt about Lee Kuan Yew during those uneasy and uncertain days.

Ong had come to Singapore from Kuala Lumpur in Malaya to help in the PAP's cause at the request of Lee, leaving behind a lucrative profession. Ong was a quiet neighbour. He went about his business unobtrusively, not bothering anyone. There were no rowdy, all-night political party meetings. In fact, I thought he was the perfect gentleman with a mild, bespectacled face to match. Being civilised ourselves, we left Ong alone. We merely viewed him with a wary eye as we continued to express our grave concerns behind his back over the PAP's grand design for Singapore.

Ong's composed manner belied his intense dedication to the mission and the fire in him. (He was to become Home Affairs Minister and later Education Minister in the PAP government.) The PAP, having performed creditably in the 1955 election for the Legislative Assembly and the 1957 election for the City Council, now targeted the landmark general election for Singapore's first full self-government scheduled for 30 May 1959.

The privileged English-educated had watched the party's successes in the previous polls with alarm and trepidation. The writing was on the wall. As the campaign for the May election gained momentum, their fears mounted. In their heart of hearts, they were not overly enthusiastic about self-government or independence.

They were happy as they were, under the British. They predicted a miserable existence if the PAP came into power. Already, the anti-colonial movement was causing the people great anguish and inconvenience with frequent strikes, bus-less days, student unrests, riots and curfews. Where would all these lead to, they wondered anxiously. One of my neighbours put the despair of the English-educated succinctly: "What's all this about independence? I want to live in peace. I want to walk the streets safely at night."

As if in a desperate, last-ditch effort to smear the PAP, many of the English-educated wrote warning letters in the newspapers. Perhaps the strongest anti-PAP sentiment was expressed by a reader in *The Straits Times'* "Forum" page on 2 May 1959: "The actions and methods of the PAP are characteristic of totalitarian parties—Fascist and Communist—and I fear that if the PAP comes into power, the people of Singapore will become victims of a state where civil liberties will be ruthlessly and systematically extinguished and the people herded and regimented into battalions of slaves for the glory of the PAP leaders."

If the English-educated had hitherto been apolitical and apathetic, the realities of the situation now woke them up. More and more began to accept that the tide could not be stemmed, unless they exercised their voting rights and blocked the PAP's onward march. This was in their interests. Most English-educated saw that Chief Minister Lim Yew Hock could be their trump card. They plumped for him because he was a moderate-left and a stout anti-communist. The mild-looking, pipe-smoking politician had proved his mettle through his tough measures during the civil commotions of 1956 and 1957. He was regarded as the best alternative to the PAP. His adamant stand against violent disturbances could serve Singapore well and provide the security it needed. No other opposition candidate deserved any worthy consideration. David Marshall had re-emerged from his "retirement" and founded a new party, Workers' Party. But he had disappointed them before and they had lost faith in him.

To be sure, the electorate in the City Council election had rejected Lim and his Labour Front party. However, Lim had formed a new political party, Singapore People's Alliance (SPA), to contest the coming polls. He was rejuvenating his political career and strengthening his position, which was reassuring to many English-educated. As the date of the election drew near, the English-educated braced themselves for the challenge. They knew what they had to do.

The election drew 12 political parties to the fray. A total of 194 candidates including 34 independents took part. At stake were 51 constituencies. The main parties were the PAP, which contested in all 51 seats, SPA (39), Liberal Socialists (32), and the Workers' Party (3). It was suggestive that the pro-British Progressive Party was again absent. They had closed shop, knowing that they had become irrelevant in Singapore politics.

Lee stood in his constituency of Tanjong Pagar where he had found victory in 1955. The other party leaders contesting included Dr Toh Chin Chye (Rochor), Dr Goh Keng Swee (Kreta Ayer), S Rajaratnam (Kampong Glam), Ong Eng Guan (Hong Lim), and my neighbour from Thomson Road, Ong Pang Boon (Telok Ayer).

Lim Yew Hock of the Singapore People's Alliance (SPA), on whom the hopes of the English-educated rested, chose Cairnhill, the old ward of David Marshall. But Marshall re-appeared to contest there again to oppose his former colleague in the defunct Labour Front.

The electorate had doubled to over 590,000. Voting was compulsory and, for the first time, the voters were citizens, not British subjects. This was the result of the Singapore Citizenship Bill passed in October 1957, one of the issues agreed to under the new constitution that Marshall had proposed as Chief Minister.

The contest was fiercely fought and the attendances at the political rallies during the month-long campaign were significantly larger than in any of the previous ones, reflecting the new political awareness. The throbbing throngs cheered, jeered and shouted slogans. Opposing candidates sold their party platforms, suggestions and comments, and threw mud at one another. In between the rallies, party supporters rode on open lorries through shopping centres, markets and residential areas, blaring their messages raucously through crackling loudspeakers, and flying their party banners. Cries of "PAP", "Singapore People's Alliance", "Liberal Socialist" and "Workers' Party" resounded throughout the island. The atmosphere was tense and frightening.

As in the 1955 general election, the largest crowds flocked to the PAP rallies. Lee Kuan Yew, Dr Toh Chin Chye, Dr Goh Keng Swee, S Rajaratnam and others spelt out what their party stood for and why it was the one to vote for. They reiterated their all-encompassing election platform. If elected, they promised to build more factories to create jobs, revamp the bureaucracy, improve inefficient government services, build more schools and low-cost public housing, raise the status of women, recognise the special position of the Malay people and other vital social issues. They would deal with the communist threat and bring peace and security.

Lee and his team drove home the message that this election was not just about ousting the British and gaining independence. It was what they could do afterwards that mattered. There were difficult and pressing problems that must be resolved before the people could have the peace and prosperity they sought. Most of the other politicians did not fully understand the deeper implications of the anti-colonial movement. Instead, they focused on attacking the PAP.

Lee was in his element. He had gained a great deal of experience from the 1955 general election and he performed like a veteran. He spoke in English, Malay and Chinese. His proficiency in Mandarin, Hokkien (the most commonly spoken Chinese dialect in Singapore) and Malay had improved considerably, enabling him to get closer to these important ethnic groups.

At a lunchtime rally at Clifford Pier on 8 May, Lee brought up the merger issue, one of his most sought-after political goals. He strongly stressed the benefits of reunion, saying it was a lifeline for Singapore. He lamented the reluctance of Federation of Malaya leaders to consider the matter because they were afraid of upsetting the voting balance between the Chinese and the Malays. He debunked Lim Yew Hock's claim that he (Lim) alone could achieve merger. Lee said Lim could not get merger by running to the airport to receive Tunku Abdul Rahman like a messenger boy. The problem was the balance of power.

Turning to the sensitive subject of the place of the Chinese in Singapore society, Lee assured the huge rally crowd that the Chinese were here to stay because they were Malayans and most of them were peaceful, law-abiding citizens. They could not be packed off to China. Politics had become a serious matter. More purposeful people had joined in to push out "scallywags and opportunists". The PAP's aim was to serve the people. No group of Malayans outside the Communist Party of Malaya (CPM) had such unity and intensity of purpose to bind the people together as the PAP had.

Another concern of the people was communism, the biggest threat to Singapore and Malaya. At a rally at the same place on 25 May, Lee dispelled the suspicion that the PAP was communist, reiterating that the party stood for a democratic, non-communist Malaya. He warned that the CPM wanted to create a Soviet Republic of Malaya. Only the PAP could defeat them. There would be a fight to establish the democratic system in the hearts and minds of the people and it would begin after the election. He declared:

> In this fight, the ultimate contestants will be the PAP and the CPM. It is a battle that cannot be won by just bayonets and bullets. It is a battle of ideals and ideas. And the side that recruits more ability and talent will be the side that wins. We shall not use the tactics of David Marshall and Lim Yew Hock in combating the communists. We shall not be intimidated or browbeaten, nor will we use repression as the means of government. We shall govern with the will and support of the people, firmly, wisely and justly.

Even Lee's wife, Kwa Geok Choo, joined in the campaign. She touched on matters close to the hearts of women to win them over. In a radio broadcast on 8 May, she said:

> Our society is still built on the assumption that women are the social, political and economic inferiors of men. This myth has been made the excuse for the exploitation of female labour. Many women do the same kind of work as men but do not get the same pay. The PAP supports the principle of equal pay for equal work.
>
> But we also face facts. We realise it can be achieved only gradually. But the PAP will do its best to see that women workers are paid a fair wage and are not exploited. We shall also introduce legislation allowing men to have only one wife except in the case of those, like Muslims, whose religious beliefs permit polygamy. Women and their families must be protected against unscrupulous husbands who treat their wives as chattels and abandon their children and families without any thought for their future.
>
> The PAP is the only party to have paid attention to the problems of human rights. We believe that women can make a valuable contribution to our political life. The PAP has done more than just talk. We are fielding five women candidates in the elections—among them the only Malay woman candidate.

The party's women candidates were Chan Choy Siong, Oh Shu Chen, Fung Yin Ching, Ho Puay Choo and Sahorah binte Ahmat. Chan had been a member of the Central Executive Council (CEC) and had given her support to Lee and his team when the communist faction had tried to topple the party in August 1957.

It was inevitable that the PAP should address the misgivings of the English-educated. K M Byrne, candidate for Crawford, put the burning topic in its proper perspective in his rally speech on 10 May at Kampong Kembangan. Byrne assured the crowd:

> The other parties have spread rumours that the PAP cares only for the Chinese, Malay and Tamil-educated people. I tell you it is a lie. The rumours have been spread around to deceive you. We are trying to give everyone an equal chance. In the past, the English-educated always had many advantages over the others. We want to do away with this.

Realising that the PAP was the party to beat, Lim Yew Hock, Chairman of the SPA and candidate for Cairnhill, launched a strong and desperate demolition exercise. He called on democratic forces to unite so that "we can be sure of defeating the PAP". At a lunchtime rally at Fullerton Square on 25 May, Lim attacked the PAP's Dr Toh Chin Chye for calling for the release of political detainees whom Lim had detained during his crackdown in 1956 and 1957. The PAP had asked for their release as a pre-condition to forming a government if elected. Lim asked, "How can they release their comrades without taking office? Do they want me to do this job for them?" He said he doubted that the Federation of Malaya whose representative had the casting vote in the Internal Security Council would be happy about the PAP's call for the release of the detainees.

At an evening rally at Dunman Road the same day, Lim predicted that Lee would lose his Tanjong Pagar seat. He charged:

> [Lee] had been in the Assembly for four years and during this time, what had he done for the voters of Tanjong Pagar? He had done nothing. Ask the voters themselves what he had done. I'm sure they won't be bluffed again.

Statements like this heartened the English-educated and raised their hopes for a PAP defeat. They hoped that those rooting for the PAP would listen and get the message and come to their senses.

Continuing with the SPA's onslaught against the PAP, Freddy Yin Ee Kheng, Administrative Secretary, predicted the PAP would lose, saying in a radio broadcast on 25 May:

> The stock of the PAP has nose-dived and it will never win enough seats to form an effective opposition, much less a majority to form a government. The PAP has come to the end of the road. The people of Singapore have awakened to the danger of this group of people, the menace that it represents. There was a time when observers feared the worst, but today, the picture is quite different.

Meanwhile, the Liberal Socialists warned the people against voting the PAP to power. E K Tan, the party's Secretary-General and candidate for River Valley, asserted at his rally on 10 May:

> If the PAP wins, there will be no human and moral values, individuality, justice, freedom, equality and democracy. Instead, there would be the establishment of privileged classes, terrorism and vassalisation of the

> mind. The communists believe that they can raise the living standards of the people by treating society as a kind of army with a chain of command comprising elites at the top and cadres at the bottom. There is no freedom in such a system. We believe that the form of socialism for Singapore should be different from what communism offers. We believe that the economic system which we have inherited from the colonial era should be modified to give the working class a more human and fair deal.

However, David Marshall of the Workers' Party thought the PAP would win. Marshall made his assessment of the situation at his rally at Buckley Road on 10 May: "Neither the SPA nor the Liberal Socialists or a combination of them, will form a government. You must face the realities." Contesting only three seats, the Workers' Party itself could not hope to form a government, but Marshall spoke his mind on several major issues:

> There must be a permanent commission of inquiry into corruption by politicians and public servants. Integration with the Federation of Malaya, though the hoped-for ideal, is a thing of the distant future now. We must learn to re-orient our policy in order that we and our children may survive independently.

He also took the opportunity to renew his attack on the new constitution over which he and Lee had clashed bitterly at the Legislative Assembly in April1957. He argued:

> The new constitution is a thing of dishonesty—a trap for young politicians. I do not think most of the candidates in the general election really understand the constitution which they ask you to let them work. It is a constitution full of dangers for our welfare, full of hidden tricks.

The election campaign reached fever pitch on the eve of the polls, as the contenders recapped their platforms and made their final appeals. Here are excerpts of the speeches of the leaders of the three main political parties.

Lim Yew Hock of the SPA:

> It is our duty to fight for the preservation of the democratic way of life and to see that Singapore remains free. We cannot afford to sit on the fence, nor can we wistfully hope that if the PAP comes into power they may adopt more moderate methods of carrying out their Marxian socialist programme. Prevention is better than cure.

Lee Kuan Yew of the PAP:

> It has been a full and exhilarating campaign. There were silly moments and some silly issues because our opponents are desperate but stupid men who believe that blabbering and lies can take the place of principles. I am confident that the people of Singapore will teach these political adventurers, and all those who hope to follow in their footsteps, a lesson they will never forget.

E K Tan of the Liberal Socialists:

> Our party has fought a clean election and we have done our best to put our party platform and stand to the people of Singapore. We are sure that all the people who sympathise with us and who want a stable government will vote our candidates in. We believe in freedom and security for Singapore. We believe in helping the people and looking after their day-to-day problems. We have always stood for the democratic ideal views.

With these opposing messages ringing in their ears, the electorate went to the polling booths on Saturday, 30 May 1959, to make their choice in this historic phase of Singapore's political transition. It was Decision Day. The weather was kind but the atmosphere was tense. Police and Special Branch men stood by to maintain law and order. My polling booth was at the Convent of the Good Shepherd at Kampong Java Road where the rambling bungalow of Lee Kuan Yew's maternal grandfather Chua Kim Teng once stood and where Lee was born. I went with my parents, brothers and some of our neighbours. Party supporters milled outside the premises. They were orderly. As we were about to enter the gate, they made their last-minute sales pitch, in soft voices, for their respective party candidates. But we, the English-educated, had already made up our minds.

We prayed that the PAP would lose.

08

BUILDING A BRAVE NEW WORLD

"Now we're finished," one of my neighbours said alarmingly.

"Looks like it," I said gloomily. "We've been overwhelmed by the masses."

"What's to become of us, of Singapore?" another neighbour asked with a sigh.

"Maybe we'd better emigrate," another suggested despondently.

It was Sunday morning, 31 May 1959, and we were in my house discussing the results of the landmark general election held the previous day, and giving vent to our feelings.

On the table in front of us lay the Sunday newspapers with bold headlines screaming across the top of the front pages that the PAP had not only won but also gained a landslide victory. We had stayed up all night listening to the announcements of the results over the radio (there was no TV then). Our hearts had sunk lower and lower as the PAP captured one constituency after another. Our worst fears had come true.

If there were any consolation to those disheartened by the PAP's triumph, it was that the election had taken place peacefully and smoothly, without any mishap. There had been no rioting, looting, shooting or bloodshed, before, during and after the elections. It was more than one can say about elections in some other countries which are often marred by deaths and injuries of politicians and voters. It was something to be thankful for.

The PAP took 43 seats of the 51 it had contested, bagging 53.4 percent of the votes cast. It was a milestone for the party. The election victory had given the PAP the mandate to govern Singapore under a fully elected self-government system. Lee Kuan Yew and the other party leaders, Dr Toh Chin Chye, Dr Goh Keng Swee, S Rajaratnam, Ong Eng Guan and Ong Pang Boon (my neighbour), were propelled into the Legislative Assembly with a big majority. All the five PAP women candidates also won.

In his Tanjong Pagar ward, Lee polled 7,617 votes. His opponent, C Subramanyam of the Liberal Socialists, got 3,105 votes; it was not a bad result for an unknown fighting against a giant politician.

Lim Yew Hock of the Singapore People's Alliance (SPA) won his Cairnhill seat at the expense of David Marshall of the Workers' Party. However, Lim was one of the only four successful SPA candidates out of the 39 who had contested. Marshall's party did not win a single seat. Neither did the Liberal Socialists. It was a crushing blow for these three parties. Out of the four remaining wards, three went to the UMNO Alliance while the other one to an independent.

In this finest hour for the PAP, Secretary-General Lee declared: "The verdict of the people is a terrifying thing. The people's verdict is clear and decisive. Nothing more can be added to it. It is a victory of right over wrong, clean over dirty, righteousness over evil."

Party Chairman Dr Toh Chin Chye observed: "The opposition will feel very lonely in the next Assembly. The PAP's victory reflects the spirit and will of the people of Singapore. We have won because our policy has been consistent."

Lim Yew Hock was gracious over his party's defeat, saying: "We congratulate the PAP and wish them luck. The PAP has made certain promises for the betterment of the people's welfare and we hope they can carry them out."

A dejected Marshall had little to say except to express his sorrow that those who had voted for him had been disappointed. He got 2,920 votes to Lim's 5,275 votes.

However, the PAP stand vis-à-vis the communists was still not clear because later that night, 31 May, Lee repeated the party's demand for the release of the political detainees, otherwise the party would not take office. He told reporters the detainees who should be freed immediately were those intimately connected with the party leadership in 1956 and 1957. This was to honour the party's election pledge. His reasons were:

> The PAP does not intend to be, or even appear to be, the handmaid of the Malayan Communist Party. But we do not intend to soil our hands by putting them in the same gloves once used by the previous

> government. We shall not continue to purge. But if the necessity arises, a PAP government would be quite capable of taking its own steps to ensure the security of the state and the survival of democracy.

Many Singaporeans failed to fathom this reasoning.

The next morning, 1 June, Lee was summoned to Government House (now called the Istana) and asked by Governor William Goode to form a government. A large crowd of supporters greeted Lee as he arrived in his black Mercedes Benz with a white top and white steering wheel, bearing an SS 6566 number plate. The press corps waited for a story. Inside, Lee reminded Goode of the PAP stand on the question of the detainees. This was the only important matter at issue, he told Goode.

The media reporters cornered Lee for statements when he emerged from the meeting. His answers clarified the current situation and gave a glimpse of the shape of things to come. Lee was his eloquent self. The PAP, he said, was ready to go. It had the Cabinet lined up. It had "all the players, the goalkeeper, the full-backs, centre-half, right and left wings, and centre-forward". Lee assured: "We have the players and I think their positions are more or less fixed. That will be known to the world at large in good time."

A reporter asked: "Will you be Prime Minister?"

Lee replied: "I have been invited to form the government. If the conditions which I indicated to the governor are accepted, I would accept the responsibility of forming a government."

Another reporter asked: "Do you know the extent of the communist underground in Singapore?"

Lee answered: "No, but I expect to find out the facts when I have access to the information. The immediate menace of violent revolution—mounting of barricades, broken heads, broken bottles, home-made bombs, bombed buses—we can deal with. This is no problem."

On the communist problem in the long-term, he said there was no danger of the communists taking over in these five years. However, if they believed that their way was the only way to bring about a powerful nation in the next 15 to 20 years, the PAP did not want to wait for them. "Therefore, we start now. We want a democratic, non-communist socialism. We believe in a non-communist, socialist Malaya."

How was he going to deal with the problems of creating jobs for the people? The unemployment rate was running at an alarming 14 percent. Lee replied: "We know what the problems are and we have assumed power because there is nobody else in the field that will attend to the problems better than we can. I am not saying we are going to solve all difficulties, but I say with all honesty and sincerity we will do our best and there are very few people in Singapore who will do better than us."

Would he make changes to the education system? Lee said the PAP had set out in considerable detail the changes needed. These changes dealt with the syllabus and the extension of school hours to Saturday so that the teaching of languages would be more effective.

On relations with the Federation of Malaya, he said: "We don't intend to jeopardise the relationship between Singapore and the Federation by going into competition with the Tunku [Abdul Rahman] across the causeway. When we get merger, the position will be different." He appreciated the Malayan leader's decision not to come to Singapore to make speeches during the election campaign. It would ease the way to a happy and cordial relationship if they said nice things to each other.

Would he take action against the English press? The English newspapers had been most vitriolic in their attacks on the PAP as seen after the inauguration of the PAP in November 1954, for example. Lee had accused them of distorting the facts about the party and its intentions. Indeed, just before the current election campaign began, he and *The Straits Times* had clashed.

Lee replied he would not like to say "take action against the English-owned press". He explained that the criterion was a foreign-owned and controlled press. Foreign capital was welcome in Singapore for doing business on a long-term basis. Foreign capital, however, which sought to exploit local capital to enter the propaganda business, would do so at its own peril. He warned: "We said that deliberately and we stand by every word."

Would he allow the British national anthem, *God Save the Queen*, to be played in Singapore?

He replied: "I have thought for a long time it is a bit silly. We will think of these little things when we come to them."

Would he be organising a national anthem competition? Lee said that, strictly speaking, there could be no national anthem while there was a foreign head of state (the British governor).

"Where will you live as Prime Minister?"

He laughed: "I don't know."

"Will you drive in S 1car?"

"You know the PAP."

The next day, 2 June, came the announcement that the British would release the detainees on 4 June. The PAP was delighted. The detainees included Lim Chin Siong, Fong Swee Suan, C V Devan Nair, James Puthucheary and S Woodhull. As they stepped out of Changi Prison, party members and supporters waiting outside gave them thunderous cheers. They issued a statement pledging their loyalty to the PAP and backing its goal of a united, independent, democratic, non-communist and socialist Malaya. Lim, Fong, Puthucheary and Woodhull were later appointed political secretaries in the PAP government.

On 3 June, the Padang opposite City Hall vibrated with life as the PAP held a mammoth victory rally. The 43 PAP assemblymen and assemblywomen gathered on the City Hall's steps. A striking feature was their dress code. They came dressed in all white. As they put it, the dress code was to signify to the people their honesty, integrity and purity.

Lee led the shouts of *Merdeka*! (freedom). Jubilant supporters responded boisterously. There were also rowdy anti-PAP supporters. Old Guard S Rajaratnam later said that half the field was filled with pro-communists who yelled anti-Lee Kuan Yew slogans. Such was the political temperature at that time. Fortunately, there were no unpleasant incidents.

Speaking in English, Chinese and Malay, Lee told the people that the new government had no future apart from the future of the people. He reminded them that the eventual enemy would still be the communists and warned them to be on their guard. He promised that the PAP and the people would not be exploited and manipulated by the communists the way they had been in the past.

Party Chairman Dr Toh Chin Chye listed the pressing problems, like the massive unemployment facing Singapore and the solutions needed. Dr Toh said Singapore's entrepôt economy must be reinforced by an industrial economy. Being a small island without natural resources, Singapore must depend on the skills of its people and these skills must be applied towards labour productivity. The task was not merely to build factories fast enough to create job opportunities. The leaders needed foresight and imagination to see other ways and means of mobilising the jobless for productive work.

The general election drew worldwide attention, particularly in Britain, of course. The ruling British Labour Party, quoted by wire services, said it had expected the PAP's victory but was surprised at the extent. The party commented:

> Some of the anti-colonial and anti-imperialist statements by certain of the PAP leaders during the election campaign have caused some concern in political quarters here. But it is possible that with the PAP's assumption of power, and its attendant responsibilities, its policies might become more moderate than the pre-election campaign speeches would suggest.

Former British Prime Minister Earl Atlee, who as Clement Atlee had headed the post-war British Labour Government that transferred power to India and Pakistan about a decade earlier, said he hoped the PAP would set a great example of responsibility.

Millions of Britons watched a television interview conducted by journalist Alex Josey in Singapore for the British Independent

Television (ITV). Among other things, Lee was asked about his attitude towards British trade, freedom of the press, and whether he was anti-white.

Lee replied that the prospects for British trade were good. He was anti-colonialism but not anti-white. He would not allow foreign capital to interfere in domestic affairs. He was a firm believer in the freedom of the local press to criticise.

The new fully elected Singapore Government was sworn in on 5 June at City Hall. To nobody's surprise, Lee became Singapore's first Prime Minister and at 35, he was the youngest ever to hold that high office. Dr Toh Chin Chye became Deputy Prime Minister in the Cabinet which comprised nine ministers. The other seven ministers were Dr Goh Keng Swee (Finance), S Rajaratnam (Culture), Ong Pang Boon (Home Affairs), Yong Nyuk Lin (Education),Ahmad Ibrahim (Health), Ong Eng Guan (National Development), and K M Byrne (Labour and Law). It was a young Cabinet, the average age of the ministers being 37.

Governor William Goode was appointed an interim Head of State, known as Yang di-Pertuan Negara, for six months. On 3 December, Yusof bin Ishak, Editor-in-Chief and Managing Director of Malay-language daily newspaper *Utusan Melayu*, succeeded Goode in a colourful ceremony at City Hall. Singapore's national flag and crest were hoisted for the first time. The national anthem, *Majulah Singapura* (May Singapore progress) composed by Zubir Said, a Singaporean of Indonesian origin, was played to replace *God Save the Queen*.

Thus Singapore saw the end of 140 years of British rule.

Without the benefit of television, Singaporeans who stayed

away from the ceremony on the Padang did not see these historic events "live" or hear the strains of Singapore's national anthem or feel the mood of the passing of an age.

Prime Minister Lee Kuan Yew began the journey to a brave new world with his first address to the nation over the radio on the evening of 5 June. The speech spelt out the government's plan of action and the need for the people's support:

> At 4 pm this afternoon, my ministers and I formally took office. The control of Singapore's internal affairs was formally transferred to the elected representatives of Singapore.
>
> Each and everyone of my ministers is acutely conscious of the heavy responsibility and great burdens with which we have been entrusted. We have taken office because we believe that the PAP is the party most capable of discharging the duties and responsibilities of the government. We are the best organised and the most coherent political leadership in Singapore. Everyone of my ministers has gone through years of political struggle before we reached this position.
>
> If we were weak or insincere we would not have survived the stresses and strains of the political struggle that we underwent. The business of a government is to govern and to make firm decisions, so that there shall be certainty and stability in the affairs of our people. We shall do our best to give you, not only a firm and stable government, but one which will carry

with it the support and cooperation of the majority of the people.

During the elections our opponents tried to frighten you against a PAP government. They spread vicious rumours that polling day would be accompanied by unrest and civil commotion. That there would be a curfew; that buses would stop running. None of these things have happened. The events of the last six days have proved the falseness of these lies. The people of Singapore went to the polls in a peaceful and orderly manner and voted in the government they wanted, a PAP government. They celebrated their victory in the constituencies and on the Padang in a joyous, sometimes boisterous but always orderly and peaceful manner. In the same way their other predictions about the terrible consequences of a PAP victory will be proved equally false.

In the next five years there may come times when we shall face difficulties and tribulations. The tasks ahead of us are not easy to accomplish. We have never pretended they would be easy. But we shall not deviate from our declared objective of bringing about a social revolution by peaceful means.

We appeal to all of you to come forward and contribute your share in bringing about this social revolution, so that the change can come about in as peaceful and orderly a manner as the changeover from the Rendel Constitution to the new self-governing

> State of Singapore.
>
> With your help and cooperation we shall discharge our duties to you, in bringing about a happier and better Singapore.

Nevertheless, there was a minor exodus of businesses to Malaya, including *The Straits Times* which moved its corporate and editorial headquarters to Kuala Lumpur, along with its top editorial staff. Many of my Eurasian friends, fearing the PAP, emigrated to Australia. The government introduced several harsh measures. One of these was cutting the variable allowances of civil servants in the higher income brackets. Another was a six-day week for schools. Those affected were angry.

The government explained that the cut in allowances was necessary for survival since the previous administration had left the coffers almost empty. The cut also applied to Lee and his ministers. The longer school week was to allow more time for the study of languages, mathematics and science. Later, the allowances were restored and the schools returned to a five-day week.

Recognising the need to be friends with all countries, Lee wasted no time in cementing relations with them. For example, Lee paid a courtesy call on his Malayan counterpart, Tunku Abdul Rahman, on 13 June, and Indonesian President Sukarno on 19 January 1960. The visits were to establish economic and cultural ties and to inform them of Singapore's policies and undertakings.

On 7 August 1959, Lee called a news conference to review the performance of his government after nine weeks in office. Lee began by painting a bright future for Singapore. The people were in good heart. The administration was sound and sturdy. If they kept going at the same steady and confident way, the next five years would be years of progress and prosperity.

Inevitably, Lee was asked about the position of the English-educated in Singapore. Lee assured the English-educated, including the top government administrators, engineers, architects, doctors, dentists and other professionals, that they had a role to play in nation-building. They could help make the social revolution work by cooperating with the government. There was sufficient resilience in them to adjust themselves to the new situation in which they had been placed. He would be sorry if they did not.

The thorny issue of the English-educated was raised again on 16 August at a luncheon held in his honour by the Singapore National Union of Journalists. Lee said this class of people had their good points. They were homogeneous, did not regard themselves as primarily Chinese, Malay or Indian. They were loyal to the community, honest and well behaved, if somewhat too obedient to the former colonial authority. Their weak points were, in the case of the English-educated Chinese and Indians, that they were devitalised, almost emasculated, because of deculturisation since they were pumped with English values and ideals. They lost their own cultures, and had, therefore, lost touch with the mass of their own people. This was a serious disadvantage in a democratic system with people who spoke the vernacular languages.

Comparing them to the Malays, Lee said: "I have not yet come across a Malay who is unable to speak or read and write in Malay. But I have come across many Chinese and Indians who are educated in English but unable to read and write or even speak Chinese or

Tamil or Malayalam or whatever their native tongue may be. Of course, there are exceptions."

Lee predicted that the present English-educated cohort would gradually disappear, to be replaced by a new English-speaking group with different characteristics in 10 to 20 years. They would have vitality, confidence and a sense of dedication to their own people. They would survive in fair and open competition. The English-educated would play their part if the challenges were put fairly and squarely to them. "I suggest to you that this is the way to the future," he said.

The blueprint for nation-building was revealed in the first sitting of the new Legislative Assembly on 1 July by interim Yang di-Pertuan Negara (Head of State) William Goode. The ingredients included a climate of confidence for economic expansion, foreign investments to build factories and create jobs, loans for private industry, better healthcare, more low-cost public housing, more schools including technical institutes, fair wages for workers, a national identity among the races, promotion of the English, Chinese, Malay and Tamil languages and cultures, closer ties with Malaya and other Southeast Asian countries, and internal security. The programme was reassuring to the public.

Not surprisingly, the subject of merger with Malaya was given a special airing. Goode declared:

> The future of Singapore lies ultimately with the Federation of Malaya as a state in an independent country. It is the government's intention during its term of office to create and bring about conditions favourable to an early re-unification with the

> Federation. The government will take firm action to prevent any irresponsible activities by individuals or organisations to negate this paramount interest of the people of Singapore and Malaya.

For now, one of the most urgent tasks was to create jobs for the large number of the unemployed and the thousands of school-leavers entering the job market each year. The answer was industrialisation. The reason was that factories employed large numbers of workers whereas trade, on which the Singapore economy had depended on for growth since the beginning of time, did not.

An organisation called the Industrial Promotion Board was established in 1959 to chart the course for the manufacturing industry. The manager was former political detainee James Puthucheary. The body was replaced in August 1961 by the Economic Development Board (EDB), with top civil servant Hon Sui Sen as its first chairman and a government grant of $100 million. Under his able leadership, the EDB performed its task successfully. (The chairman is now Dr Beh Swan Gin, who was appointed in December 2014.)

The father of Singapore's economic development was Dr Goh Keng Swee, then the Finance Minister. Dr Goh was Lee Kuan Yew's former economics tutor at Raffles College and member of the Malayan Forum in London. Prime Minister Lee placed his complete trust in him to build up the economy. Dr Goh was known for his comprehensive grasp of economics, enterprising spirit and foresight. One of the boldest decisions he made was to turn a large expanse of swampland in Jurong into an industrial site, pre-empting the demand for factory space. He later admitted that if his plan had failed, the project would have been scoffed at as "Goh's Folly."

The EDB opened offices in rich catchment areas, such as Europe, the United States and Japan, to woo investors to Singapore. It was gruelling work for the field officers, especially in Europe and the United States. At that time, investors there knew nothing or very little about Singapore so appointments to see them were hard to get. But the EDB officers never gave up and the factories did come, slowly at first and rapidly thereafter. First came the labour-intensive, low-skilled projects, the perfect cure for the high unemployment rate of about 14 percent, then the capital-intensive, highly-skilled operations and then the high-technology, knowledge-based establishments one sees today. Investors were offered tax-free status for a certain number of years, soft loans for manufacturing, research and product development, engineering support and many other types of assistance. By the early 1970s, the unemployment problem had been solved.

Another urgent task was building homes for the people. The agency in charge under British rule, Singapore Improvement Trust, had built only 23,000 units in its 32 years' existence. A new authority, the Housing and Development Board (HDB), was formed to take over the critical task. The HDB targeted 51,000 high-rise apartments under its first five-year plan. At the height of the construction period, the completion rate was one unit every 45 minutes. Later, the HDB offered the flats for sale, enabling the people to build up their assets and a stake in the country. The government made home financing easier by allowing buyers to use a portion of their savings in the public pension scheme, Central

Provident Fund (CPF), to defray the purchase price. The scheme also applied to buyers of private properties.

To create a literate society, a new education policy was formulated to provide education for all children in four language streams (English, Chinese, Malay and Indian) with a common syllabus for all four streams. New schools were built, teacher-training was intensified.

A special education programme was drawn up for the Malays, the largest and poorest of the minority races. A Malay Education Advisory Committee was set up in 1959, and the first Malay secondary school opened the following year. Free education was offered up to tertiary level. Malay was made the national language and the language for the national anthem.

A bilingual policy was introduced, with English as the common language, to improve the people's proficiency in their respective mother tongues and help them keep their roots. Facilities were established for the study of local languages. The government started integrated schools, enabling students of different language streams to intermingle and study under the same roof, and to appreciate one another's language, culture and religion.

The government made sure of the success of the bilingual policy by introducing a double-weightage system for the study of the mother tongue, where 200 marks were allotted. The high marks were a great incentive. But the system proved to be a bane for those who found it difficult to master their mother tongues as they could lose a lot of points all at once, bringing down their overall score. This was one of the most contentious policies.

The learning of Chinese in particular was difficult and the high marks required caused many students to fail to gain entry to local junior colleges or universities. Those whose parents could afford it went overseas for their tertiary education. Families have been known to emigrate because of the bilingual policy. The double-weightage system was abolished in August 1985, but a pass in Chinese was still a must.

Another important key to Singapore's success was an efficient and honest civil service. Adjunct to this, a Civil Service Political Study Centre was set up on 15 August 1959 to educate senior officers and political leaders. Addressing them on 16 November, Prime Minister Lee told them:

> As political leaders, your duty is to see that the corrupt are isolated and removed. But it must be done in a way that the innocent are not so terrified that they are hiding under the table. I must emphasise the urgency of the necessity to get the political leadership to understand the administrative machinery, and the administrative machinery to respond to its fullest capacity.
>
> You must have had your bellyful of complaints of inadequate supervision and corrupt practices among contractors. I would not say they were unfounded. And I would not say what corrupt practices should be brought to light.

Taking the lead, Lee resigned from his post of legal adviser to the numerous trade unions he had served, explaining to them that as Prime Minister, he had to be neutral and fair to all, not to just one section of the populace, although the government's attitude towards workers had not changed.

Over and above all these elements necessary for nation-building that the government particularly emphasised was the spirit of national unity and loyalty to country. The multi-racial population must be moulded into a cohesive unit so that they would think and work for the country as one people. The importance of national unity was reinforced by the Loyalty Week organised on 3 December 1959 following the installation of Yusof Ishak as the Yang di-Pertuan Negara. Lee said:

> Without this quality, we shall never build the foundation of a stable society for ourselves and our children. Few people in the world have ever been asked to undertake a more difficult task. Diversity of race, language and culture is part of the richness of Singapore. But in one thing we cannot afford—diversity in loyalty. If our new citizens are loyal not to Singapore but to the countries of their origin, then the state will run into difficulties. But all work and no play makes for a dull life. We must never overdo things. Whilst we live and work and sacrifice for the next generation, let us not banish all pleasures and happiness from our own. So let us make this week [Loyalty Week] a week of rejoicing and relaxation.

The government made sure of securing undivided loyalty from its people by amending, in May 1960, the Citizenship Bill first passed in 1957 under the Lim Yew Hock government. Under the new ruling, Singaporeans had to choose whether they wanted to stay in the country or elsewhere. They could not have dual citizenship.

For a time, as part of the national unity programme, cultural shows featuring Chinese, Malay, Indian and English skits, dances and songs were staged on the Padang and other venues. The shows were billed as *Aneka Ragam Ra'ayat* (People's Cultural Concerts). One held on the Padang on 16 August 1959 attracted an audience of over 50,000, including Prime Minister Lee, Culture Minister S Rajaratnam and other dignitaries.

From 20 August 1960, the various races had a permanent and central location to intermingle and enjoy cultural and sports activities with the formation of the People's Association (PA). Lee was the chairman. From the PA sprang community centres (called community clubs today) that later proved to be more than just gathering places for social functions. They became a bastion against hostile elements attempting to wreck the new nation.

Getting down to the grassroots, PAP ministers and assemblymen held meet-the-people sessions to listen to and solve the people's problems, while at the same time explaining various government policies. In fact, it was David Marshall who initiated these sessions when he was Chief Minister. Lee and his colleagues went one step further by starting regular walkabouts in housing estates, which have since become a regular feature of today's Singapore.

The government also organised a clean-up campaign to beautify the country. Ministers and assemblymen rolled up their sleeves over several weekends, leading Singaporeans to clean littered streets, dirty housing estates, choked and smelly drains and filthy beaches with brooms, rakes and other implements.

As the tasks of nation-building proceeded, a new perception of the PAP began to dawn among Singaporeans. They saw that the PAP government was serious, honest and sincere about improving the welfare of the people, although some of its policies were unpalatable. There were no signs of the oppression, the destruction of civil liberties, the enslavement of the people and other social evils that many, especially the English-educated, had feared.

Instead, although he ruled with a firm hand, Prime Minister Lee constantly challenged Singaporeans to be creative, to break new ground, to dare to excel. He expected only the best from them and made them alert all the time to new opportunities, or dangers facing them. He would assess the local and world situations, expressing his optimism or warning of perils ahead as the case may be.

Delivering his first National Day Message on 3 June 1960, Lee predicted a bright future for Singapore, encouraged Singaporeans to keep up their morale and confidence and make the year ahead a year of consolidation. The economy grew steadily, with home-grown businesses expanding and new ones starting up, and new investments pouring in from foreign countries, mainly from the United States and Japan, all bringing greater affluence to the people.

But the communists had not given up the pursuit of their avowed goal of a communist Malaya. They had failed to usurp the PAP in 1957 and to influence the outcome of the landmark general election of 1959. Underground, they were planning other tactics. Lee and his colleagues knew that they must crush them to prevent the new nation from falling into their hands. The time for the final showdown must come. As Lee was to admit later, he was apprehensive of the prospect.

09

PLOTS AND COUNTER-PLOTS

Lee Kuan Yew's apprehension about the communists was understandable. They were a powerful force and die-hard revolutionaries. Their comrades had won colossal revolutionary battles in China and the Soviet Union. In Singapore, they commanded a huge following from the Chinese-educated and the communist-controlled trade unions. The PAP needed the support of these sections of the population and so had worked alongside the communists. Hence, the PAP did not adopt an anti-communist stand, but positioned itself as being non-communist.

Conversely, the communists needed a strong, legitimate political party they could use as a front. The two sides share a common platform—anti-colonialism. Although their final objectives differed, the PAP for a non-communist Singapore and the communists for a communist Singapore, they decided to work together as a united front.

But relations soured following the pro-communists' abortive attempt to topple the PAP's Central Executive Committee in August 1957. In a bid to re-establish goodwill, the underground Communist Party of Malaya (CPM) led by Chin Peng sent a top emissary to see Lee several times. The envoy was Fang Chuang Pi whom Lee nicknamed the Plen (plenipotentiary). The Plen told Lee that there was no need to fear the communists and that they could form a united anti-colonial front to fight in the 1959 general election. Among other matters, he asked Lee to abolish the Internal Security Council. Lee refused.

Tension mounted. What followed was as Lee described it, a series of plots, counter-plots and sub-plots that would have made an Oppenheim thriller read like a comic strip cartoon.

Ironically, it was the PA's own Ong Eng Guan who unwittingly started the test of strength and endurance. Ong, who had been the Party Treasurer and Mayor of the City Council and was now Minister of National Development, managed his ministry with an iron hand as he had done in the City Council. But he was not performing his job of building more public housing as well as he should. Lee took over the portfolio.

Unhappy with this, Ong challenged the party leadership and criticised their policies. He was expelled from the party, along with two sidekicks, and replaced by Tan Kia Gan as National Development Minister. In December 1960, Ong resigned from his Hong Lim constituency and formed the United People's Party. The by-election for the vacant Hong Lim seat held on 29 April 1961 was a disaster for the PAP. Ong won with a majority of over 4,900 votes against the PAP's candidate, Jek Yeun Thong.

The defeat alarmed not only Singapore but also Malaya. Tunku Abdul Rahman, now Malaya's Prime Minister after gaining independence in 1957, saw the loss as a sign that the PAP was unable to control the situation in Singapore. However, this turned out to be blessing in disguise for Singapore at that time. The Tunku, who had been against merger fearing it would upset the racial balance, now began to have second thoughts. He feared the communists would overrun his southern neighbour and turn it into a communist base, like Cuba, and undermine the mainland. He decided that a large Chinese population was a better proposition.

The Tunku first made public his new stand and his proposal in his address to the Foreign Correspondents' Association of Southeast Asia held in Singapore on 27 May 1961. His concept was a grouping comprising not only Singapore and the Federation of Malaya but also Sarawak, Sabah (then known as British North Borneo), and Brunei. Later, at an UMNO general assembly in Kuala Lumpur, he developed his ideas. He told the Malays that he had considered the prospect of being swamped by the Chinese from Singapore but argued that this was preferable to a communist coup.

Lee and his colleagues heartily welcomed the Tunku's change of mind and accepted his proposal in principle. Merger had been their long-cherished dream and now it was coming true. The communists, of course, were vehemently against merger because it meant that Malaya would take control of Singapore's security and crush them. Then began a series of attacks to discredit the PAP and shake the government. The assault was the more shocking as it was led by Lim Chin Siong, Fong Swee Suan and S Woodhull—political secretaries in the government. Among other things, they opposed independence through merger, demanded the release of all political detainees, the abolition of the Internal Security Council, press freedom and free speech. They mustered the support of all trade unions, even PAP assemblymen and supporters. Lee denounced their agitations as acts of treachery.

Then eight PAP assemblymen, led by Dr Lee Siew Choh, Parliamentary Secretary in the Home Affairs Ministry, joined in the rebellion by declaring that there was no democracy in the PAP.

The crisis deepened with the death of the PAP Assemblyman for Anson on 26 April1961, Baharuddin bin Mohamed Ariff. The by-election took place on 15 July. It was a five-cornered fight. The surprise was the return of David Marshall of the Workers' Party who challenged the PAP's Mahmud bin Awang, President of the Trades Union Congress. The communists backed Marshall and during the campaigning, he attacked the PAP as Lim Chin Siong and his comrades repeated their demands and accusations.

In his rally speech at Shenton Way on the eve of the by-election, Marshall said Lee should resign if he won. He shouted:

> Whether it is Goh Keng Swee or Toh Chin Chye who will replace him is irrelevant. We have had enough of being treated like blind chicken with humbug about merger in the never-never future. We want practical results in the field of freedom from imperial rule, freedom for our people and our working class movement to evolve according to our genus.

Prime Minister Lee assured Singaporeans at a PAP rally at Maxwell Road the same night: "Whatever happens in Anson, whether we win or lose, we will never let the people down." He accused the three rebel political secretaries and the eight assemblymen of trying to destroy the PAP's chances of winning the by-election by issuing damaging statements. He said their schemes showed their utter disregard for any principles of party comradeship and rules of decency. He advised them to resign if they disagreed with party and government policies. That was the decent thing to do.

The by-election was again a disaster for the PAP. Marshall won, although with a small majority of 546 votes. In his moment of glory, he brandished a hammer (the Workers' Party symbol) and exclaimed above the rousing cheers of his supporters at the counting centre, Victoria Memorial Hall: "We say to Emperor Lee Kuan Yew: Resign and may you in your retirement learn humility and humanity so that in the years to come your undoubted abilities may unselfishly and honestly serve the people."

The same night, the eight rebel assemblymen issued a statement declaring that the PAP had reduced intra-party democracy to a mockery by flagrantly disregarding the majority view among party executives and rank-and-file. The statement was a riposte to the PAP's accusation that they were stabbing the party leadership in the back by their public criticisms.

The next day, Lee dismissed Marshall's call to him to resign, saying whether he resigned or not was a small matter. The PAP would carry on with its duties of running the government. He attributed the defeat in Anson to disloyal party members, rather than to rival parties. But the following day, 17 July 1961, came a bombshell that sent shockwaves across the nation and made headline news.

Lee had sent his letter of resignation to party Chairman Dr Toh Chin Chye. In the letter, Lee spoke of the grave difficulties that lay ahead of the government and of the danger of industrial unrest stirred up for political motives. He mentioned the treachery of the three political secretaries and the eight assemblymen. He explained that with the defeat in Anson, the PAP now faced trials and tribulations. Now that an open confrontation had occurred, he believed Lim Chin Siong and his confederates would mount their politically-motivated industrial action. Because of this imminent threat, the PAP and the government needed firm and resolute leadership to withstand the assault. He reminded Dr Toh:

> You will recall that in May 1959, I had asked you as Chairman of the party, to lead the government as Prime Minister, but you had insisted that it was not your desire to assume the leadership of the government, although you were quite willing and happy to continue your leadership of the party. Now you know that those who have broken away from us are calling for my resignation. I have carefully considered the matter and I feel I must write to you to say that I am placing my Prime Ministership of the government at the disposal of the Central Executive Committee.

Lee said his resignation did not mean that he was washing his hands of his responsibilities to carry out the many unpleasant and awkward tasks the government had to do to maintain the economy of the island, the livelihood of the people and the peace and order of the state. He ended his letter with: "I am quite prepared to assume the leadership of the government on behalf of the party provided it is the clear wish of the party executive and of the assemblymen who will have to follow us into battle."

Dr Toh promptly gave him the party's blessings, saying in his reply made the same day:

> The Central Executive Committee was unanimous in choosing you as Prime Minister to lead the government to fulfill the political programme of the party. We have always believed in collective leadership and we must share the responsibility for successes or mistakes that have been made.
>
> The call for your resignation as Prime Minister by our opponents is only a cloak to confuse the people over the vital issue of merger between Singapore and the Federation, an objective upon which the party was founded and from which we cannot deviate. Suggestions have been made that I should be Prime Minister in your place. Let us not be deceived by this attempt to split the unity of the party and its leadership. The Central Executive Committee have every confidence that you will be able to lead the government and party out of its present difficulties.

Dr Toh, who was Deputy Prime Minister and Leader of the House, then called for a crisis meeting of the Legislative Assembly to debate a motion of confidence. The sitting on 20 July presented the

PAP with the opportunity to force the issue on the communists and to flush out any remaining disloyal PAP assemblymen. Presenting the motion, Prime Minister Lee enumerated before a hushed House the details of the political drama. In a speech lasting over an hour, he revealed a cloak-and-dagger plot of the British and the communists to overthrow the PAP government.

Lee said that there had been friendly fraternisation between the British and Lim Chin Siong, S Woodhull and company after the Hong Lim by-election in April. They had visited the British High Commissioner, Lord Selkirk, at his home at Eden Hall for consultations. Lee added that it was curious to see the great anti-colonialists and revolutionaries consulting with the British lion, instead of with the PAP.

The British had tried for two years, with "every blandishment and argument, every device and seductive manoeuvre", to manipulate the PAP into a position where the party would become the successor to Lim Yew Hock's policy. Their attempts were to ensure that the Communist Party of Malaya would be attacked not by British imperialism, which was the supreme power in Singapore, but by the locally elected government with limited powers.

The British plotted to engineer an open collision between the non-communist left in the PAP and the communist left. They wanted the PAP to remain in office, committed to defending British colonialism, or to resign and thereby dispose of a non-communist government not amenable to British pressure. They made the pro-communists believe that a non-communist government was no longer necessary and that a pro-communist government was possible. Hence, the communists made a bid to capture the PAP and the government in 1957. The PAP moderates, however, did not want to fit in with the scheme to beat the communists for the benefit of British colonialism.

Lee said the British had also tried to put the British Borneo territories into a position where they would come together immediately in a federation under British tutelage, but ready to be transferred to a nationalist government of Greater Malaysia if the international situation turned delicate. The British had failed on all these counts. He warned:

> If we get no independence through merger, we will leave the British with the predicament of having to deal with the communists themselves, even in an elected government. It is the duty of the PAP, as a political party, to hasten independence which will benefit the people.

S Woodhull later denied there had been a plot. He and his friends had visited Eden Hall merely to clarify their position since the PAP had threatened that the British would finish them off.

A heated debate over the confidence motion ensued. Dr Lee Siew Choh, one of the eight disloyal PAP assemblymen, condemned the proposal for merger as a sell-out. He harangued the PAP and the government for over six hours, the longest marathon speech ever made in the House. Behind the scenes, while he rattled on, S Woodhull, James Puthucheary and other comrades, furiously composed pointers to keep Dr Lee going. In all, the sitting lasted 13 hours, until 4 am the next morning. Never before nor since then has there been a longer Assembly session.

Before the division vote took place, another high drama unfolded. The PAP needed every vote it could get for the vote of confidence was extremely crucial. But one of its backbenchers, Sahorah binte Ahmat (Assemblywoman for Siglap) was in hospital. In desperation, party officials fetched her in an ambulance and brought her to the House to cast her vote. The tension mounted. In the end, the motion was carried by 27 votes to eight, with 16 abstentions. Among the 16 was Ong Eng Guan, a former PAP stalwart who now bore the banner of the United People's Party and winner of the Hong Lim by-election in April. David Marshall and Lim Yew Hock were among the eight who voted against.

Lee Kuan Yew had survived another baptism of fire. Reassured of his position, he paved the way towards consolidating the strength of the party and the government.

Not surprisingly, Lim Chin Siong, Pong Swee Suan, S Woodhull (the three rebel political secretaries), Dr Lee Siew Choh and 12 other dissident PAP Assemblymen were dismissed from office and expelled from the PAP soon after the crucial debate, and 14 branch officials suspended from duty. This marked the end of the acrimonious relationship between the moderates and the extremists in the party. The ex-PAP men then formed the Barisan Sosialis, with Dr Lee as Chairman and Lim as Secretary-General, to continue their struggle.

Altogether, the PAP expelled 16 PAP assemblymen, including Ong Eng Guan and two others sacked earlier. With the dismissals and the loss of the Anson seat in the by-election, the Lee Kuan Yew government now had only 26 representatives in the 51-seat Legislative Assembly, a majority of one. The number became 25–26 in July 1962 when PAP assemblywoman Ho Puay Choo crossed the floor to become an independent, later joining the newly formed Barisan Sosialis. The position see-sawed back to 26–25 when a sacked PAP assemblyman rejoined the party, then became 25–25 with the death of Health Minister Ahmad Ibrahim (Sembawang constituency) on 21 August. Wisely, Lee realised that the ground was not sweet to hold a by-election to fill the vacant Sembawang ward. Had he done so and lost, the communists would have toppled the government. The government survived this voting crisis to the next general election in 1963. As we shall see later, that was the crucial year in the PAP-communist struggle. Meanwhile, Lee took the opportunity to explain in detail to Singaporeans the grand designs of the communists, why the PAP worked with them and the PAP's strategy, in a series of 12 radio talks between 13 September and 9 October 1961.

The PAP found it necessary to work with the communists as an anti-colonial united front mainly as the latter were a formidable force and commanded a mass following among the Chinese-educated people and trade unions. The story began when he and his team made contact with one Laniaz in 1953. Laniaz had started as a nationalist in a group fighting against the British. The group happened to be communists. He had been detained by the British in 1951 along with John Eber, Devan Nair, James Puthucheary and several others. Here are excerpts of the radio broadcast of 2 October:

> We knew he [Laniaz] wanted to establish an independent communist Malaya and he knew we wanted to establish an independent democratic Malaya. But neither of our two different objectives

> would ever come to anything as long as the British were here. We never forgot that once the British were out of the way, there would be trouble between us and the communists as to what kind of Malaya we wanted to have in place of the old British colonial Malaya.
>
> We have now fallen out because we have disagreed on our next objective. We want merger and independence. The communists do not. They have a vested interest in continuing the anti-colonial struggle so that under cover of anti-colonialism, they can advance communism. They want the anti-colonial struggle to go on and on, meanwhile using Singapore as a base from which to undermine Malaya.

Lee explained that his government did not lock up Lim Chin Siong and associates now because the PAP would lose the open argument of who was right and who was wrong. This was the battle for the minds of the people, for the people's support for what the government believed was right for the country. Singapore was a multi-racial city with four major language groups: the English-speaking, Malay-speaking, Indian-speaking and Chinese-speaking. Although the first three classes were convinced that Lim and his communist friends were up to no good and should therefore be put away, the Chinese-speaking Singaporeans had to carry the opinion of all the people with it. He mentioned two crucial factors:

> The first is that to take stern action against the communists while Singapore is still a semi-colony, with ultimate power still vested in the British, would

be to open ourselves to smear and misrepresentation that we are just stooges of the British and have acted to preserve British interests. British power is supreme in Singapore. The sovereignty of Singapore is still vested in the British. In the last resort, it is they who have the final say on what happens to Singapore.

The last government under Tun Lim Yew Hock took massive action against the communists. The government failed in the eyes of the people. They failed not because they had taken action against the communists, but because their action was deliberately misconstrued to the people by the communists as having been done under instigation by the British. As a result, the government lost out.

The second factor we have to bear in mind is this. It is unwise to take stern immediate action against subversion in the unions, cultural organisations, old boys' associations and even in the universities' student clubs, because the action will be very largely against the Chinese-educated who have penetrated the leadership in these unions and organisations. Unless there is a clear distinction made between the communists and the non-communists, we would merely create resentment against the government and sympathy for the cause of those detained. To purge the communists, we have to be careful that we make it clear that we are not purging the Chinese-educated. This is a trap into which we must never fall.

Lee recalled that the Lim Yew Hock government fell into the communist trap by allowing themselves to be represented as anti-Chinese culture and education. The communists wanted the PAP government to do the same thing, but the party was not going to oblige them. He said:

> Because we are not likely to play into their hands, Lim Chin Siong and his friends know that they are in serious trouble. They realise they have made a grave error of judgement and have been taken for a ride by the British. They know that they are in trouble with the British and with the Federation. Their objective is to involve us in their trouble and do us the greatest amount of damage in the minds of the people, to paint us as rightists, reactionaries, stooges and a host of other abusive terms. This trouble is of their own making.

In an another radio broadcast two days later, Prime Minister Lee revealed how, during the critical 25-25 voting position, the communists had induced PAP assemblyman Chor Yeok Eng (Jurong) to defect to tip the balance towards the opposition. The Barisan Sosialis could then bring the government down. Lee said there was the veiled threat of what would happen to those who did not follow the mass line. But Chor was neither persuaded nor intimidated. They also tried to cajole several other PAP assemblymen who similarly stood their ground. Lee never forgot them for their bravery and loyalty, saying that without stalwarts like them, the PAP would have disintegrated as a government in 1961 and 1962.

These abortive attempts led Lee to re-think a section in the Singapore Constitution that allowed members of the Legislative Assembly to change sides without losing their seats, as the sacked PAP assemblymen had done. He argued "this political musical chair charade" was disruptive and even dangerous given the prevailing unstable situation. He advised the British to amend the constitution to stipulate that henceforth, those who wished to transfer their party affiliations must resign their seats and stand for re-election. It was a brilliant tactical move. The British were initially aghast, telling Lee that his proposal was undemocratic. But Lee warned them that without the constitutional change, the communists would take over the country. The British finally agreed.

As Lee said, the communists' methods were crafty. On the surface, the communists made themselves appear to be reasonable people and claimed they were always ready and willing to accommodate the employers. Yet at the same time, they worked behind the scenes to direct people and organisations, including the People's Association, the Business Houses Employees Union and even the English-stream school teachers, to create trouble on their behalf. They exploited every issue to foment bitterness, frustration and hatred among the people towards established authority. They formed local working committees in each district and constituency to organise house-to-house campaigns, public meetings and political education of the rank-and-file.

In his broadcast on 6 October, Lee revealed the communist link by showing that these organisations had pro-communist cadres such as S Woodhull, Dominic Puthucheary (younger brother of James Puthucheary) and others. Citing an example, he related how the Secretary-General of the Singapore Teachers' Union (STU) and a communist cadre had tried to exploit the unhappiness of English school teachers over the six-day week introduced soon after the 1959 general election. Not only did they rally the teachers to demand the demolition of the new work schedule, but the language they used in their circulars also contained Marxist terms such as:

> Campaign to seek support of the public and the working class movement. A massive appearance of an army of teachers will ensure the annihilation of the six-day week. One cannot but arrive at the irresistible conclusion that political expediency led the government to impose the six-day week.

Lee said these political phrases were not those of the President of the STU, or of the Central Council. The phrases were inspired by the pro-communist cadres behind the scenes. The teachers, realising the true meaning of the circulars, refused to support the campaign. The Central Council issued a statement clarifying its position in the matter and demanding that the petition be taken away.

Lee declared in the radio broadcast:

> We will always view with sympathy any genuine unhappiness of the English school teachers over the six-day week, but we cannot be expected to view with sympathy the efforts of the pro-communist cadres to heat up and exploit this unhappiness.
>
> The communists' devious ways were also apparent on the subject of merger with Malaya. At first, they vehemently opposed the arrangement. Then, when

> they realised that going against the tide was futile, they switched tactics to say that they were opposed only in form. They wanted Singapore to be the 12th state in the grouping and sharing the same position as Penang, where education and labour would be controlled by the Central Federation Government. In other words, their aim was complete merger.

Delivering his radio broadcast on 9 October, Lee Kuan Yew explained why the communists' merger proposition was unacceptable to Singapore. If they had their way, it would mean that only people born in Singapore would automatically become Federation citizens, like those born in Penang. As about 325,000 adult Singapore citizens out of the 650,000 were born in Singapore, this would mean that half of the population would promptly lose their citizenship rights on joining Malaya. An even more difficult condition of complete merger was that since a person must have knowledge of Malay (the national language in Malaya), most of the 325,000 Singapore citizens who had come from China, India and other parts of the world, would not get Federation citizenship.

His government's intention, Lee said, was for all Singapore citizens to retain all the rights and privileges they enjoyed, regardless of whether they were born here or elsewhere. The government had also proposed that the citizens of the new and larger Federation should be called Federal nationals so as not to confuse people by using such phrases as new Federation citizens.

Lee went on to highlight several sectional interests in Singapore to be protected on merger. He said the English-educated needed the assurance that the 4:1 ratio between the Malays and the non-Malays would not apply in the Singapore section of the civil service. Businessmen, contractors and bus companies wanted the same treatment as before with regard to tenders and licences, with no priorities or special rights for anybody. Chinese parents who wanted their children to attend Chinese schools expected the policy of equal treatment of all streams of education to continue. Singapore wanted also to retain its pro-labour policy and its free port status. Lee said:

> Every legitimate interest will be protected. But in the end, the communists will still find merger unpleasant, because security comes under Central Government control. However fair and just the arrangements on citizenship or Federal nationality, and every other matter, they will still oppose. Their real objection is that security will be in the hands of a strong Central Federal Government. Unfortunately, they cannot admit this selfish interest publicly, so they will find fault with every conceivable other point to achieve their aim to block merger.

Lee described the break-away Barisan Sosialis as the main open front communist organisation, with Dr Lee Siew Choh as their front leader. The communists had a subsidiary body in the Party Rakyat, and a few cadres planted in David Marshall's Workers' Party. They tried to penetrate Ong Eng Guan's United People's Party. They tried to get these four parties into the Singapore Socialist Front so that they could control the organisation, just as they controlled the Federation Socialist Front. In the Federation of Malaya, the communists had heavily infiltrated the Labour Party of Malaya.

He named the front leader in the Federation as Lim Kean Siew, Secretary of the Federation Socialist Front. Lim talked in the same vein as Lim Chin Siong. They wanted Singapore and the Borneo territories to get independence separately first, before they would discuss merger. Their reason was simple. As long as Singapore remained a colony, the communist struggle could be disguised as an anti-colonial fight.

The communists in Malaya and Borneo assembled their open front organisations. They maintained contact with Lim Chin Siong through Dr Lee Siew Choh whom Lee described as "the post office box". (In an interview reported in the *Guardian* on 22 September, Dr Lee had denied he was a communist, saying that if he became convinced there were communists in the Barisan Sosialis, he would expose them and let the people decide.)

The communists knew they could not stop merger or Malaysia, no matter how hard they tried, Lee Kuan Yew said. However, their cadres would continue organising and trying to capture the leadership of trade unions, political parties, cultural associations, old boys' associations and student clubs. As they lost old cadres, they recruited new ones. The Singapore government would not be complacent. The government was equally determined to see merger through and that "we shall be patient and forbearing".

He promised that merger would solve many problems. Other than security, reunion meant a larger market for Singapore and hence, a solution to its economic and social problems. The long-term solution was to present the people with a clean and effective alternative to a rigidly disciplined communist society.

Lee's revelations over the radio erased once and for all any lingering suspicion of the PAP being communist or a communist base that had been hanging over Singaporeans, including the English-educated who had previously shown their hostility towards the party. The disclosures reaffirmed the party's genuine intentions of improving the people's livelihood. The fresh perception of the party proved to be the turning point in its political fortunes.

But the communists were not finished yet. In November 1961, about a month after Lee's radio broadcasts, they brewed student unrest among Chinese middle school students. This was over the new policy on Chinese education that brought the system of four years primary, two years senior primary, three years junior middle and three years senior middle (known as the 4-2-3-3 system) in line with that practised in the English, Malay and Tamil language streams, that is, six years primary and four years secondary.

Clearly, the fewer years Chinese students would have to spend in school would be a welcome advantage to them. But the communists exploited the issue by denouncing it as a lowering of standards and an attempt to destroy Chinese education. Falling for the bait, militant students called for a boycott of the first Secondary IV competitive examinations under the new system held that November, and picketed the examination centres. A melee ensued, as students keen to take the examinations forced their way in, helped by their parents. The boycott failed.

The communists also went abroad, condemning merger that would create Malaysia as a neo-colonialist plot. Some foreign countries, particularly in Asia and Africa, became suspicious of the real intentions. To clear the air and allay their fears, Lee took it upon himself to visit several Afro-Asian countries including India, Burma and Egypt, in April 1962. He was accompanied by government officials and journalists. He spoke to their leaders, assuring them that merger was not a neo-colonialist scheme. The tour lasted six weeks which Lee declared a success as these countries now knew what Malaysia meant.

Malaya's Prime Minister Tunku Abdul Rahman was pleased with Lee's initiative and the favourable publicity it generated. However, the Tunku was annoyed by the visit Lee made to Moscow in September that year on his way home from the Commonwealth Conference in London. Said the horrified Tunku:

> It came as a surprise to me to know that he has gone to Moscow. From what I know, he has been attacking the communists and those parties which he suspects of having connections with the communists. His visit to Moscow will naturally nullify what he has said. Perhaps he has gone there to see for himself how bad the communists can be. Until I have seen and heard from him the reason for his visit, it is not possible for me now to say whether he is right or wrong in going there.

Lee, who stayed three days in Moscow with National Development Minister Tan Kia Gan, explained that it was an unofficial visit, without political purpose. It was a fact-finding mission, "to see something of what, after all, is one of the biggest countries in the world". He was received by Soviet First Deputy Foreign Minister, Vasily Kuznetsov. Lee held talks with him, enlightening his host about the proposed Malaysia, visited the Kremlin and Moscow University, rode on the city's famous subway and attended a Bolshoi Ballet performance. He did not meet Prime Minister Nikita Khruschchev. He told reporters before flying home:

> I do not know what it was like in 1917, but 45 years after the revolution I find their officials a very sophisticated and competent lot and in some cases men of great ability. But nevertheless, their information on Malaysia and their analysis of Malaysia as a simple piece of neo-colonialism is utterly wrong. I told them it is too simple to say that Malaysia is just neo-colonialism. They heard my piece and I hope it rang a few bells with them.

On his arrival at Paya Lebar Airport, Lee assured everyone that he had not been brainwashed by communism, saying: "I know what I am and the Russians know it." On Tunku Abdul Rahman's suspicions, he mentioned the advantage of knowing the Russians "to tell them where they get off". As he put it:

> We must be sufficiently mature to see and judge for ourselves. If we have sufficient conviction and belief in our principles, we can go around the world and we can come back true to our beliefs, true to our principles, because of what we have seen. We are neutral, where it is a collision of the big power blocs because we are not sure who is on our side, but we are not neutral where our interests are concerned. And if we are threatened, we shall defend ourselves.

Lee reiterated the wisdom of merger, saying: "It would be utterly ridiculous for us, with 1.6 million people, to try to chart our own way in this world."

His Moscow visit came under heavy fire from none other than the Barisan Sosialis. The party, which opposed merger in its present form, charged that Lee went to Moscow as "a rabid anti-communist just to further his ulterior motives". Claiming that he had embarrassed Malaya, which had announced further restrictions on student travel, the party said: "Mr Lee's trip to Moscow immediately after rendering his services to the British Colonial Office is another indication of his political opportunism. It is sheer hypocrisy and arrogance on the part of Mr Lee for him to dub all those whom he refuses to grant the same freedom of travel as he has granted himself, as being immature and gullible."

Communist opposition and snide remarks notwithstanding, Lee proceeded to complete the work on merger. Independence through merger was the big prize he had long sought. During the next few months, he held a series of discussions with Tunku Abdul Rahman and the British to sort out and finalise the details. Among the most difficult issues standing in the way were finance, education, labour and a common market. Malaya drove a hard bargain, such as maintaining its right to decide what products should enter the common market. Singapore had no choice but to agree.

Finally, 16 September 1963 was set as the date for the creation of Malaysia. At last, Lee's long-cherished dream was about to be realised. Unfortunately, the dream soon turned into a nightmare for him.

10

BIRTH OF A REPUBLIC

Water-boats sprayed the Singapore harbour with multi-coloured water. A thousand bulbs bedecked the ships and boats riding in anchor, and fireworks mushroomed into a myriad of little colourful stars, illuminating the evening sky with a brilliant glow. Yachts, sampan and other small vessels raced through the waves in a sea carnival. At the airport earlier in the day, the RAF (Royal Air Force) had given a spectacular air display. Thousands had come to watch in wonder. Thousands more had thronged Kallang Park to patronise a food and fun fair. The event was opened by the First Lady, Puan Noor Aishah, wife of the Yang di-Pertuan Negara, Yusof bin Ishak. Singapore was ablaze with joyous celebrations lasting a week. North of the causeway, the festivities were equally crowded and lavish.

The day was 16 September 1963. It was a day of national pride, the day Singapore became a part of an independent Malaysia. Singapore had entered a new era. Reunification of the two countries, separated by the British in 1946, had been Lee Kuan Yew's long-cherished dream and now it had come true. Coincidentally, it also marked Lee's 40th birthday. No birthday present could have been more meaningful for him. All the planning, the hard negotiations and the frustrations had come to fruition. He shed tears of joy as the historic moment overwhelmed him.

Much water had passed under the bridge before this event. On 6 July 1962, the Legislative Assembly had passed the Referendum Bill on merger by 29 to 17 votes. The victory for the PAP government could not have been more decisive and sweeter. With the passage of the Bill came Referendum Day on 1 September. The electorate's endorsement was equally decisive, with 70 percent of them saying "Yes". In a desperate effort, the Barisan Sosialis had exhorted the electorate to cast blank votes. However, their wheedling had been in vain because the government had quickly countered it by amending the Referendum Bill to stipulate that blank votes would be regarded as approval of reunion. The rationale behind the counter-measure was that anyone who cast a blank vote would be deemed to be unable to make up his mind and he should therefore follow the majority.

As it turned out, however, only 25 percent of the electorate cast blank votes, and even fewer (1.6 percent) obliged the Barisan. It was a resounding victory over the communists. After the Referendum, Prime Minister Lee had taken further steps to ensure that the communists' fortunes continued to dwindle. Grassroots support was rebuilt and strengthened. Lee toured all 51 constituencies to win the hearts and minds of the people. He explained government policies and listened to their problems. He reassured them that Malaysia offered a better and more secure future. The marathon constituency tour ran from November to the following September.

Having failed to win local support, the Barisan Sosialis turned to external forces, such as the Partai Kommunis Indonesia (PKI) and Party Rakyat Brunei (PRB). The PRB President, A M Azahari, had staged an abortive revolt in Brunei on 8 December 1962. Azahari was an anti-communist but had consorted with the communists to achieve his ambition. The communists found him a useful ally for their scheme and together they conspired to launch violent demonstrations in Singapore to support the Brunei revolt.

Alerted to the scheme, Singapore police, assisted by their counterparts from the Federation of Malaya, launched Operation Cold Store on 2 February 1963 and detained 107 subversive elements. They included Lim Chin Siong, Fong Swee Suan, S Woodhull, Dominic Puthucheary and Said Zahari who had connived with Azahari to create civil disorder. Lim, Fong and Woodhull were back in jail. The police sealed the Barisan Sosialis headquarters at Victoria Street.

Operation Cold Store broke the camel's back. Communist Party of Malaya (CPM) leader Chin Peng admitted in *My Side of History*: "Operation Cold Store shattered our underground network throughout the island. Those who escaped the police net went into hiding. Many fled to Indonesia." But, he said, he "continued to work at how best we might raise the impact of our activities on the front line in Malaya".

Despite the mass arrests and the crippling of the communist underground network, the Barisan Sosialis continued with their agitation. On 22 April1963, the party brought some 300 supporters, including its own assemblymen, to demonstrate at City Hall to protest against the alleged ill treatment of the political detainees. Bearing placards with anti-PAP slogans, they surged into the building, disregarding police orders to disperse. The police guarded the entrance to the Prime Minister's Office. A scuffle ensued. The angry mob attacked the law officers with their placards, injuring many. After some 15 minutes of skirmishing, the police arrested seven Barisan Sosialis assemblymen. They were charged in court with attempting to overawe the Prime Minister and other ministers, rioting and unlawful assembly. Party Chairman Dr Lee Siew Choh and another assemblyman were charged with abetting the offence.

The hearing before Chief Justice Wee Chong Jin lasted 17 days, until 29 August 1963. It made headline news. Dr Lee Siew Choh and another assemblyman were acquitted. The others were found guilty and were each sentenced to a month's jail for rioting and three weeks for being members of an unlawful assembly, the sentences to run concurrently. They gave notice of appeal. The appeal was heard a year later, on 17 and 18 August 1964. In its judgement the following day, the Court of Appeal dismissed the appeal and set aside the sentences. The appellants were discharged but were bound over for $1,000 to be of good behaviour for six months.

But Singapore kept the situation under control and Malaysia Day on 16 September 1963 reflected the communists' failure to block merger. A colourful giant billboard erected at the front entrance of City Hall with the words "Majulah Malaysia" (onward

Malaysia) trumpeted the new era. The billboard depicted a picture of a happy people of various races with arms linked. The Padang across the road was filled to capacity.

The ceremony began with the arrival of Yang di-Pertuan Negara Yusof Ishak and his inspection of the guard of honour mounted by the Singapore Volunteer Corps. The VIP guests, who included Cabinet ministers, members of the diplomatic corps, Dato (Dr) Ismail bin Abdul Rahman representing the Central Government, and Duncan Sandys, British Secretary for Commonwealth Relations and the Colonies, exemplified the importance of the occasion.

Prime Minister Lee proudly read the Malaysia Proclamation that ended with these words:

> Now I, Lee Kuan Yew, Prime Minister of Singapore, do hereby proclaim and declare, on behalf of the people of Singapore, that as from today, the sixteenth day of September 1963, Singapore shall forever be a part of the sovereign democratic and independent state of Malaysia, founded upon the principles of liberty and justice and ever seeking the welfare and happiness of her people in a more just and more equal society.

In his speech, Lee regarded the day as a day of fulfillment, a day offering promises of a greater future. He dismissed charges that Malaysia was a neo-colonialist plot. He warned, however, that new perils beset Singapore. The communists and anti-national elements were not giving up the fight. He declared:

> We have decided this day to go into it in unity, willingly and freely with our brothers in Malaysia,

> Sabah and Sarawak and we shall help bear our share of the burden that independence brings to us. In return, all we ask for is an honourable relationship between the states and the Central Government, a relationship between brothers, not a relationship between masters and servants. We pledge our loyalty to the Central Government, to Tunku Abdul Rahman, Tun Abdul Razak and their colleagues in power. It is a loyalty which transcends party rivalries and petty personal differences. It is an unswerving loyalty to an unalterable principle of unity for the prosperity of Malaysia.

After the speech, Lee led the shouts of "*Merdeka*!" three times to a roaring response. A march-past followed, performed by uniformed and civilian groups headed by members of the Ex-Services Volunteer Corps Association, men who had fought the Japanese. The day's celebrations ended with a float procession.

Britain's Queen Elizabeth II sent her congratulations and good wishes to the Yang di-Pertuan Negara, through Lord Selkirk, the Commissioner-General for Southeast Asia: "At this moment it is fitting to remember those of every race who, over the past 144 years of close association between Singapore and Britain, have contributed to the development of the greater commercial centre and industrial complex into which this City State has now been fashioned."

However, the Barisan Sosialis was not finished yet. One hour after the proclamation, the party held a mass rally at the public housing estate of Tiong Bahru where chairman Dr Lee Siew Choh denounced merger as neo-colonialist. He vowed that his party would continue to oppose the new federation and to support the demand of the people of Sarawak, Sabah and Brunei for self-determination and independence.

Actually, most Singaporeans were beginning to get bored with such diatribes, repeated over and over again like a broken gramophone record. They viewed them as pointless, good only as light-hearted reading at breakfast. More serious, to them, was Singapore's prospects in Malaysia. Would they indeed enjoy a better and more secure life as Prime Minister Lee Kuan Yew had promised? It remained to be seen as Singaporeans geared up to live as Malaysian citizens.

To get a fresh mandate from the people to run the country under the umbrella of the Federal Government, the PAP Government called for a general election to take place on 21 September, five days after the proclamation of merger. Nomination day was 11 September. The election saw two watershed political developments. First, it was the first clash between the PAP and the breakaway Barisan Sosialis. This was a fight between the non-communists and the communists. It was a test of strength for them. All eyes were focussed intently on this battle of the giants. The other contenders were irrelevant. The tensions and fearful anticipation that ensued were understandable.

Thanks to the exposé by Prime Minister Lee in the Legislative Assembly, in his radio broadcasts and elsewhere, Singaporeans now knew the PAP was not communist or a communist base, whereas the Barisan Sosialis was communist-dominated. Furthermore, the PAP's good track record for the past four years testified to its honesty and sincerity in wanting to improve the people's livelihood. This knowledge was particularly significant to the English-educated who had suspected the PAP of being communist bent on breaking their rice bowl. Their choice was therefore clear: the PAP or the Barisan Sosialis.

It was the turning point in the relationship between the English-educated and the PAP and their support strengthened the party's position at that crucial time.

The other pivotal development was that the election spelled the end of the political careers of former Chief Minister David Marshall and his successor Lim Yew Hock of the Singapore People's Alliance. Lim had reigned from 1956 until 1959 when the PAP assumed power that year. In the 1963 general election, Marshall stood at Anson but surprisingly, not on a Workers' Party ticket but as an independent. Lim did not even take part.

Marshall lost to the PAP's P Govindasamy. He got only 416 votes and lost his deposit. That was his swansong. Thereafter, he concentrated on his law practice. From 1978 to 1993, he served as Singapore's Ambassador to France, then Spain, Portugal and Switzerland. He passed away in 1995 of lung cancer.

Lim had made valuable contributions to Singapore's decolonisation process and deserved some credit. He was the Chief Minister who led the all-party Singapore delegation to the successful Merdeka Talks on the new Singapore Constitution in London in 1958 that eventually paved the way to full self-government for Singapore. Apparently, he had now decided to rest on his laurels. Thus exited another prominent politician of the 1950s.

In the 1963 general election, the PAP went for all 51 seats in the Legislative Assembly and the Barisan Sosialis 46. The Barisan launched its usual invectives, and accused the PAP of selling out

Singapore to Malaya. The PAP spared no efforts to publicise its track record and reiterate the benefits of reunion.

Ultimately, the PAP won the day.

The scoreboard read: PAP – 37 seats with 47.4 percent of the vote cast, and Barisan Sosialis – 13 seats with 32.1 percent. The result correctly reflected the actual strength and ground support of the two rival parties at that time. However, such was the Barisan's power and influence over the electorate in certain constituencies that PAP leaders Dr Toh Chin Chye and S Rajaratnam won by the skin of their teeth, while K M Byrne and Tan Kia Gan lost the fight. The remaining seat went to PAP dissident Ong Eng Guan of the United People's Party.

Prime Minister Lee described the PAP victory as a vote of confidence. The fight was not between the PAP and the Communist Party of Malaya (CPM), but between the rest and the CPM.

He declared:

> The communists are an endemic threat. You are not going to cure it by having a jab of penicillin or taking a dose of atremyacin. The moment your health goes down, your resistance goes down. They come up, but if you keep fit, the country sound, employment is full, houses, schools, homes, clinics, hope of a better life and immediate tangible results, then we can fight them openly and win.

Sadly, Lee's dream of life in Malaysia was soon to be shattered. Merger proved to be far more complex than Singapore and Malaya had imagined. Relationships were stormy from almost Day One.

Externally, Malaysia was beleaguered by Indonesian President Sukarno's policy of confrontation. Sukarno had launched this policy on 20 January 1963, charging that Malaysia was a neo-colonialist plot designed to destroy his country. He sent commandos to Singapore and Malaysia to take lives and destroy property. The most destructive for Singapore was the bombing of MacDonald House at Orchard Road on 10 March 1965 that killed three innocent office workers and injuring 33 others, seven of them seriously. Two Indonesian agents were caught, found guilty and hanged.

Internally, misunderstandings arose between Singapore and Malaysia. The fire of conflict was first lit during the sitting of the Malaysian Parliament on 21 December 1963. This was over the tax provisions in the Budget. Lee Kuan Yew pointed out that the provisions would make the rich richer and the poor poorer. There were other bones of contention. For example, the proposed common market that would have given Singapore bigger trade opportunities did not materialise. Singapore investors grumbled that the Central Government favoured those setting up plants in the mainland. Singapore was asked to contribute more towards defence. Malaysia closed the Bank of China in Singapore. It accused Lee's Press Secretary, Alex Josey, of interfering in domestic affairs and expelled him.

The discord worsened when the PAP took part in the Malaysian general election in April 1964. Even though it was only a token participation with 11 candidates fielded, UMNO and the MCA (Malayan Chinese Association) objected, arguing that the PAP's entry would jeopardise their positions in the Malay and Chinese communities. The PAP explained that it had as much right to participate in Malaysian politics as the UMNO Alliance had in Singapore. The PAP was not challenging anybody. All it wanted was to be a loyal opposition and to help build a united, non-communist and non-communal Malaysia. As it turned out, the PAP fared badly in the election, winning only one of the 11 seats it contested.

Fears over the PAP mounted when the party decided to open branches in all the 11 Malaysian constituencies it had contested. Lee's repeated assurances that the PAP would serve all races were taken as a criticism of UMNO. Lee also talked about a Malaysian Malaysia, a concept they disliked. The friction then became a communal one. UMNO's extremist leaders held rabble-rousing meetings in Singapore. They made inflammatory speeches accusing PAP's Malay leaders of being anti-Malay, anti-Muslim and anti-religion. Lee labelled these UMNO leaders ultras.

Then, one of the worst racial riots in Singapore broke out.

It was shortly after 5 pm on Tuesday, 21 July 1964. Singapore Malays were marching in procession in Geylang, a traditionally Malay district, to celebrate Prophet Mohamed's birthday. A member of the Federal Reserve Unit asked a group of stragglers to rejoin the main stream. What followed was mayhem. Instead of obeying, they set upon the policemen. In the blink of an eye, the marchers began attacking spectators and passers-by. By nightfall, the riots had spread to the city. An all-night nation-wide curfew was imposed. The violence continued for a week, leaving 23 people dead and over 450 injured in its wake.

Lee went on the air immediately after the riots erupted. He said there was organisation and planning behind the outbreak to turn it into an ugly communal clash. He appealed to the people to stop "this stupidity" and to help the government restore law and order. They should ignore rumours and wild talk of revenge as this would only inflame men's minds. He said: "What has happened cannot be undone. What will happen depends upon what you and the government can do. We shall make it clear that lawlessness does not pay. But more important, harmony between our communities must be preserved. This you can help me do."

Goodwill committees were formed in every constituency. Lee toured the areas to calm the people and to warn them to be on guard against extremists who were determined to destroy the country. Malaysian Prime Minister Tunku Abdul Rahman and his deputy, Tun Abdul Razak, flew to Singapore to try to help alleviate the volatile situation. But two months later, Indonesian agents lit the spark that plunged Singapore into another week of communal clashes. The trouble began with the mysterious death of a Malay trishaw-rider near Geylang. The grim list of casualties showed 12 people killed and about 100 others injured.

To prevent future racial incidents, the Tunku and Lee agreed to stop talking about sensitive issues publicly. Still, the UMNO extremists persisted in causing trouble. They accused Lee of being a communalist and an enemy of Malaysia. The marriage blew hot and cold. At one point in April 1965, hopes were raised that the ongoing problems might have been resolved. But a month later, Lee took another step to advance the call for a Malaysian Malaysia that rekindled the fires of animosity. Along with four opposition parties in the mainland and in Sarawak, the PAP formed a Malaysian Solidarity Convention designed to realise the goal of a Malaysian Malaysia. The Malaysian government considered this a brazen attempt to topple them. The rift widened. As the tension built up, there were rumours of a move to arrest Lee. The Malaysian government denied this.

By August, the relationship had become so bad that the Tunku told Lee that the only way to prevent a communal bloodbath was for Singapore to leave Malaysia, the sooner the better. In vain, Lee suggested alternative solutions, such as a looser federation. The Tunku stood firm and on 9 August, Singapore became a separate entity once again. It was a crushing blow to Lee. However, the separation automatically gave the nation independence, which had been the ultimate objective in any case. To a shocked nation, he intoned the Proclamation of Independence at 10 am that day at City Hall, before a gathering of journalists and the diplomatic corps:

> Now I, Lee Kuan Yew, Prime Minister of Singapore, do hereby proclaim and declare on behalf of the people and government of Singapore that as from today, the ninth day of August in the year one thousand nine hundred sixty-five, Singapore shall be forever a sovereign democratic and independent nation, founded upon the principles of liberty and justice and ever seeking the welfare and happiness of her people in a more just and equal society.

Singapore had entered another era in its history.

The TV news conference that afternoon (TV had been introduced on 15 February 1963) was perhaps one of the most moving given by a national leader anywhere. Lee's strong voice faltered as he said: "For me, it is a moment of anguish. All my life, my whole adult life, I have believed in merger and unity of the two territories... We are connected by geography, economics and ties of kinship... It broke everything we stood for."

Then he wept. He sat back in his chair, asking for a few minutes' adjournment as he wiped away his tears. When he was able to resume, it was 20 minutes later.

Lee outlined the basis for Singapore's survival:

> What has happened has happened. But be firm and calm. We are going to have a multi-racial nation in Singapore. This is not a Malay nation, not a Chinese nation, not an Indian nation. Everybody will have a place in Singapore, and we will continue helping the Malays in competition with UMNO. We unite regardless of race, language, religion or culture.

The official reason given for the separation was the need for friendship, security and peace of Malaysia as a whole. But former Social Affairs Minister Othman Wok and a member of the Old Guard, still believes that there was another reason. This was to prevent the publication of a report of the Royal Commission of Enquiry on the violence in Singapore. Addressing Tampines Junior College students to mark Racial Harmony Day on 21 July 1997, Othman said the report would have pointed accusing fingers at the Malaysians guilty of the troubles. With Singapore out, the Commission was dissolved automatically.

With independence came the birth of the Republic of Singapore. The Legislative Assembly became Parliament. The Yang di-Pertuan Negara was renamed President of the Republic of

Singapore and 9 August was declared National Day and a public holiday. International recognition came quickly, led by Malaysia, of course. Among other things, Singapore adopted a policy of non-alignment. A Ministry of Foreign Affairs and a Ministry of the Interior and Defence were created, with S Rajaratnam and Dr Goh Keng Swee in charge respectively.

Peace returned to Singapore, Malaysia and Indonesia on 12 August 1966 when Indonesia stopped its confrontation policy after Suharto had overthrown Sukarno in a bloody coup. Singapore's external relations took a significant step forward when the Republic, Malaysia, Indonesia, the Philippines and Thailand formed Asean (Association of Southeast Asian Nations) on 8 August 1967 to promote regional cooperation.

The task of nation-building in the choppy sea of politics was enormous. The Republic of Singapore was a small nation, with a population of less than two million, a small domestic market and no natural resources. Almost everything for its needs had to be imported. The only asset it had was its people. Then there was the perennial threat of a communist takeover.

One of Lee's first tasks was to boost the people's confidence and morale, using inspiring words of encouragement. He urged Singaporeans to stand united as a multi-racial nation, promising a place for everybody. Singapore wanted to be friends with Malaysia and trade with them and anybody else, including Russia and China and even Indonesia, he said.

Lee deemed unity as an essential pillar of a dynamic Singapore he was trying to build. He repeated the call in many of his public speeches to stir up the people's courage and confidence. In an address at the 111th birthday of the Indian saint Sri Narayana on 12 September 1965, he positioned the Republic not as a vanquished and broken nation but as one that was still strong and important in Asia. In the area of trade, he said that the trading community in Malaysia could not afford to ignore Singapore's potential purchasing power, since more than 40 percent of the purchasing power in the whole of Malaysia was in the Republic. He explained:

> We may be 20 percent of the population of Malaysia, but the purchasing power, the capacity to buy goods like microphones, clocks, drinks, fans, lights, television sets and transistors, the money is here because here they work. If people do not want that 40 percent to 44 percent market, that is their business. We want to open the market with them, but if they do not want it, we will make our own soap.

On another occasion, a mammoth agricultural exhibition on 18 September, Lee stressed that size was less important than quality. It was the quality of the people, the mettle in them that counted. Singapore did not believe "in shaking knuckle dusters" at others because Singaporeans were polite, but they were determined to survive in Southeast Asia for the next 1,000 years. He vowed: "Nothing will hold us back. We have thick skins and necks. Even our chickens have thick necks."

On 21 September 1965, Singapore took its place as the 117th member of the United Nations with unanimous approval, and as the 22nd member of the British Commonwealth the following month. In December the same year, Parliament passed the Singapore Army

Bill and in March 1967, the National Service Amendment Bill as well. The Bill made it compulsory for all male citizens reaching the age of 18 to register for national service.

Lee also touched on tourism, which he regarded as an essential driving force for the country's economic progress. His message to commemorate Tourism Week in September 1965 reminded Singaporeans that the industry was a fast-growing source of foreign exchange for the country. Every citizen must make visitors welcome, Lee reminded, saying: "This makes life better for all of us in Singapore, with more trade and tourists spending foreign currency. They can return with experience of time spent in Singapore in which they had a fair deal for their money and with courtesy as well. The range of Singapore's cuisine is a reflection of the nation's multi-racial society."

Lee again rallied Singaporeans forward when he opened the Everton Park Housing Estate on 9 November 1965. Making it clear that Singapore did not want to be anybody's stooge, he declared:

> We don't want to fight anybody. We intend to be ourselves and to hold this part of Southeast Asia. We intend to stay. Anybody who thinks we can be made pawns is making a very big error of judgement. We are sovereign, independent—forever and ever. We dig our toes in and fight. Anybody who thinks they can push us around, I say, over my dead body. I know in 10, 15 years, I can breed a generation that can man missiles.

However, while Singaporeans deserved a good life, they must not be selfish and self-centred, as Lee pointed out in his Chinese

New Year message on 20 January 1966: "But in the midst of this rejoicing, abundance of good food and good clothes, and free from the stifling shroud of silent intimidation and the threat of oppression, let us remember our friends and relatives who are struggling to achieve the ideals of human equality and justice which guide our own society. For in the end, our destinies cannot be separated."

Lee did not forget to reassure the minority races of their place in society. In his Hari Raya Puasa message on 22 January 1966, he gave this pledge: "In independent Singapore, all men are brothers. All men are equal citizens and their cultural, religious and linguistic heritage will be respected. On this Hari Raya Puasa I send my good wishes to all Muslim citizens and wish them security, progress and happiness in the years ahead. The happiness of the various communities in Singapore depends on their ability to be tolerant of each other as well as the different habits of life and religion."

As a great visionary and long-term planner, Lee was already thinking about self-renewal, which he considered vital to Singapore's continued success. This entailed broadening the talent base. He revealed his succession plan during a National Day celebration dinner at Queenstown on 11 August 1966. He said: "You cannot breed it too quickly, but one year has shown what is possible. And in three years, we will have a new system, a new generation of leaders of men able to look after themselves, with the brains, the guts and the industry. This is what we have to do."

Thereupon, self-renewal became part of the political system.

Meanwhile, as the process of building the Republic of Singapore went apace, the Barisan Sosialis continued to incite troubles. This time, the party turned its attentions to independence, which Singapore had gained following separation. They were the only major political party that opposed it. Chairman Dr Lee Siew Choh denounced independence as "phoney" and "a British plot to perpetuate colonialism." On 17 October 1965, about 1,000 supporters marched through the town, protesting against "undemocratic acts of the government". They distributed leaflets portraying a huge fist punching Lee Kuan Yew in the face. Armed policemen used tear gas to disperse them and arrested 19 trouble-makers. Later, the Barisan egged on Nanyang University students to condemn the university's proposal to improve standards and to use more English in the lectures. Several students boycotted classes and intimidated their lecturers. The university hit back by expelling 85 of them, while police arrested 44 others.

Reinforcing their protest against independence, the Barisan Members of Parliament boycotted the House when it sat in December 1965. Actually, the Barisan had by then lost a lot of its strength. Of the 13 MPs who had won in the 1963 general election, three had been detained that year and another two had left the country. The remaining seven began resigning to carry on their "struggle against imperialist aggression in the streets". The exodus was completed on 8 October 1966. Hundreds of their supporters paraded along High Street towards Parliament House, carrying banners proclaiming: "Parliamentary Democracy is Dead" and "Support Barisan Sosialis".

The Barisan MPs' resignations contributed to the PAP's good fortunes for in the by-elections that followed, the PAP candidates filled the 13 vacant seats, giving the party a total of 50 seats in

Parliament, with the sole remaining seat still held by the United People's Party. This was the beginning of the end for Barisan Sosialis and the dawn of a brighter day for the PAP.

Out in the streets, the Barisan Sosialis flogged other matters, such as national service and the amendments to the Trade Union Ordinance. The party charged that national service was a colonial device and told eligible boys not to register, and that the new trade union laws allowed only Singapore citizens to be members. On 3 April 1967, the party called for a general strike to protest against the measures. The government deemed the strike illegal and de-registered three trade unions which had joined the industrial action. These were the Singapore Commercial Houses and Factory Employees' Union, Singapore Rubber Employees' Union and Singapore Shoe Factory Employees' Union.

The Barisan Sosialis intensified its "struggle in the streets" with more demonstrations during which its supporters attacked the PAP's branch offices, government offices and even the US Embassy. They staged a sit-down protest outside Changi Prison against the alleged ill treatment of political detainees, shouting slogans and reciting Mao's quotations. Police arrested over 300 of them. Most of the accused were found guilty in court of unlawful assembly. They were sentenced to between three and six months' jail while the others were given a conditional discharge.

In the midst of these political disturbances, the British unexpectedly announced the early withdrawal of its armed forces from Singapore. They had hinted about the move in April 1967 and confirmed it on 16 January 1968. The withdrawal was to take place in 1971, instead of in the mid-1970s as originally scheduled. The proposal was ill-timed and a setback to the new Republic. For one thing, the nation now had to build up its own defence capability in four years instead of the targeted 10 years. For another, the economic vacuum created was immense.

The British military had been an important source of income, employing some 30,000 Singaporeans directly and thousands more indirectly, and contributing about 15 percent to the country's Gross Domestic Product (GDP). The early pull-out would retard the growth of the fledgling economy. It was a dilemma.

Raising this issue in his New Year message on 1 January 1968, Prime Minister Lee Kuan Yew told Singaporeans to be brave and strong in the face of the new adversity:

> Changes are going to take place in our economy and the pattern of employment as the British armed services begin their run-down. Britain has promised to help, but they can help only as much as their economy will allow them. More important is that we help ourselves. Our citizens in the armed services, some 30,000 civilian employees, must be ready and willing, over the next few years, to refit and retrain themselves to become the skilled and semi-skilled workers we need even now in Jurong (Singapore's first and largest industrial estate). And more factories are being planned by industrialists. Only a rugged, disciplined and closely knit community, aware of her problems and seeking rational, not irrational solutions, can create this climate of confidence, internally and internationally. Never forget that only

> intelligent anticipation, purposeful planning and determined leadership will guarantee our economic growth, industrial expansion and prosperity.

The government swiftly took remedial measures to recoup the expected 15 percent loss in GDP. As examples, the former British naval bases were converted into commercial establishments to service merchant ships plying between the West and the East. Singapore had the good fortune of being in a strategic location. Promotion of the manufacturing industry, one of the main engines of growth, was intensified here and abroad. More technical training institutes were set up to improve the people's skills and productivity.

Steadily, the economy took off. The economic expansion played a large role in rendering the communists' onslaught irrelevant. They began to lose their grip on trade unions and other front organisations as well as on the political scene. This was evident from the Barisan's absence in the general election of 1968 held to give the government a fresh mandate to resolve the problems facing the new Republic. Having boycotted and resigned from Parliament two years earlier, Dr Lee Siew Choh and comrades were not interested, preferring to continue their struggles in the streets.

The number of seats in the new Parliament had been enlarged from 51 to 58. On nomination day, 17 February, Singaporeans gasped with surprise when the PAP got a massive walkover, with 51 of its candidates returned unopposed. This was unprecedented in the history of local Parliamentary elections. The PAP had won even before it had started campaigning. The phenomenon reflected the PAP's growing popularity and the absence of an opposition equipped to challenge the party. On election day, 13 April, the party took the remaining seven seats.

Thus began the so-called one-party rule in Singapore. With the Barisan Sosialis out of the political scene and no formidable opposition in sight, the PAP swept the board in the next three general elections—in 1972, 1976 and 1980.

Obviously delighted by the colossal swing towards the PAP in the 1968 polls, Prime Minister Lee deduced that the communists had given up the fight. They knew they had no chance because the government's policies of the past 10 years had effectively removed the people's resentment, frustration and bitterness of unequal opportunities and unequal rewards. The ground had been taken away from them. In his victory speech on the steps of Raffles Institution, the counting centre, Lee told Singaporeans:

> People in Singapore know what is at stake—their lives and the future of their children. We, the People's Action Party, will never break faith with our people. We shall take steps to ensure that we ride through the storms and squalls of the crucial years ahead. A vigorous and resourceful people given a determined and dynamic lead will overcome the problems they know are ahead in the 1970s. We shall triumph.

Indeed, the economy of the new Republic of Singapore grew from strength to strength, increasing the affluence of the people and enhancing their skills. Political stability became the norm. Industrial strikes, demonstrations and street violence were bad memories of the past. The PAP reigned supreme until 1981 when it got a jolt.

11

WHEN THE OPPOSITION CAME

For 13 years, the PAP was the only political party in the Singapore Parliament. The absence of an opposition on the stage meant a clear road for the PAP government to formulate and implement policies without distractions and interruptions. The total monopoly in Parliament horrified some observers, particularly those from the West, who condemned it as undemocratic. But although Prime Minister Lee held a tight rein, there was no abuse of power and no deprivation, degradation or oppression of the people.

The government kept its election promises to raise the people's living standards and make Singapore a happy place to live, work and play in racial harmony. Challenged to dare to excel, Singaporeans put their shoulders to the wheel. The nation-building programme was tremendously successful during the 13-year one-party rule. There were more and better factories, trading and financial institutions, hotels, restaurants, shops and other commercial establishments, producing more well-paid jobs and therefore higher income. More public housing and schools sprouted up. The transportation system, public utilities and other types of facilities and infrastructure were improved. Singapore was becoming a global city, wealthy, literate and world-wise, ahead of many Asian countries, and even some European nations.

Singaporeans were grateful for the harvests, but they had one complaint. The PAP administration appeared arrogant and paternalistic. "This is good for you, so don't argue," they seemed to be saying. There were hardly any consultations with the people when drawing up policies, and without an opposition in Parliament, there were no checks and balances. Most people feared to criticise the government openly.

Some policies were harsh, controversial and therefore unpopular. Examples were birth control, legal abortion, higher vehicle road taxes, streaming in schools, a "Stop at Two" family planning programme, preference for children of sterilised parents and later, graduate mothers, the "Speak Mandarin" campaign, and cars having to have their petrol tanks half-full and later three-quarter full, when going to Malaysia.

Then in 1981, a lawyer named J B Jeyaretnam came into the picture to drive in the first wedge since 1963 that broke the PAP's total stranglehold.

However, it must be said that Singapore had never been a one-party state. At various times, there were several registered political parties. Many took part in the general elections and by-elections before and since 1968 when the PAP first swept the board. The reasons for their failure in getting into Parliament time and time again were simply that their candidates lacked the necessary calibre and credentials, and that their platforms offered no credible, alternative policies. They failed to match the PAP's package deal.

Lee said the Singapore electorate was not gullible. The people knew a good government when they saw one, and if the PAP ever broke faith with them, they would kick the party out of office through the ballot box.

Nevertheless, the population profile had changed over the years. A younger generation of Singaporeans was growing up. They were more sophisticated and demanding than the older Singaporeans, although it is true that their elders lived in an uncertain political climate where they had to depend very much on the government. Today's young citizens want a greater say in the decision-making process in this democratic society, or at least be consulted for their views first, whether the government deigns to accept their opinions or not.

Thus, the coming of Jeyaretnam was like a breath of fresh air.

Jeyaretnam was Secretary-General of the Workers' Party, which David Marshall founded before the landmark 1959 general election. J B, as he was popularly known, was a seasoned politician who had tried in vain five times previously for a place in Parliament. His moment finally came in the 1981 by-election held on 31 October. The Anson seat had been vacant after its incumbent, C V Devan Nair, was appointed to become the third President of Singapore. Jeyaretnam faced a PAP newcomer, Pang Kim Hin, lauded by the party as a young man of high integrity with strong academic qualifications, and an unknown politician in lawyer Harbans Singh, Secretary-General of the United People's Front.

The electorate also saw a new political party, Singapore Democratic Party (SDP), making a bid for the vacant Anson seat. The party was formed by another seasoned campaigner, lawyer Chiam See Tong. Chiam, the Secretary-General, and Fok Tai Loy, the Chairman, went to the nomination centre on 21 October to register their names. Then came a surprise. A hurried hush-hush consultation with Jeyaretnam ensued. Afterwards, Chiam emerged to say: "We have graciously withdrawn." The *volte face* was to avoid splitting the opposition vote. Jeyaretnam wanted to win badly.

The battle centred on J B and Pang of the PAP and was keenly fought. Both sides blew their rallying calls and hurled the usual brickbats at each other. PAP leaders advised the Anson electorate to be wise and elect Pang for continuity and a more stable and prosperous future. They believed they still held the ground and were confident of winning. J B urged the voters to elect him if they wanted democracy and launched his election theme, "A More Caring Society".

The atmosphere at the counting centre, Gan Eng Seng Secondary School, after the polls had closed was tense, as the restless supporters from both camps eagerly awaited the outcome. Interested Singaporeans watched the proceedings in their living rooms. Some hoped that the Anson electorate would vote for J B, if only to tell the PAP that an opposition in Parliament would be quite beneficial. Indeed, the Anson electorate gave J B their votes. The win was a minor miracle for him and the Workers' Party. In their hour of glory, J B's supporters were delirious. They triumphantly waved the party flags, and cheered and shouted themselves hoarse.

The result was close, though, with J B scraping through by 653 votes over Pang. In total, he amassed 51.9 percent of the valid vote cast, a swing of about 35 percent against the PAP. Harbans Singh got only 131 votes and lost his deposit. What mattered was victory. As in soccer, a win by a solitary goal is a win. Jeyaretnam had made it at last, at his sixth attempt. He had created political history in Singapore and broken the monopoly of the PAP. He became something of a folk hero. Those who had hankered for an opposition would now hear a dissenting voice in Parliament to bring up on their behalf matters they had feared to express, even if the new MP was overwhelmingly outnumbered. They hoped this would be the shape of things to come in local politics.

Beaming broadly, J B declared amid the cheers of his supporters:

> This victory is yours. It is not mine. It is the people's victory against the might of the PAP and all government agencies. I thank God for answering the prayers of not only myself but also of hundreds of thousands of Singaporeans. I pray to God that I will have the strength to serve not only the people of Anson but also the whole of Singapore. I am sure the Anson voters want me to regard myself not only as their MP but for the silent majority. There is a new sun breaking out tomorrow morning. Let us welcome the dawn of a bright, prosperous, happy Singapore, a Singapore we can call our own.

Only one thing was missing to complete his happiness, his wife Margaret, who had been a fervent supporter in his past election campaigns. She had died in 1980. Jeyaretnam expressed his sadness as he said:

> This is also my saddest moment. One person who had fought for your cause as fiercely as I did is not here. But I know that although she is not here physically, she is here in spirit. I am sure she will rejoice tonight, seeing you all here cheering me.

Then he hugged his son, Philip, standing beside him, and whispered: "We've won, son." They remained in embrace for a while and shed silent tears of joy. It was a poignant moment for the family.

What were the PAP's comments? Goh Chok Tong, Organising Secretary of the party's by-election campaign, made the point that the people of Anson had a lower threshold of pain. Brushing aside his deep disappointment, Goh affirmed the party's efforts to continue on with its long-term policy of self-reliance. The party would not go soft in order to win back the votes. He declared: "Let us show the people of Singapore what policy will work for us in the longer term." Meanwhile, Prime Minister Lee, expressing surprise at the PAP's by-election failure, said:

> I had expected a shift of about 15 percent. I never expected 35 percent. We'll have to find out why it happened and take the necessary measures. We'll win Anson back.

Jeyaretnam's election victory stirred a new political awakening in Singapore. It opened the eyes of Singaporeans to the fact that the PAP was not invincible after all. This was again evident in the general election of 1984 held on 22 December when the crack in the PAP's armour became a little wider.

For this election, the number of seats in Parliament had been further increased to 79. In addition, an unprecedented scheme was implemented in the Parliamentary system—the creation of seats for Non-Constituency Members of Parliament (NCMPs). The aim was to allow defeated opposition candidates polling the largest number of votes nationwide a place in the House, provided they got at least 15 percent of the ballots cast. But they would have no voting rights. Also, the number of seats reserved for NCMPs would be proportionate to the number of seats won by the opposition in Parliament. The maximum was three, which was later raised to four, with provisions for up to six.

Lee had mooted the idea of an NCMP back in 1982. His rationale was that he wanted several better and more intelligent opposition members as sparring partners for the younger PAP ministers and MPs. Moving the NCMP Bill in July 1984 which was eventually passed, Lee gave more insight into the purpose of the concept. He explained that the younger ministers and backbenchers needed training in Parliamentary debate. The NCMP scheme would provide a means of giving vent to "any allegations of misfeasance or corruption or nepotism", thus dispelling suspicions of cover-ups of alleged wrongdoings.

Lee argued that the NCMP idea would also serve as an education for the younger generation of voters who had missed the political conflicts of the 1950s and 1960s. They had been toddlers or teenagers then, with no idea of how destructive an opposition could be, and who now felt they were missing something. He was thus giving them the opportunity to experience some of the excitement of political combat.

The NCMP proposal proved to be a controversial one. Opposition parties decried it as another political deception of the PAP to fool the people. They accused the government of trying to mislead the public into believing that they could have an opposition without having to vote them in and therefore, there was no need for them to vote for the opposition. The NCMPs could be the opposition, said the PAP. The critics snorted that NCMPs, with no voting rights, were just mere decorations in Parliament. They were not genuine representatives of the people who could take their multitude of problems of housing and education, for example, to the ministers concerned for the solutions. NCMPs were not even postal boxes.

The 1984 general election saw more new PAP bright sparks as part of the party's ongoing process of self-renewal. Most notable was Brigadier-General Lee Hsien Loong, Prime Minister Lee's eldest son. BG Lee stood in Teck Ghee and was a big hit at once, especially among the young. The other new PAP blood included Mah Bow Tan and Ng Pock Too, both from the civil service. Mah was placed in Potong Pasir and Ng in Anson. The PAP had won 30 of the 79 seats in a massive walkover on nomination day, 13 December, leaving 49 to be contested at the polls. The huge PAP walkover was reminiscent of previous hustings.

The opposition candidates included Chiam, Secretary-General of the SDP, who had given way to Jeyaretnam in Anson in 1981, Jeyaretnam himself standing in his constituency again, and Dr Lee Siew Choh of the Barisan Sosialis, still very much in the picture after his boycott of Parliament in 1965 and the mass exodus of his colleagues in 1966.

Chiam chose Potong Pasir to stand against Mah Bow Tan. He had once stood against PAP heavyweights Lim Kim San in Cairnhill in 1976 and Howe Yoon Chong in Potong Pasir in 1980 and had lost both times. He was an independent then. Now he had a political party which he hoped had raised his political profile and the electorate's confidence. Jeyaretnam stood in Anson against Ng Pock Too, while Dr Lee Siew Choh went for Boon Teck to oppose the PAP's Ho Tat Kin.

Chiam, Jeyaretnam and Dr Lee were experienced campaigners who many Singaporeans thought would probably make good Parliamentary material. Would this be the day for them? The verdict rested in the hands of those living in the constituencies the opposition candidates were contesting.

Jeyaretnam repeated the Workers' Party platform of "A Caring Society" and of the aim to fight for the people's rights as citizens of Singapore. They had rights, he thundered at his rally speeches, the right to be consulted on any decision affecting them. They had the right to demand that all decisions be taken with the wishes of the majority. They had the right to live in dignity as human beings and to receive protection under the law.

Chiam's message urged the people to "Stop the PAP". He challenged the people to decide what sort of society they wanted. They must know that a one-party rule could lead to a totalitarian state. The coming election was a watershed. The mild-looking politician was coming into his own as an honest and dogged fighter.

Dr Lee was as vocal as ever in his condemnation of the PAP.

He castigated the party with his favourite line of fire: "Political deception, threats and suppression." He called on his electorate of Boon Teck to wake up and fight the PAP for freedom. He made the sales pitch that he could teach the younger upstarts in Parliament the finer points of political debate and of politics in general.

The PAP fought for continuity of leadership for greater prosperity. The counter-attacks on the opposition candidates were hard and systematic as usual. The opposition were men of no substance, the party leaders charged. They flogged dead issues. They had no policies or programmes worth considering. They were poor Parliament material. At an election rally in Fullerton Square, Prime Minister Lee even went so far as to compare Chiam's 'O' level results with those of his opponent in Potong Pasir, Mah Bow Tan. He denigrated Chiam's academic results because he had only six credits, and lauded Mah for his string of distinctions. (Lee later retracted, saying Chiam had in fact seven credits and not six.)

Lee probably did not expect his remarks to have an adverse effect on the PAP's campaign in Potong Pasir. At election time, the electorate of Potong Pasir registered their support for Chiam by accepting him as their MP. Political observers believed that Lee's ridicule of Chiam was the deciding factor for the latter's victory. Certainly, it failed to advance Mah's cause.

Chiam had succeeded at last, in his third attempt. Like those in Anson in 1981, the electorate of Potong Pasir had demonstrated that they were not afraid of the PAP. Chiam and his supporters were over the moon with the victory. Waving the party flags of a white triangle over a white circle against a red background, they cheered and chanted: "Chiam See Tong! Chiam See Tong!"

The beaming victor in a voice charged with emotion thanked the people of Potong Pasir for their confidence in him, and paid tribute to his supporters:

> This victory is not the achievement of one person. It is the result of a good team that I have. I am fortunate to have a very capable and hardworking team without which I would not have succeeded. I thank every member of the team. It is also their victory.

In Anson, his constituents returned incumbent Jeyaretnam of the Workers' Party, rejecting PAP newcomer Ng Pock Too. The second election success in a row proved that Jeyaretnam's 1981 victory was not a fluke.

This time, both his sons, Philip and Kenneth, were there to embrace him in his victory. In his victory speech, interrupted by tumultuous cheers from his supporters, he said:

> My dear, dear voters of Anson, you have made it again. You have withstood the onslaught of the mighty PAP and I salute you. It's your victory and yours alone and you can take pride in the fact that you have again set Singapore on the road to democracy.

Chiam and Jeyaretnam were the only two successful opposition candidates, making the final score in Parliament 77-2. Veteran Dr Lee Siew Choh lost. His failure indicated that the once powerful Barisian Sosialis no longer appealed even to the working class. The party just floated on the waves of politics after that, before finally sinking under in 1988. It was the end of any communist and pro-communist involvement in local politics.

Lee Hsien Loong won comfortably in his first election. But the results were very close for several other PAP candidates. The narrowest margin was in the battle in Jalan Kayu between the PAP's Heng Chiang Meng and the Workers' Party's M P D Nair, a veteran and aged politician. Heng squeezed through by only 571 votes. It was like 1963 all over again when some PAP stalwarts breasted the tape just centimetres ahead of their opponents.

Nair's good performance was significant in that it reflected Singaporeans' dissatisfaction with the PAP. The extent of the hostility and protest vote was evident also in several other constituencies where the opposition candidates garnered massive votes without their need to hold too many rallies, or go house-to-house canvassing.

A good example was the contest between unknown politician Lee Chin Teck of the Singapore United Front, and Labour Minister and Second Minister for Law and Foreign Affairs Prof S Jayakumar in Bedok. During the hustings, the PAP revealed that Lee Chin Teck had been receiving psychiatric treatment and was therefore unfit for Parliament. His family then withdrew him from the polls. Thus, he did not campaign and his constituents never saw him. But his name was not removed from the register, making him still a candidate technically. At election time, nearly 5,000 of them voted for him, about half the number they gave to Jayakumar.

The opposition rebuffed the NCMP concept. M P D Nair, who emerged as the top opposition loser in the final count and was therefore most eligible for a seat in Parliament, refused the offer. Neither did the next top losers who could have accepted it in Nair's place. They maintained the argument that the scheme was a

PAP gimmick crafted to perpetuate their reign. They preferred to win their seats in the polls and be genuine representatives of their constituents. That was the democratic way, they insisted.

Overall, the election results reduced the PAP's popularity from 77.7 percent to 64.8 percent. It should be mentioned that there is a big difference between the groundswell of today and that of yesteryear. In the 1950s and 1960s, when the communists were in their heyday in Singapore, they made attempts to instigate the electorate to vote for the communist-supported party or parties. In later years, without communist influence, the people made up their own minds. Many opposed the PAP simply because they were fed up with its domineering attitude and its unpopular policies.

However, the negative impact on the PAP was the same—a loss of ground. The 1984 election results told the party to return to the drawing board, look deeply into the people's unhappiness and adopt remedial measures.

A disappointed PM Lee realised this need as he analysed the outcome of the general election at his post-mortem news conference in the early hours of the next morning, 23 December. He said:

> I see a more fluid transition from the amalgam, the coalition that was forged in the battle for merger with Malaysia, then separation, then withdrawal of the British armed forces. That generation provided a very firm, secure solid base for high endeavour. That generation has grown old, diminished in numbers. A younger generation has got to find its own goals, decide what it wants out of life in Singapore and what there is to put in.

> The results of the elections show a highly sophisticated electorate. They wanted to put pressure on the PAP. They wanted more people in Parliament to get us to either go slower, if they don't like to go as fast, or to be more generous in policies, less austere and so on. In no case did they take a chance. The results showed an unexpectedly subtle understanding of how to use the vote to maximum effect. The signal has been sent.

The election marked the beginning of a transition to a new team. The team would be led by Goh Chok Tong, who was appointed First Deputy Prime Minister and earmarked to succeed Lee as Prime Minister. Goh had been Defence Minister and Second Minister for Health. He promised that he would address the demands of the younger generation, have more dialogue and put important national issues for public discussions before implementing them. He would also present a softer face than Lee did. As a line of communication, a Feedback Unit was set up to provide a listening ear to the grouses of disgruntled Singaporeans for appropriate action. The changed official attitude was reassuring to the people.

As expected, Chiam and Jeyaretnam made Parliament sittings more exciting. They posed probing questions and made vitriolic comments on many government policies, rattling the PAP ministers and backbenchers in the House. They alerted the ruling party to the true picture on the ground. They were thorns in the flesh of their PAP counterparts. Singaporeans hailed them as their spokesmen to bring up issues they themselves dared not express. The sight of

Chiam and Jeyaretnam challenging the indomitable PAP beamed on TV gladdened their hearts. Good, they said, at least they kept the PAP on their toes. They hoped this would be the beginning of a multi-party Parliament since 1963.

Of course, the two brave opposition MPs were out-voted all the time. Still, they fought hard for many important national issues. One of the hottest topics was the government proposal to push back the age of people allowed to withdraw their savings from the public pension scheme, Central Provident Fund (CPF), from the official retirement age of 55 to 60 and later to 65. The scheme formed part of the paper on the problems of the aged prepared by Health Minister Howe Yoon Chong. The government reasoned that those aged 55 were unable to take care of their hard-earned money. The CPF would do that on their behalf until they were 60 and above, thus ensuring their financial security in their twilight years.

The anger generated was understandable and Chiam had exploited the issue during the election campaign. Contributors to the CPF held that it was their money and that they should be allowed to withdraw it at the retirement age of 55 as the government had promised. They argued that if they were unable to look after their money at 55, how could they be more capable at 60 or worse, 65? Many would probably be dead by then. They should be allowed to enjoy the fruits of their labour while they could. Chiam and Jeyaretnam championed their cause. They pointedly warned that the government would be committing a criminal breach of trust if they implemented the scheme. The opposition MPs expressed their suspicion that the government was short of money and needed the people's savings for public expenditure. The government categorically denied the accusations. Even several of the PAP's own backbenchers opposed the plan.

After much debate and feedback from the ground, the government finally gave in. The withdrawal age remained at 55, but CPF contributors must leave $30,000, or $45,000 for husband and wife combined, in what was called the Minimum Sum Scheme, as security for their future. As an alternative, they could withdraw all their savings and pledge their home to the CPF. This sum has since been increased gradually in tandem with inflation.

Jeyaretnam performed like a veteran parliamentarian from the very beginning, with his eloquence and fiery oratory. But the same could not be said of Chiam, at least in his first few appearances. Those who watched him on television saw a timid and confused person, blinking his bespectacled eyes, looking around and groping for words. Once he fumbled on one important national matter and was criticised for failing to do his homework. The encounter took place during the Budget debate in April 1985 when Chiam alleged that the Housing and Development Board (HDB) did not subsidise its public housing which was why the flats were expensive. He claimed the subsidy was a myth and questioned the HDB's accounting and land valuation system.

National Development Minister Teh Cheang Wan took pains to explain to Chiam how the HDB worked out its costing to prove there was a subsidy. After Teh's lengthy explanation, Prime Minister Lee stepped in to reinforce the argument and debunk Chiam's allegations. Conceding defeat, Chiam uttered what became a classic one-liner from Parliament: "Well, if the Prime Minister says so, it must be so." The Member of Parliament for Potong Pasir later confessed that experience gave him his "first great political lesson" he would never forget. Henceforth, he learnt never to speak in Parliament or anywhere else without being fully prepared first.

Although he was steady, Jeyaretnam tended to overstep his line in his exuberance to push his views across. Several times he made remarks and accusations in Parliament which were deemed improper. He was brought before the Parliamentary Committee for Privileges and censured. One of the most serious remarks he made was his allegation of executive interference in the judiciary. Prime Minister Lee promptly got the Chief Justice's assurances that there was no interference. Jeyaretnam's downfall came when he was charged in court in 1986 with false declaration and manipulation of his party's funds. He was found guilty and fined $5,000 plus a jail term of one month. Under the Constitution, an MP loses his seat if he is fined $2,000 or jailed for one year. He is also disqualified from taking part in Parliamentary elections for five years. It was an unhappy end to Jeyaretnam's parliamentary career.

Because of his conviction, the court ruled that Jeyaretnam was unfit for the legal profession and he was later barred from practising as a lawyer. In October 1988, the Privy Council in London allowed his appeal and restored him to the rolls of lawyers. In their judgement, their Lordships recorded their "deep disquiet" over what they described as "misjudgements" and said the accused had "suffered a grievous injustice".

Chiam was now the sole opposition voice in Parliament. He showed a brave front. He had improved his performance after that "first great political lesson" in 1985. He ignored the heckles and jeers of the PAP backbenchers whenever he rose to speak. He was the butt of their jokes. But one could see that these were friendly jibes and he knew it. He just blinked and smiled. They all liked him and even Lee once said: "I like him, you know. He is so childlike."

Certainly, his Potong Pasir constituents were proud of him whom they affectionately addressed as "Ah Chiam".

His electorate demonstrated their affection by returning him in the 1988 general election held on 3 September. Chiam defeated another new PAP bright spark, Kenneth Chen, a businessman. The Potong Pasir incumbent not only beat Chen, he also increased his majority from 60.3 percent in 1984 to 63.1 percent. Elated by his second successive victory, he told his constituents as his exultant supporters cheered and waved the party flags:

> Thank you, thank you, the courageous voters of Potong Pasir. I thank you once again for returning me as your representative in Parliament. You have increased your votes to me and I thank you for it.

Then he promised them what he would do to make life better for them. Later, he told reporters: "I think I have become some sort of symbol for democracy, to show that other Singaporeans can also be elected and remain in Parliament."

Chiam was the only successful opposition candidate, though, despite the growing groundswell against the PAP. It was a poor crop for the opposition. Perhaps the government's remedial measures were working nicely.

The 1988 election marked a further transition in leadership. There were 17 new PAP faces. This leadership was given the responsibility of taking Singapore to the year 2000 and beyond. Prime Minister Lee defined the election as "truly a watershed".

Introducing the new PAP candidates at a rally, thanking and bidding farewell to those stepping down, he advised Singaporeans:

> Vote for the best candidate. If the non-PAP candidate is better than the PAP candidate, will do a better job in the Town Council and in Parliament, vote him in. In that way, Singapore is safe. If you vote the wrong man, then I wish you well. You will soon find out.

The number of seats in Parliament had been increased to 81 and the electorate had swelled to 1.45 million.

Another new concept, Group Representative Constituencies (GRCs), was introduced to add to the NCMP scheme. The purpose of the GRC, or team MPs, was to ensure continued representation of minority races in Parliament, particularly the Malays. Each team would consist of three, one of whom must be a Malay or an Indian. For the 1988 election, 13 constituencies were designated GRCs.

The opposition denounced the GRC scheme as another PAP tactic to perpetuate its rule. In keeping with its promise for consultation, the government held a public hearing on the matter before the general election. Speaking his mind, Chiam argued that Singapore was trying to build a cohesive society from among the different races. The multi-racial community was beginning to think as one nation. In his law firm, he employed staff from various racial groups. Being a Singaporean, he did not regard them as Chinese, Malay or Indian. Now the government was making the people more conscious of their ethnicity and splitting them apart. It was an about-turn. Despite objections from the opposition, the scheme was implemented.

During the campaigning, one of the most heated rallies was in Eunos, one of the 13 newly created GRCs. Here, lawyer and newcomer Francis T Seow led the challenge against the PAP. A former solicitor-general who had gone into private practice, he had a veteran team-mate in none other than Dr Lee Siew Choh, although the third man in the three-man GRC team was an unknown figure, Khalid Baboo, a part-time television comedian. They stood on a Workers' Party ticket and faced the PAP's Dr Tay Eng Soon, Zulkifli Mohammed and Chew Heng Ching.

Seow was eloquent and outspoken in his criticisms of the government, which he directed mostly at Prime Minister Lee. In October 1986, they had clashed during the Commission of Inquiry convened to study the operations of the Law Society of which Seow was then the President. The proceedings were televised and the public saw the lawyer fearlessly facing Lee. He soon became a popular figure among those Singaporeans who were unhappy with the PAP and saw him as good opposition material in Parliament. His rallies in Eunos drew huge, throbbing crowds each night. Some estimated the number at 50,000. As he blasted the PAP, they chanted: "Francis! Francis!"

Dr Lee Siew Choh was another crowd-puller, with his vociferous attacks on the PAP. He was still a much-admired politician for his courage in standing up to the PAP. There was a general sense that the Workers' Party GRC team just might carry the day. They nearly did, gaining almost half of the 75,000 votes cast. It was a close shave for the PAP.

Had the Workers' Party won, the PAP would have lost a heavyweight for Dr Tay Eng Soon was the Senior Minister of State for Education. In fact, the party had deliberately put him in Eunos to blunt Seow's teeth. Nevertheless, the enormous amount of votes Seow and his team harnessed was the biggest eye-opener for the PAP. The effect of the tremendous support for the opposition was evident in the final count. Although the PAP won all the wards except Chiam See Tong's Potong Pasir, it lost further ground overall. It collected 63.1 percent of the valid votes cast, a setback of 1.7 percent on the 1984 results.

However, Prime Minister Lee was not perturbed. At his post-election news conference, he viewed the election success as a solid victory. His assessment was:

> This is the people's verdict on the New Guard. Their consultative style has won their support. To lose only one seat is a landslide victory. The drop in the percentage of votes is not particularly significant. The younger electorate had not voted too differently from their elders. This is reassuring. The transition is now complete. The future is up to my younger colleagues.

Based on the results, the Workers' Party was the losing opposition with the highest number of votes and so was entitled to the NCMP seat. The party would undoubtedly have chosen Seow as its representative. But unhappy events befell him, including alleged tax evasion by him. The fallen would-be politician then left the country. The Workers' Party chose team-mate Dr Lee Siew Choh to take his place. The former Barisan Sosialis chief was back in Parliament after an absence of 23 years. He had aged but his voice was still strong, as were his criticisms of the PAP. Together with Chiam, Dr Lee kept Parliamentary debate alive.

Having been disqualified for five years, Jeyaretnam did not take part in the general election. But he incurred more problems. As Secretary-General of the Workers' Party, Jeyaretnam had helped the party's candidates in their electioneering. In one of the rallies at Bedok Town Centre on 26 August, he defamed Lee Kuan Yew by imputing that Lee had contributed to the death of National Development Minister Teh Cheang Wan. The minister had committed suicide in December 1986 while he was under investigation for corruption.

Lee sued Jeyaretnam, who denied he was seeking to defame the Prime Minister. The hearing took place in July 1990 and the High Court, ruling that Lee had a case, awarded him $260,000 in damages, plus costs and 6 percent interest from 1 September 1988. The court also ordered Jeyaretnam not to repeat the slander. But that was not all. Jeyaretnam also defamed Law Minister Prof S Jayakumar, four former Indian PAP MPs and eight organisers of the 1995 Tamil Language Week in an article published in the Hammer, the Workers' Party organ. In an election rally in January 1997, he defamed then Prime Minister Goh Chok Tong. Unable to pay damages running into several hundred thousand dollars, he was declared a bankrupt in 2001.

Singaporeans who had regarded him as a worthy opponent of the PAP were disappointed with him. They found it hard to believe that a lawyer of his experience did not know better than to cast aspersions on other people.

Following the 1988 general election, the PAP government introduced yet another Parliamentary concept. This was the Nominated MP (NMP) scheme. The idea was to allow leading citizens to say their piece on affairs of state in Parliament and to inject fresh ideas in Parliament debates. NMPs would be selected from prominent people in business and government through recommendations. Several of them have since been appointed. The opposition comments can be summarised thus: "This is another PAP design to perpetuate its rule."

After a poor crop in 1988, the opposition made inroads again in the 1991 general election on 31 August, and gained a larger harvest. Chiam not only retained Potong Pasir but two of his Singapore Democratic Party comrades standing in other constituencies romped home, too. In fact, party Chairman Ling How Doong was the giant killer. Standing in Gombak, he defeated PAP incumbent Seet Ai Mee, Acting Minister for Community Development. Seet was the only minister to lose. She had beaten Ling in 1988.

Another successful party was the Workers' Party. Its new member, Low Thia Khiang, a Nanyang University graduate and a building contractor, won in Hougang, defeating PAP incumbent Tang Guan Seng. Low's team-mate, NCMP Dr Lee Siew Choh, lost in Eunos yet again. In all, the opposition won four seats, the largest number since 1963 when the Barisan Sosialis took 13 seats and the United People's Party one.

For the 1991 election, the PAP had changed the electoral boundaries and increased the number of GRCs from 13 to 15 by grouping several single-seat wards, one of which was Tanjong Pagar, Lee Kuan Yew's fort since 1955. The number in each team was increased from three to four.

The opposition saw the scheme as another PAP attempt to dilute the opposition's strength. But this election was most memorable for the unique strategy adopted by the opposition to gain more seats in Parliament. They decided to call the general election a by-election. It was an innovative tactic not seen before or after. The PAP dismissed the idea as a desperate move.

The opposition's reason was simple. They knew that they had no chance of forming the next government and that, in their heart of hearts, most Singaporeans still wanted a PAP government whatever its faults. Led by MP for Potong Pasir Chiam, the opposition agreed to field only 45 candidates for the 81-seat Parliament. They stayed away from 36 wards, including all the 15 GRCs, thus handing the PAP 36 seats on a platter. As a bonus, the opposition deliberately gave the PAP a walkover in five other wards on nomination day, 21 August. This brought the party's total to 41 seats, thereby automatically returning it to power. So the opposition told the electorate in the remaining 40 constituencies to be contested that it was safe to vote for all the opposition members there.

As in previous elections, the rallies were electrifying. Larger attendances were seen at those of the opposition. Oddly enough, the PAP organised few rallies, preferring to campaign through dialogue sessions which they considered to be more effective. The opposition's main line of attack was the rising cost of healthcare, education, transport and other social facilities. The PAP must be checked or life in Singapore would become increasingly more expensive, they told the people. As electioneering reached fever pitch, some Malay opposition members touched on communal matters. The PAP sternly warned them to be careful.

The strategy of naming the general election a by-election did not work as expected. Still, although the 1991 results indicated that the pro-PAP sentiments were still strong, the scale of protest votes was higher. This was reflected in the reduction of the PAP's majority from 63.1 percent in 1988 to 61 percent.

However, the PAP must have done its homework well for the opposition's fortunes declined in the next general election on 2 January 1997. Only the Singapore Democratic Party's Chiam See Tong of Potong Pasir and the Workers' Party's Low Thia Khiang of Hougang won. The victory was the fourth in succession for Chiam and the second for latter-day politician Low.

Then Chiam faced a rebellion in his party. In an internal power struggle in 1993, a new member, Dr Chee Soon Juan, a former National University of Singapore lecturer, replaced him as Secretary-General. Chiam left and formed another party, Singapore People's Party. A similar power struggle took place in the Workers' Party. Here, Low Thia Khiang ousted J B Jeyaretnam as Secretary-General in 2001, much to the veteran politician's dismay.

Chiam and Low repeated their performance in the 2001 general election on 3 November. Chiam's electorate of Potong Pasir kept their "Ah Chiam", while the Hougang voters returned Low as their MP. The PAP not only captured all the other constituencies but also increased its majority to over 70 percent, an excellent performance indeed. The swing-back showed that the PAP's consultative style of government was bringing results. However, it could also be that Singapore still lacked opposition politicians worthy of the electorate's trust and confidence.

The PAP has always warned Singaporeans that an opposition in Parliament would drive foreign investors away and frustrate the government's plans for a better Singapore. But events have shown that these have not happened. Singapore continued to attract foreign investments and increase the affluence of the people. These achievements came despite the presence of an opposition. Indeed, the coming of the opposition has brought several benefits such as a change in the government's paternalistic style of governance and uncompromising attitude, and a greater willingness to listen to the people's ideas. All these changes are to the nation's good.

Chiam See Tong and Low Thia Khiang have opposed and will continue to oppose and criticise government policies they think are wrong. It is the duty of the opposition to do so. But they have proved to be loyal citizens. They have shown that their only interest is the betterment of Singapore. They have demonstrated their support on many occasions when the nation faced internal and external threats to its security, such as international terrorism and the SARS (severe acute respiratory syndrome) outbreak that ravaged the country in 2003. Lee Kuan Yew himself said he liked Chiam and admired Low. He once described Low as a man of depth and substance, saying: "I listen to him, all the others I switch off."

Singaporeans want more opposition in Parliament but are discerning enough to distinguish the wheat from the chaff. On the other hand, they still prefer a PAP government, as exemplified by the successive general election victories since 1959, because it has not broken faith with them. On this basis, the PAP will continue to govern until more opponents like Chiam and Low, or better than they are, enter the political theatre. At the moment, the crystal ball shows a blank.

12

LEE ATTACKED

Probably no other profession in the world bears such a bad name as politics. Examples of the derogatory definitions are: "politics has always been the systematic organisation of hatred", "politics is too serious a matter to be left to politicians" and "politics is blood sport". Whatever the portrayal may be, politics is indisputably a tough, rough and dangerous game. In some countries, politicians are assassinated and voters bribed, cajoled, threatened, injured and killed during election time.

Singapore, too, sailed in the stormy sea of politics, especially during the tumultuous mid-1950s and some years after that. However, it must speak volumes of the situation here that no politician or voter has died or been injured in battle. Although the early days of the social revolution were turbulent, all the general elections since 1955 have taken place peacefully. Still, there had been dangerous and traumatic moments for many of the local politicians. Lee Kuan Yew was no exception. Lee was harassed, intimidated, jeered and spat at, cursed, and physically attacked on a number of occasions during those dark days. Even today, there are people who hate him.

Some of the worst assaults on Lee took place during his marathon walkabout from November 1962 to September 1963 when he toured all 51 constituencies (the total number at that time) after the Referendum for merger with Malaya. His goal was to reassure Singaporeans that reunification would greatly benefit them economically, get the people's views and consolidate the government's strength against the communists who were dead set against reunion.

For example, in Toa Payoh, a Barisan Sosialis stronghold which Lee visited on 11 August 1963, a large, unruly and angry crowd gathered at the branch office of the Singapore General Employees' Union. They comprised adults as well as boys and girls, their faces masked. It was reported that they were anti-merger elements. They locked the gate of the union's premises and stayed inside. There was also a crowd outside, many of them Lee's supporters. The demonstrators inside strung black banners and posters, scrawled with abusive words likening Lee to Hitler. To complete the bizarre picture, they carried an effigy of Lee flanked by tiny Swastika paper flags. They booed and hurled abuse when Lee arrived in his Land Rover just after 5 pm. The police, with pre-knowledge of the ugly mood, were already there to keep law and order.

Unable to get in because of the locked gate, Lee challenged the demonstrators to come out and discuss what their problems were.

When they refused to come out, Lee shook the gate. His supporters surged towards the gate and joined Lee in shaking it. Lee was in a nasty situation. He finally gave up. The booing and jeering stopped, only to resume when he returned to his Land Rover. Speaking to the accompanying reporters later, he said the communists knew exactly what they wanted—a communist Malaya. But they would have it "only over my dead body".

Another hostile reception greeted Lee two days later, at the Siong Hoe Biscuit Factory at Ah Hood Road. The factory was not operating as its workers were on strike engineered by the Singapore General Employees' Union. The union was the industrial backbone of the Barisan Sosialis. As Lee passed by, the picketing strikers booed and jeered him. He stopped and told them the government wanted to help them, but they must not allow themselves to be used by the communists. He invited them to an open discussion on their grievances. They refused, and continued booing and jeering. He told them: "You are all like parrots." Realising that they were not in the mood to listen to reason, he continued on his tour.

The most dangerous encounter Lee had was at Towner Road about a month later. It was here that he was physically assaulted. The time was 11pm and he had finished addressing a large crowd at a market and was leaving the place. Opposite the market were the head offices of the Singapore Business Houses Employees' Union and the Singapore School Canteen Vendors' Association. Both organisations displayed hostile banners attacking Lee. As he passed by, a small group, some of them masked, booed. He stopped and approached them to ask what the problem was. Union President Foo Yoon Fong, Secretary-General P Govindasamy and several other officials emerged from the building and started accusing Lee of being a traitor. One of them even shouted obscene words at him. They demanded to know why the government was trying to close down the union. Lee replied that the union had broken the law. He invited the officials to his Land Rover to talk about it. They refused.

A crowd surrounded them and began shoving. A melee ensued and angry hands pushed Lee into a monsoon drain. Someone pulled him out. He was not hurt. A television reporter was also pushed into the drain and a cameraman was punched in the face. At one point during the scuffling, Lee caught hold of Govindasamy's wrist and shouted: "Stop using your hands on me."

After the police had restored law and order, the belligerent union officials retreated into the union premises, while continuing to accuse Lee of being a traitor.

Shaken by the physical attack, Lee said afterwards: "Luckily I am agile and I take no chances. I make no secret of the fact that I am prepared for trouble. I have done unarmed combat training and know how to look after myself. If you show fear, they will really go for you. They are toughs, and you've got to be tough with them."

Then there was the hate campaign mounted by ultra-extremists when Singapore was part of Malaysia. They denounced Lee Kuan Yew as a communalist and an enemy of Malaysia who was trying to challenge Malay rights and destroy peace and harmony. As tension built up, the Singapore Government heard a rumour of the Federal Government's attempt to arrest Lee. Denying the rumour, Acting Malaysian Prime Minister Abdul Razak said: "The allegation by the PAP is too wild and mischievous to merit any comment. The people of this country know that the Alliance government is a responsible, just and fair government. We do not go about arresting people without sufficient grounds or reason."

Singapore and Malaysia were not the only countries with anti-Lee Kuan Yew elements. Lee met some even in Cambridge in April1969. He was there to deliver the James Smuts Memorial Lecture before some university dons. In the audience was the Cambridge University Vice-Chancellor, Sir Eric Ashby. While Lee was speaking, about 40 left-wing students demonstrated outside. They waved red flags and yelled slogans from Mao's thoughts. They banged the windows and threw tennis balls about the lawn. Suddenly, a ball crashed through a window, landing about 10 feet away from Lee.

Lee was unperturbed. He interrupted his talk and calmly said to his audience: "I am quite happy if you can hear. I have considerable experience in these matters. From the feeling one gets of it, this is synthetic revolution. If we can ignore the people outside, and as long as the audience is prepared to go along with me, I think we should go on with the proceedings."

He received a standing ovation for his calmness. Then rain dispersed the rabble students. Later, they denied Lee was the object of their scorn. They claimed they were after the dons.

Besides disgruntled trade unionists, workers and students, the Western press appeared to feel duty-bound to launch their tirades, too. Lee knew only too well that the pen is mightier than the sword and that if used recklessly, it could destroy Singapore. He had drawn the line back in 1959 after he had been asked to form the government and warned journalists not to cross it. He had made it clear that foreign capital that sought to exploit local capital to enter the propaganda business would do so at its own peril. What was important was accurate and fair reporting. He had been consistent in his stand since and he would not let the foreign press forget it.

He made the point strongly on 9 June 1971 during his address to the conference on The Mass Media and New Countries. He reminded journalists that the freedom of the press in Singapore must be subordinated to the over-riding needs of the nation's integrity and the primary purpose of an elected government.

He told the writers: "We want the mass media to reinforce, not to undermine, the cultural values and social attitudes being inculcated in our schools and universities. The mass media can create the mood in which people become keen to acquire the knowledge, the skills and disciplines of advanced countries. Without these, we can never hope to raise the standards of living of our people."

Lee warned that an irresponsible press could, over a sustained period, influence the behaviour of people and spark off political action. He cited the racial riots of 1950 and 1964, and the communist-inspired violence by young Chinese workers and students, as examples of the destructive events in which the newspapers and broadsheets played an important role.

He asked not only for fair and accurate reporting but also for the right of reply on misleading articles. His message was clear: "Don't engage in domestic politics. That is for the citizens of Singapore. Give us the right of reply. You come to my market on my terms. Doing business here is a privilege, not a right." When the foreign press continued to defy him and took their chances, Lee had the Newspaper and Printing Presses Act tightened. Several reputable publications, such as *Time*, *Wall Street Journal Asia* and *Far Eastern Economic Review*, were taken to task and their circulation in Singapore curtailed.

The attacks of the foreign media centred on Lee's style of government. They dubbed him a dictator and accused him of stifling the freedom of the press. In a BBC radio interview in November 1971, he was asked why he was tough. Lee replied that he was not taking a tough line, but he had to be firm on certain things. He could not allow the communists to run wild and ruin the country. In another BBC interview in 1977, he denied being a dictator, saying: "I am on parade all the time. Why need I be a dictator? They come to violent ends."

The *Washington Star* touched on the subject of political detainees while interviewing Lee in November 1978. Lee put the case in its proper perspective:

> We know that if our foe wins, we die and die painfully. But when we win, our foes live comfortably, even in prison, with butter and eggs and meat according to the special rations which the rules of the game lay down upon us. This is in part an unequal conflict, because on one side is terror that is absolute, on the other side which is not really terror. It is just a deterrent, and often no more than soporific. You put a man in, you feed him, he studies, he writes his memoirs, he comes out and fights. If his side wins, he pulls your fingernails out and you are dead.

There were also charges that Singapore had no human rights.

Former US President Jimmy Carter was one of the most vehement critics as he championed the democratic cause for small non-communist nations. Lee gave his answer in an interview with *Time* magazine in May 1977: "President Carter should accept the world as it is—many different societies, cultures, stages of development. Now we hear that we have to be like you, or else we are not civilised."

Lee added that he believed the United States was in danger of setting a narrow definition of democracy with which only a few Western European nations could possibly comply.

Lee's definition of democracy is a society where there is access to information on world affairs other than information the government gives, and where dissent is allowed, provided it does not express itself in violence against established society. Speaking to a group of Australian journalists in May 1977, he put the case as such: "When we talk about human rights, we are really talking about different things in developing countries." That same month, the *Times* of London jumped into the act to question him about his style of democracy. Lee told the newspaper that developing countries sometimes had to sacrifice certain liberties for the sake of development, security and to prevent communist oppression. He argued: "You cannot expect to find in Asia or Africa norms and standards which did not exist in Western Europe 30 years ago under Hitler or even in the southern states of America in the 1950s."

The newspaper asked why ballot papers were numbered and why political detainees were not brought to trial. Lee explained that the British started the idea of numbering ballot papers, but that did not prevent the communists in Singapore from getting 30 percent of the vote in 1963 (through the Barisan Sosialis). He said: "I do not want to get into the situation where we remove the numbers and then, after the opposition lose, they will accuse me of stuffing the box with ballot papers marked in our favour."

On detention without trial, Lee posed the rhetorical question: "Do you believe we will get witnesses to go up and swear on oath to be identified by those in court? Half the strength of the Malayan Communist Party is the awe and fear which they have established in the minds of the people. That is, if you betray them then some time, some place, they will settle the score."

Lee assured the newspaper that he was prepared to release the political detainees if they renounced the Communist Party's policy of overthrowing the government by violence. (Indeed, all political detainees have since been released and many of those exiled have been allowed to return to Singapore. They included James Puthucheary and his brother Dominic, Fong Swee Suan and S Woodhull who were arrested under Operation Cold Store in February 1963.)

The Socialist International, of which Singapore was then a member, was equally vociferous in its attacks against the alleged lack of human rights. In 1977, the organisation voted to expel Singapore. But Lee had already decided earlier to leave the hostile group anyway.

Lee could also throw comments and criticisms as well as he could take them, and they ruffled feathers. One of his favourite topics was Britain's welfare state. Although he held affection for the nation, the erstwhile mighty empire was not a good example Singapore should emulate, he was wont to say. That caused a lot of unhappiness among the British. On one occasion, he really twisted the British lion's tail. This was during the state dinner in Singapore on 8 April 1985 given in honour of Margaret Thatcher who was then the British Prime Minister.

Speaking before the distinguished dinner guests, Lee praised Thatcher's attempts to change the direction Britain should take and predicted that privatisation of major sectors of the British economy would bring back vigour to British industry. Singapore, he said, had used to advantage what Britain had left behind, including the English language, the legal system, parliamentary government and impartial administration. Then came the bombshell:

> However, we have studiously avoided the practice of the welfare state. We saw how a great people reduced themselves to mediocrity by levelling down. The less enterprising and the less hardworking cannot be made equal simply by cutting down the achievements of the enterprising and the striving. And we have seen how difficult it is to dismantle a system of subsidised living once people get accustomed to a government providing it.

The rejoinders came fast and furious the next day, with several British politicians wielding the hammer. Shadow Health Minister Frank Dobson blustered: "Mr Lee should keep his stupid mouth closed. I hope Mrs Thatcher has not learned too much in Singapore, otherwise she will be putting opposition leaders in jail when she returns."

Labour MP Allen Adams hotly decried Singapore as a model state. He scoffed: "If we are going to take his state as a model, the country (Britain) would be going back to 1870 when people worked in sweatshops round the clock for virtually nothing."

Labour's Foreign Affairs spokesman George Robertson said: "I do not think the British people would want to make the choice to turn Britain into an offshore capitalist enclave. Singapore is hardly a model for democratic choice."

All this banter was part and parcel of Lee's politics. He took the rough-and-tumble in his stride. He had his own mind and ideas about world affairs. He was not sensitive. In an interview with the BBC in December 1987, during the height of the press freedom controversy, it was suggested that he was over-sensitive and over-reacting. He retorted: "No, no. I have a pretty scarred hide. I am accustomed to arrows and bolts of lightning."

He was also unconcerned by being labelled a bully, saying in another BBC interview in October 1989: "If little things like that anger me, I'll be running out of energy. No. People can say what they like. But I am what I am, and I don't want to waste time chasing phantoms."

Despite the warning of punishment for inaccurate and biased reporting, some foreign press continued to do so. The *Far Eastern Economic Review* (which has since closed shop) defamed Lee. In an article published on 17 December 1987, the Hong Kong-based weekly accused Lee of being intolerant of the Roman Catholic Church and of persecuting the clergy. In response, Lee sued the magazine. The hearing in the High Court ran from 25 September to 14 October 1989. The judge found in Lee's favour and awarded him $230,000 in damages, plus costs.

Following the court case, the *Review*'s sister publication, the *Wall Street Journal Asia*, published a report in which it implied that the judge had not been impartial because the plaintiff was the Prime Minister of Singapore. The daily newspaper was charged with contempt of court and found guilty in a 43-page judgement delivered on 11 January 1991.

In its defence, the *Wall Street Journal Asia* had argued that its article was not meant to attack the judge or the judiciary. It was merely a newsworthy story of public interest.

In May 1990, Lee visited London during a European tour. Sky TV seized the opportunity to get an interview with him. Host Frank Bough could not resist the temptation of asking his Singaporean guest about his style of government and the one-party rule. Here are excerpts of the interview:

Bough: In 1981, Jeyaretnam won a seat in a by-election as an opposition MP.

Lee: Yes.

Bough: The only opposition MP in the entire Parliament.

Lee: Is that wrong?

When Bough hesitated, Lee pursued the issue: Is that wrong?

Bough: There is no opposition. Why was there no opposition to you?

Lee: Because I won 75 percent of the vote in 1980. Is that wrong? Is that wrong?

Bough tried to evade the issue, but Lee persisted: Is that wrong? Is it wrong to win 75 percent of the vote in a free and fair election?

Bough: Not at all.

Some Western journalists even tried to presume to know about Singapore politics and its problems, to the extent of having the audacity to criticise and offer suggestions. Once, during a news conference, Lee had to cut down to size one such misguided journalist. Looking him in the eye, Lee told the newsman sternly that he had been governing Singapore for 15 years and he still had not been able to solve all the problems. The journalist (and a foreigner at that) could not know what the problems were exactly and therefore he should not be telling Lee how to do his job.

In May 1990 while on a visit to Paris to address the Institute of International Relations of France, Lee met journalists who inevitably broached the subject of his style of government. He asked those who had not visited Singapore to do so and then "we can talk". He told them:

> The Western press has an insidious tendency of living up to show solidarity. *Dow Jones* was wrong! The *Wall Street Journal Asia* was wrong! So is the *Far Eastern Economic Review*, in interfering in my daily politics and refusing me a right of reply. They lost the argument but the Western press is not interested, they just repeat that I am shutting up the press.

Those who worked with and for him vouchsafed Lee was never a dictator. Former Law Minister E W Barker who had known Lee since his schooldays and who had studied with him in Cambridge, once said: "He is not a dictator. He listened to us. My other colleagues of my age would not be in the Cabinet if he were so. He has been out-voted on occasions. When we are against him, in the end he's with us. But he is a strong leader."

Another long-standing comrade, former Deputy Prime Minister and Senior Minister S Rajaratnam, described Lee as tough, firm, authoritarian, a man who did not trust easily. He qualified this by saying: "But he is neither rigid nor intolerant of opposite points of view. Argue a case properly and show him the facts, and he will reconsider his own viewpoint."

Rajaratnam said that Lee had such a sharp mind and debating skills and was so well-prepared that any minister with a different point of view must be prepared to challenge him and meet his rebuttals. He explained: "Mr Lee doesn't argue because he wants to argue. He wants to know why you say this, have you got the back-up to say so. In that sense, he's overpowering because he's so well-prepared."

Former diplomat George Seow put it dramatically: "He is never a dictator. Former Cabinet ministers like Dr Toh Chin Chye and Dr Goh Keng Swee would pound the table and challenge his views. In the end, it's a Cabinet decision."

Lee was also criticised for his habit of making public the reasons for removing his colleagues from office. It was like hitting a man when he was down, some people complained. Lee's reply was that sometimes, the truth had to be told to preserve the integrity of the government. Perhaps the most disquieting of such revelations was the unfortunate case of C V Devan Nair. A former trade unionist, communist and detainee, Nair was one of the early PAP Central Executive Committee members. When Singapore was in Malaysia, he was the sole PAP MP in the Federal Parliament. After separation, he was appointed Secretary-General of the National Trades Union Congress (NTUC). In 1979, he was fielded to contest in a by-election in Anson. He won his seat.

When Benjamin Sheares, the second President of Singapore, died in 1981, Lee recommended Nair for the highest office in the land. Lee had once publicly praised Nair for "his intense dedication and honesty", pointing out that once in a long while, Singapore could get a person of his calibre. Lee moved the motion for Nair's appointment at a Parliament sitting on 23 October 1981 where he enthused:

> Those of us who have known him well are confident he will rise above his loyalties to the NTUC and the PAP to embrace a broader spectrum of loyal Singaporeans. We cannot change his character, his way of life, or the habits of a lifetime. Indeed, they are his strengths. What will change is his role. From defender and champion of the workers, he must now become a focal point for all Singaporeans to identify themselves with.

Singaporeans, and not less Lee himself, were therefore shocked when Nair tendered his resignation in March 1985. More shocking was the news of his alcoholism. Before a hushed Parliament on 29 March, Lee read out the letter of resignation. He confessed that he and his Cabinet colleagues had not known of the President's problem. Nearing the end of his address, Lee was overcome with emotion. He choked several times as he asked the House to join him in wishing Nair "fortitude in his task of rehabilitation". He added in a quivering voice: "With the help of his wife and family, he must find the strength and the stamina to break his dependency."

Unfortunately, the unhappy story did not end there. It eventually blew up into one of the most sordid episodes of the decade. It began when Nair started attacking Lee and calling for his resignation. Lee had no choice but to put matters in perspective. In a White Paper published on 20 June 1988, he bared it all. Giving his reasons in Parliament, he said he did not want to do this, but Nair's "recent public statements on political developments in Singapore as an active participant have made it necessary to put the facts on record so that Singaporeans can understand his motives and see through his statements".

The White Paper unearthed all the shocking details. Examples were Nair's "uninhibited" behaviour with various women while on a visit to Sarawak in March 1985, his association with a German woman, ill-treatment of his wife and his drinking habits. Nair, in statements following the disclosure, accused Lee of seeking political revenge by releasing the sordid details and said that "it is with history that I will now rest the matter". Lee later remarked that he was disappointed with his old comrade and that he was not the man he used to know.

However, Lee was sympathetic towards his family and showed deep concern about their welfare. He had a soft heart behind that stern face. He wrote a letter to Nair's son, Janadas, made public on 3 July 1988 in which he said:

> I fear not for your father, because he no longer knows what is good for him. I fear more for your mother. She is a loyal Indian wife, who will keep suffering for his sake. You can minimise that suffering if you are very firm, and whenever necessary, brutal and tough with your father. You must face this reality quickly, or you will not be able to cope with him.

The attacks by the Western press followed Lee even after he had resigned as Prime Minister, and the object of their scorn was always the same—a dictatorial government. Somehow, they appeared unconvinced by Lee's assurances repeated over and over again that he was not a dictator, or by the civil liberties Singaporeans were enjoying, or the well-fed and well-dressed people they could see for themselves. One school of thought has it that Western newspapers hate good news about Singapore or anywhere else in Asia. They want to see violent anti-government demonstrations, economic crises, people rummaging among the rubbish bins for food, people being tortured, and the like. They seem to have a penchant for putting Asia in a bad light. Then they can tell their readers back home: "There, you see. They can't do without the West."

Several newspapers and politicians in Malaysia took issue with Lee's memoirs, *The Singapore Story*, when it was published in 1998. The *New Straits Times* said it was saddened that Lee had chosen to vilify some of Malaysia's former leaders, describing it as bad taste because they were dead. "The dead don't tell tales and cannot possibly defend themselves, even when lies are told, in a futile attempt to rewrite history," said the daily.

In its editorial, the *Utusan Malaysia* charged that Lee might be trying to disrupt Malaysia's efforts to repair its floundering economy because Singapore did not want to see Malaysia become more prosperous and developed. "Singapore must realise that it is in more need of Malaysia and its neighbours to maintain its economy, as it is devoid of natural resources," said the newspaper.

Former senior journalist Samad Ismail was quoted by *The Sun* in September 1998 as saying that Lee had a jaundiced view based on a faulty memory. “He fights against imaginary enemies and tells people that he has won. If there is no enemy, he creates one to show he is a warrior, a knight in shining armour,” said Samad.

Malacca’s Chief Minister Abu Zahar Isnin urged Lee to promote friendly ties between Malaysia and Singapore instead of harping on history and dwelling on old issues. Malaysian Chinese Association Youth chief Chan Kong Choy said he was shocked that Lee had described former MCA President Tan Siew Sin as “short-sighted” and “stupid”. Chan, who is also Deputy Energy, Telecommunications and Posts Minister, said: “The reality today shows that the position of the Chinese in Malaysia is not as bad as Mr Lee made it out to be.”

Joining in the chorus, Malaysian Chinese Association’s International Youth Bureau Chairman Lee Hwa Beng urged Singaporeans to stop all action and statements from politicians that would damage Malaysia’s sovereignty and image. Johor State Executive Councillor Jimmy Low even suggested the banning of the memoirs from Malaysia as “they would poison the mind of a younger generation of Malaysians”.

Then there was the interesting encounter with William Safire of the *New York Times* in February 1999. The interview took place at the side of the World Economic Forum in Davos, Switzerland. Inevitably, the topics on dictatorship and freedom of the press cropped up. Safire is no fan of Singapore and his comments have always been acrid. Here are edited excerpts of the interview:

> Safire: I’ve often written that you’re a dictator.
>
> Lee: Yes. But if that makes me a dictator, well, you’ve won. So, am I a dictator? Do I need to be a dictator

when I can win hands down?

Safire: Why don't you permit competition politically if you can win hands down?

Lee: I do permit competition.

Safire: You don't feel that you have abused, or misused, the law to intimidate people into not running against you?

Lee: No, no. I don't think so. They can run against me, but it's an effort to gather enough people to make that consistent try year after year, to build an organisation.

Safire: You're trying to leave me with the impression that there is an open, free, political competition, backed up by a free press in Singapore. That is just totally at variance with the facts.

Lee: I do not agree with that. You called me a dictator. My answer to that is you are entitled to call me whatever you like, but that doesn't make me one, because I don't have to be a dictator. I can get a free vote and win. We do not own the press, as they do in Malaysia. Nobody is allowed to own more than 3 percent of the shares. The management of the press is in the hands of our four big banks.

> Safire: And that makes them terrified of crossing you?
>
> Lee: No. That makes them have a vested interest in stability and growth, and they support parties that will bring about stability and growth.
>
> Safire: But what about truth and freedom? Isn't that just as important as stability?
>
> Lee: Our press does not lie. It does not. Nobody is shut off.

Among other issues, Safire charged that Singapore's judges were compliant and used corruptly to bankrupt Lee's opponents. Lee replied that he took his opponents to court when they libelled him and they paid damages for that.

> Safire: That was because of your corrupt judges?
>
> Lee: Now, just a moment. The World Economic Forum and its rival organisation, Emet, listed us in their competitiveness report, and confidence in our judicial system, compared to all the other countries, is right on top.
>
> Safire: That's on economic...
>
> Lee: No, no, no, no. You don't have judges who are honest and competent in economics and dishonest

> and corrupt in libel cases.
>
> Safire: Why not?
>
> Lee: Because that's not the way we run our system. That's not the way we appoint judges. A judge has been appointed...we have inherited the British system. Once appointed, he cannot be removed. His salaries are guaranteed under the Constitution. All his perquisites cannot be diminished.
>
> Safire: Is there any harsh question I have not asked that you were prepared for and would like to unload your answer to me?
>
> Lee: Well, I think I don't have any answers to give. I am not a model of anything. I just want to make Singapore work.

One of the most fundamental principles on the role of the press he laid down was that they should not denigrate and downgrade Singapore's political leaders as this would destroy the people's respect of them. If that happened, they would not be able to govern effectively. He made it clear that only those elected by the people could set out-of-bounds (OB) markers. Lee recalled, in an interview with *The New Paper* in February 1993, his clash with Leslie Hoffman, Editor-in-Chief of *The Straits Times*, in the mid-1950s. The newspaper was "gunning for us day by day", he said. "I reminded him (Hoffman) that he was not elected and that when I win the coming election, I will show him who runs Singapore—he or me. I said: "Look, I'm putting my life at stake, if I lose and the communists win, I'm in real trouble. You are sitting on the sidelines tapping away on your typewriter, what gives you this God-given right? Who gave you this right? I am seeking this right and when I get it, I'm going to tell you how you should not run your paper." And I won that right and he ran away."

Indeed, Hoffman went to Kuala Lumpur when the PAP won the historic 1959 general election to manage the newspaper's editorial operations there. "So we settled the OB markers. In the end, *The Straits Times* had to come back to Singapore and run it on our terms. That's how it has been and that's how Singapore progressed," Lee said in *The New Paper* interview.

Lee's ability to stand up to onslaughts from anywhere impressed Singaporeans, even those who disliked him. Everybody loves a strong leader and Lee fitted the bill perfectly. He was fiercely determined about safeguarding Singapore's honour and position and of making the nation a success. He was neither defensive nor apologetic. He was beholden to nobody. And he was nobody's fool. Plaudits and flattery never influenced his thinking.

Like all politicians, Lee had enemies in the stormy sea of politics. He experienced verbal and physical attacks here and abroad, and survived. Politics may have earned a bad name, but it is safe to say that Lee amply demonstrated that it could be a noble profession working for the common good—in the right hands.

13

MOULDING A NEW SINGAPOREAN

The year was1990. Singapore was celebrating its 25th year of independence. Lee Kuan Yew had been Prime Minister for 31 years and would soon step down. A huge sum was spent on the festivities, which included an open-air night party at the famous shopping belt of Orchard Road. The newspapers and television network produced special editions and programmes recounting the nation's dynamic history. A fund was set up for charity organisations. A slogan was crafted that proclaimed boldly: One People, One Nation, One Singapore. The merriment culminated on 9 August, the day the Republic acquired nationhood, in a massive and glittering parade at the National Stadium.

Singaporeans rejoiced. And well they might. They had a great deal to cheer about. They were an independent people with their own identity. Under the British, they were faceless. They were British subjects, not even citizens, in their own land. When the PAP formed the government in 1959, it set out to establish a Singaporean identity. This was the most essential ingredient for nation-building. What is a Singaporean? How did Prime Minister Lee and his colleagues undertake the consuming task in his 31 years as premier?

By legal definition, a Singaporean is a citizen of Singapore whether by birth and upbringing, or by residence. By history and tradition, he is an immigrant from Malaya, Indonesia, China, India and other countries who has made his home here. Singapore is cosmopolitan, not homogeneous.

Lee once painted the picture like this:

> This is not a homogeneous society. Disparate groups of people came to make a living under British rule. They remained themselves in separate distinct compartments. It's like an aquarium, with different glass partitions and different salinity of water. We're trying to form one nation out of them, by removing the glass partitions and gradually equalising the salinity.

The PAP leadership wanted Singaporeans not only to be united but also highly educated, productive, rugged, confident, cultured, gracious and above all, loyal to the country. In this respect, they introduced the emotive definition of a Singaporean.

The government created public awareness of what Singaporeans should be through speeches, media programmes, community clubs and other channels. A national pledge, "We, the citizens of Singapore, pledge ourselves as one united people, regardless of race, language or religion..." was composed. Schools were encouraged to introduce the study of the arts. Programmes were launched to promote the arts industry. Slogans such as "One People, One Nation, One Singapore", "Be gracious", "Dare to excel" and "Be the best one can be" were produced. Then there were the "Courtesy", "Keep Singapore Clean and Green", "No Littering" and "No Spitting" campaigns.

Lee elaborated on the emotive definition while addressing the reunion dinner of the St Andrew's Old Boys' Association on 8 September 1968:

> The acid test of who is a Singaporean is whether the person is so committed to Singapore that he is prepared to stick out and fight for Singapore. An emotive definition, a qualitative not quantitative test of a Singaporean is a person who either by birth and upbringing or residence in Singapore feels committed to upholding this society as it is—multi-racial, tolerant, accommodating, forward-looking—and prepared to stake his life for this community.

Lee told the guests he found it strange that some of the people most willing to stake their lives for Singapore were those born and brought up outside and who had settled here. The reason might be that they knew how unpleasant life could be in other societies which were neither tolerant nor accommodating. These were the people most prepared to fight for Singapore, for a multi-racial community. He admitted that all new countries faced the "grave problem of identity". They invariably had more than one race or tribe within their natural boundaries inherited from the colonial power. In Singapore, the people did not want to be Singaporeans; but Malayans and later Malaysians. Then merger ended abruptly without the people being Singaporeans. His government was not going to pretend that these differences did not exist and that was why Singapore had achieved relative success. He said:

> But having admitted these distinctions, we go on to provide each his place in the sun in an open competitive society, whilst ensuring that the collective group interests of all are not jeopardised by any sectional selfishness. If by the year 2000 St Andrew's School is still known by the same name, then the Singaporean has already been clearly defined.

His vision was a fair percentage of Chinese ethnic descent, a good mixture of Indians, Ceylonese, Eurasians, Malays and others, each with a lifeline to his cultural and linguistic past. This was to provide some ballast in the traditional values of his own cultural heritage. All would seek the widest common area of understanding in language, in values, in emotional attitudes. Most important was a common and undivided loyalty to the integrity of a society which offered them "the maximum of personal freedom of choice compatible with the maximum of equal opportunities for economic advancement and fulfilment".

Defining the characteristics of a Singaporean was difficult, although Lee thought Singapore already had a hard core of people who knew exactly the attributes the Singaporean must have to protect the country's collective interests. Schools like St Andrew's had "a responsibility to transmit and nurture these attributes". They must inculcate the same basic values and attitudes to life and proficiency in a common language. They should "help jell the various ethnic linguistic and cultural groups into a uniform distinctiveness separate from the rest of Southeast Asia".

Lee regarded this as "particularly vital in a country with a one man, one vote system where the temptation to get votes on the basis of ethnic, linguistic or religious loyalties often became irresistible".

The promise of "the maximum of personal freedom of choice" was key to securing loyalty. The government delivered the promise by, for example, providing equal education and job opportunities for everyone, establishing a meritocratic system, and introducing the popular home ownership scheme under the Central Provident Fund (CPF). In short, the ultimate goal was to build the best home possible for its citizens to work, live and play under the principle of a fair, just and equal society. It would be a nation Singaporeans would be proud to own and to defend to the hilt.

Singaporeans took the point to be citizens worth their salt and became more aware of their role in society. In a message before the general election of 1968, Lee made the heartening remark that since 1959, the Singapore landscape had been visibly transformed.

He added:

> But more important is the transformation taking place in our younger generation growing up educated, healthy, vigorous, conscious of their responsibility to each other and society. It is they who will maintain

> Singapore's position as a great centre of civilised and cultivated living with the highest standard of living in Southeast Asia.

One aspect that worried Lee was the high birth rate. In 1965, for example, the rate was 29.9 percent per thousand population. It was feared that the demands for economic, social and other services of a large population would over-stretch Singapore's existing resources, thus depriving the people of the good life they sought. To address the dilemma, a Family Planning and Population Board was set up on 12 January 1966 and a "Stop at Two" policy implemented. It was a controversial policy. Nevertheless, the strategy succeeded. By 1970, the birth rate had dropped to 22.1 percent per thousand population.

But, as the economy continued to boom in subsequent years, with new factories and commercial establishments opening, and bringing with them the multiplier effects, Singapore found itself suffering from acute labour shortage. Lee had no choice but to reverse the policy. The people were now encouraged to produce more babies and given a variety of incentives, such as special income tax relief. In addition, foreign workers were invited to work in the country to enlarge the manpower pool. However, Singapore needed not only a large labour force but also superior brains.

In a speech at a seminar on communism and democracy on 28 April 1971, Lee surprised the public by revealing how small the base of superior brains in Singapore needed for leadership in politics, economics and security was. The main burden of running the nation rested on the shoulders of some 300 key people, including those in the PAP like MPs and cadres. He sounded a warning note: "If all the 300 were to crash in one jumbo jet, Singapore would disintegrate." The government therefore had the duty to expand the number of what he termed "key digits".

To speed up the development of more "key digits", several initiatives were introduced on the education front in the 1980s. These included the Gifted Education Programme, the Special Assistance Plan (SAP) schools and streaming.

Under the streaming policy, pupils were classified into "fast learners" and "slow learners" based on their academic performances. The former went into the "special" or "express" course and the latter into the "normal" course.

This was a touchy issue. Many parents argued that it was wrong to categorise pupils at such an early and most impressionable age. Pupils consigned to the "normal" course earned the stigma "stupid". As one parent put it succinctly, it was "a terrible label to slap on a child". On the other hand, some students in the "special" or "express" course felt a sense of superiority, an attitude hardly in keeping with the move towards a just, fair and equal society.

Making Singaporeans gracious and cultured was also a difficult task to accomplish. One of the greatest obstacles hindering the process was the pressing need for economic survival that was taking precedence over cultural development.

Lee advised the people to strike a balance between work and play. As he put it during the 9th Anniversary Dinner of the Tiong Bahru Community Centre in October 1969, Singaporeans enjoyed little of the pleasures of life and overlooked their social and cultural goals. He called for a more gracious living as otherwise, life could become "mean and ugly". He said: "Life should be more than just existence, the business of making a living. This is the new way of life."

Lee again pressed for cultural development in his address at a Chinese New Year and Hari Raya Haji function in March 1970. He said he was dismayed to see the absence of books, paintings and magazines, the symbols of a cultured person, in the many homes he had visited. For instance, out of the 10 flats in Queenstown he had visited, only two families had literature and art pieces in their living rooms. In every flat, though, there were Hi-Fi sets and radios. He reminded the people:

> In schools, we are trying to teach our boys and girls music, painting, art—a little bit of culture, so that they can do more than just press a button, see a picture or hear a sound. This is absolutely crucial because in that way you may have a creative, imaginative society. You want invention, you want to progress. The human mind must be creative, must be self-generating. It cannot depend on just gadgets to amuse itself.

Obviously, most Singaporeans were so engrossed at making a decent living that they paid little or no heed to his exhortation to indulge in the arts. This was evident by the fact that 10 years later, Lee found the mark of a cultured man still missing from among them. He bemoaned the fact in May 1980 when speaking about how educated parents could help speed up the learning process of their children:

> What has struck me again and again when visiting is that I see Hi-Fi, marble or terrazzo tiles, expensive

> furniture, colour television. But I have never seen a bookcase or a bookshelf. I have seldom seen a painting. They have photographs of fathers and mothers, of grandfathers and grandmothers. One home had books and paintings. He was a returned student, Chinese-educated, from a Japanese university. He had a Japanese wife. He was a cultivated man with a cultivated wife.

Similarly vital to the Singaporean character that Prime Minister Lee frequently advocated was the practice of Asian values of thrift, discipline and industry. Lee adopted the Confucius philosophy as it fitted his own concept of politics, filial piety, hard work, loyalty and submission to authority. He considered the value system necessary for building a strong and progressive nation, and as a safeguard against undesirable Western practices. The system must be passed on from generation to generation. Parents had the duty to inculcate it in their children. He emphasised that the mother tongue was the channel for transmitting these values and it must be preserved. Hence the introduction of the bilingual education policy. "Keep your roots," he often said.

At the same time, knowledge of the English language was necessary. Lee put the point across strongly in his talk to students and lecturers of the Nanyang University's Historical Society in February 1978:

> Be fluent in the English language so that you can step into the world of science and technology, but know enough of the mother tongue to preserve your Asian

> values to acquire sufficient ballast to withstand the onslaught of passing Western fads and fancies. We have developed and progressed not because we were a Western-Occidental-type society, but because we were an Asian-Oriental-type society, hardworking, thrifty and disciplined. That we can also use English is an added advantage.

Lee conceded that the study of the mother tongue was a painful process for many, especially for those brought up in a Western-type environment and exposed to Western influences. But it had to be done quickly. For the Chinese, the mother tongue should be Mandarin as the *lingua franca* and not Hokkien (the most widely spoken Chinese dialect), as the latter was "not congruent" with the written Chinese script. If Hokkien prevailed, the standard of written Chinese would deteriorate. He said the human brain could handle two languages. As he put in a speech in March 1978:

> Your child has a brain bigger than the biggest computer man has ever built. Whilst the world's biggest computer cannot handle two languages, most human beings can, especially if they are taught when young.

The drive towards bilingualism at first caused confusion and misinterpretation among the ethnic groups. This was because of the overwhelming "Speak Mandarin" campaign and the large-scale attempt to convert dialect names of the Chinese and of certain streets and public places, into Mandarin. Was the Prime Minister trying to force every race to learn Chinese, since the Chinese formed the majority of the population? Lee assured Singaporeans that was not his intention. The government was implementing the bilingual policy fairly and equally for all races. For example, as he explained during a seminar organised by the Malay Teachers' Union in June 1978, every Malay would learn Malay and English, and no Malay needed to study Chinese.

Lee also stressed the importance of upholding family ties and obligations. The family was the basic unit and building block of Singapore society. Observance of family ties was part of the Asian value system that would create a civilised character. He was concerned to see that modern lifestyles were breaking up the three-tier family. He took pains to explain why strong family bonds were essential.

On one occasion, in his Chinese New Year message in February 1981, Lee cited as an example the solidarity of the family which had held Chinese societies together through the last 4,000 years. He described China as "a civilisation unique in its continuity and one which had survived in recognisable form despite the ravages of flood and famine, fire and pestilence, wars and earthquakes" and which "after each catastrophe, people picked themselves up, dusted themselves and cleared the debris".

Such was the importance he attached to the value of strong family relationships that he dwelt on the topic again in his Chinese New Year message the following year:

> The old cannot be discarded because they are old. If sons and daughters treat their parents this way, they are encouraging their own children to treat them

> likewise in turn. This practice must be avoided at all costs.

Lee's hard work of fashioning the new Singaporean identity showed good results, especially in the area of cohesiveness. He was delighted with the progress. As he described it in his Hari Raya Puasa message in August 1980: "We are becoming one people much sooner than I had dared to hope. We must safeguard and foster this growing unity." He regarded the improvement as a significant achievement over the situation 15 years before when the nation had faced an uncertain future.

But while the trend was encouraging, Lee suggested that being cohesive as one nation also meant playing good music in concert by striking their notes in unison as in a symphony orchestra, in other words, teamwork. Getting people to study and work hard was not a problem. Getting them to pull together was. He drove home the point colourfully during his National Day Rally in August 1981 where he likened the government to a conductor and every company to a musician. If they coordinated well, they could raise productivity. He said: "To have a better life, all must play good music."

Another major national problem that Lee had to confront was the low procreation rate. It seemed that not enough Singaporeans were responding to the call for more babies. He was dismayed by the lukewarm reaction. Of greater concern to him was the low birth rate of bright babies needed to expand the number of "key digits". The lack of sufficient manpower, especially the bright ones, would retard economic growth.

Lee discovered after a thorough study that one source of the problem was the trend among graduates of marrying late, not marrying at all, or of graduates marrying spouses with lower academic qualifications. In his mind, this was a lop-sided pattern of procreation and was wrong. The situation must be corrected at once because otherwise, Singapore's talent pool would shrink in 25 years' time, while the proportion of the less bright would rise.

Lee used the occasion of his traditional National Day Rally in August 1983 to bring the matter into the open. The subject became known as The Great Marriage Debate. He entreated graduates to marry graduates and have children, the more the merrier. It was their duty.

Quoting from studies made through research on the subject of Nature vs Nurture, there was mounting evidence that nature, or what was inherited, was the greater determinant of a person's performance than nurture, or education and environment. Research on identical twins, who were given away at birth to different families of different social and economic classes, showed that their performance was very close, although their environment was different. He said the conclusion drawn was that 80 percent was nature and 20 percent was the differences from different environment and upbringing.

The message was not well received. The public argued that there had been dull children born of brilliant parents, and brilliant children born of seemingly illiterate parents like hawkers, washerwomen, road sweepers and garbage collectors. It was an insult to these people because, although they did not go to university, they should not be dismissed as morons. Was the Prime Minister trying to build an elitist society? Procreation was a private and personal matter. People thought they should be left to decide for themselves when and with whom they should tie the knot, and whether to have children or not.

A woman graduate, piqued by Lee's supposition, shot an angry letter to *The Straits Times'* Forum Page a few days later, fuming: "I am not going to jump into bed with the first man I meet."

The controversy raged for a long time. The temperature on the ground rose higher when Prime Minister Lee pursued the matter by introducing incentives, such as admission preference to schools for children of graduate mothers over children of non-graduate mothers. He was convinced that this punitive measure was the only way of inducing graduates to have more children and discouraging non-graduates from multiplying. To persuade male and female graduates to meet, socialise and hopefully marry, a body called the Social Development Unit was set up. People dubbed it a match-making agency for the elite.

Lee appeared to have scored a point when he announced the results of his efforts at his National Day Rally in August 1986. He reported an increase in graduate marriages since he raised the topic three years before, citing figures from the Registry of Marriages. With a triumphant smile, he exhorted: "Don't give up. Facts and figures do not lie." At a similar rally two years later, he reported more progress, although the development was "very slow and very painful". The public reaction was: Sure, more graduates were marrying graduates. But would they all produce brilliant children?

The debate on procreation, or the lack of it, continues to this day. Carrots, such as a baby bonus, are dangled. Despite these incentives, the public reaction remains more or less the same.

Procreation is a private and personal matter. No one can force anybody to marry and produce babies.

Aggravating the problem of low procreation rate was emigration, which was reported to be rising during Lee's watch. It was negating the attempt to widen the pool of labour. The outflow must be stemmed as the nation could ill afford to lose precious local talent. Economic needs aside, it seemed that, to Lee, emigration went against the spirit of loyalty to country, the emotive definition of the new Singaporean he was trying to mould. He voiced his concerns at his National Day Rally in August 1989. Describing the trend as alarming, he revealed that the brain drain was negligible in the 1960s but by 1988, the number had soared to about 4,700. Young Singaporeans were "creamed off" by countries looking for able and talented Asians to contribute to their development.

Lee said he failed to understand why these young people left Singapore, despite all the efforts to provide them with one of the best homes on earth, equal education and job opportunities and social, health and other essential services that are second to none. His generation had a different outlook on life. Relating his own experience, he assured Singaporeans that he never felt he belonged to England where he studied for his law degree. This was despite the fact that he spent four years there and that he did not return to Singapore in the intervening years because airfares were costly and sea travel took too long. Although life in England was not bad, he was sometimes uncomfortable.

Before the rally, Lee had asked some of his ministers and other people for the reasons why they would remain in Singapore. Then he produced a letter he had received from a young man who gave his reasons: "But speaking for myself, the single most important reason is that Singapore is my place. It is something I call mine, never mind the constraints."

The man was a returned Cambridge scholar in his 30s. Lee was moved to tears when he read the letter. In a faltering voice, he told his audience:

> I had never expected this quiet, very prosaic, scholarly type, with glasses, had passion. To build a country, you need passion. If you just do your sums—plus, minuses, credit, debit—you're a washout. When we fought in 1962, '63 against the communists, when we went through hell in 1963–65, many people thought we were crazy. We could lead peaceful quiet lives. Why were we doing this? It was an act of conviction. This is my country. This is my life. This is my people. You will trample over us over our dead bodies. We dug our toes in, we built a nation.

Lee also strongly advocated bonding among the races. To him, this was an indispensable quality all Singaporeans must have. By bonding, he meant a chivalrous attitude where ethnic groups would help one another in a national crisis, regardless of race, language or religion. He believed this element was crucial for strengthening the spirit of cohesiveness. While cohesiveness was becoming discernible, he was not sure if bonding existed or when it would be welded. One of the occasions where he brought up the matter was during a talk to National University of Singapore students in December 1986. He posed the question:

> How long will it take before we become all Singaporeans? I have no idea. It will improve with another generation. But are we sure that in a moment of crisis, when the heat is on, we are all together, heart to heart? I hope so. But we ought to have a fall-back position and quickly fill up all the missing hearts if some go missing. It is in the nature of our society.

Lee repeated his anxiety in an interview with a West German magazine, *Zeitmagazin*, released in Singapore in February 1988. He told the publication he could not say how Singaporeans would react in a difficult period such as a world depression and when the country had to eat up its reserves to buy essential items. He asked:

> If the national cake gets smaller and smaller, can we share the burdens and eat less? That is a problem. For Singaporeans to face difficult periods together, they must feel that they were one people, despite their different races, languages or different histories.

He admitted that the Asian traditions of hard work, mutual help and strong family ties would help, but:

> The Chinese families will cling together. But there are seven major dialect groups, and during their history in Singapore, mutual help had always been within each dialect group. The Indians and the Malays likewise. Will they share what they have and help each other in adversity? If it turns out there is no common sense of nationhood, that's very sad and troublesome.

Nevertheless, there are those who still prefer to emigrate. Emigration was one of the realities of life that Lee seemed unable to accept. He would speak his mind against it whenever the opportunity arose. A recent case that ruffled his feathers occurred in May 1996 when a young woman wrote in the Life! section of *The Straits Times* of 29 May bewailing her "dream of a car and a house getting out of reach" .

Lee took the chance to rebut her in his address to the Singapore Press Club and the Foreign Correspondents' Association meeting on 7 June that year. In his speech, he disputed the woman's contention that the grass was greener on the other side of the fence. The pot of gold at the end of the rainbow was in fact in Asia. The region was enjoying phenomenal growth. American, European and Australian professionals were flocking to the region to look for work, and Singapore was one of the choice locations for jobs. Even many Singaporeans who had migrated to Australia had returned for jobs, or sent their children after university to work here, he said. He cited poor, backward communities in China, Vietnam and the rest of Asean as examples of those who would become middle-class industrial societies like Korea, Taiwan, Hong Kong and Singapore. They were going to experience what Singapore underwent in the past 30 years. East Asia was "entering a golden age, an economic and cultural renaissance". The young should not worry over prices of private properties and cars. They should instead seize their opportunities which their fathers never had. Prices of properties and cars would never be out of reach for those who seized their opportunities. He struck this optimistic note: "Our present is better than our past. But, believe me, the best is yet to be."

These were some of the more difficult problems Lee Kuan Yew and the Old Guard encountered in the process of shaping the new Singaporean, to make them loyal and give them a face after 140 years of British rule where they were merely British subjects. Overall, the results were encouraging. A new national identity has emerged, although perhaps not yet the splitting image of Lee's original emotive definition.

So what is the Singaporean of today like? He accepts his place in his cosmopolitan society, respects his political leaders (sometimes overly obedient), and is loyal. The new Singaporean is literate, bilingual (some even trilingual), intelligent, brand-conscious, efficient, confident, law-abiding and world-wise. He has "the maximum of personal freedom of choice" as Lee had promised long ago that he would have. Under the British, he was poor, illiterate and ignorant, his future determined by them. Today, he can get what he wants in life, knows what he has to do to achieve his goals and is wealthier than most of his counterparts in the region. He is in a position to aspire for the 5Cs (cash, credit card, condominium, car and country club membership), although the trend changed to replace country club membership and either condominium or car with career and children because of the hard times.

Contrary to popular belief, the new Singaporean is enterprising and creative. There are several hundred thousand Singaporeans who own and/or manage large, medium and small corporations in a diverse range of economic sectors, plus thousand others running family-owned businesses throughout the island. Hundreds of new businesses are registered every day. All these manufacturing and commercial establishments form the backbone of the economy.

The R&D incubators have hatched inventions, many of them world firsts. The Singaporean dares to venture abroad, too, and to take risks, to multiply his economic fortunes. The large number of overseas branches set up in the East and the West testifies to that. He is like his forefathers.

A leaf from Dr C F Yong's highly informative book, *Chinese Leadership and Power in Colonial Singapore*, shows that Singaporean businessmen of the 19th century and early 20th century established branches in other Asian countries long before the word "regionalisation" was coined and became fashionable. Prominent among these pioneers were Tan Kim Ching, Seah Liang Seah, Lim Nee Soon, Tan Kah Kee, Aw Boon Haw and Tan Beng Swee. A few even went to Shanghai, and that in the days of sailing ships. They set a fine example of bold entrepreneurship to succeeding generations of Singaporeans.

The new Singaporean has other praiseworthy characteristics. He is courteous, gracious, helpful and generous. He respects his elders, fellow-citizens and visitors, supports charity causes, visits old folks' homes and hospitals to comfort the aged and the infirm, renders assistance to those in distress and similar acts of charity.

The best examples were seen during the 2003 Severe Acute Respiratory Syndrome (SARS) outbreak that caused several deaths and crippled many businesses, and the collapse of Nicoll Highway and a construction site at Ayer Rajah in April 2004. At great risk to themselves, rescue workers of various races found common ground to aid the victims.

Another major test of Singaporeans' generosity was seen during the tsunami disaster that took place on 26 December 2004. The killer waves swept through southern Thailand, north Sumatra, Sri Lanka, India and even as far as east Africa, killing more than 200,000 people, washing away coastal towns and villages, and leaving hundreds of thousands homeless. Singaporeans donated money to the tune of S$150 million, food, clothing and other items.

Prime Minister Lee Hsien Loong described this spirit of voluntarism and compassion as a "precious and valuable" trait.

Interestingly, too, for good or bad, there has been a paradigm shift in cultural preferences, at least among the English-educated. During colonial times, they were Anglophiles since English culture and values predominated. They lost their mother tongues and cultures. Many behaved like Englishmen (Westernised Oriental Gentlemen or WOGs) and Englishwomen (Westernised Oriental Women or WOWs). After World War II, American culture and values flooded the country and washed away much of the English mode of life. Thus, today's English-educated Singaporean is largely Americanised. He imbibes American music, dances, movies and literature. Some even resort to using American lingo and speaking with an American accent.

Old Guard S Rajaratnam summed up the new Singaporean succinctly while addressing Lee Kuan Yew's 60th birthday celebration function in September 1983. Rajaratnam, then Second Deputy Prime Minister (Foreign Affairs), said:

> Mr Lee Kuan Yew's greatest achievement is not the physical transformation of Singapore but the transformation of the mind and character of the average Singaporean. The docile, self-centred, money-grubbing and rootless colonial slave of a few years ago

> has, under his leadership and in a very short time, been transformed into an uncringing Singaporean who is today reaching out confidently for a place in the 21st century.
>
> His goal is not a nation of rabbits led by lions, or a nation of lions led by rabbits or, worse still, rabbits led by rabbits but, as befits the Lion City, a nation of lions led by lions.

Alas, no one is perfect. There are pictures of the "Ugly Singaporean". These are painted by both locals as well as foreigners, such as former Chinese Ambassador to Singapore, Chen Baoliu. In her speech at the China-Singapore Business Forum in Beijing in November 2003, she portrayed Singaporeans as "an arrogant lot". The general perception is that the Singaporean tends to think too highly of himself. When he is overseas, he behaves badly, is condescending and inclined to criticise the shortcomings of the host country, comparing them with Singapore's great accomplishments and smooth efficiency.

Among other disparaging adjectives bandied about are: materialistic, discourteous, ungracious, aggressive, grumpy, impatient, selfish, greedy and *kiasu* (a Hokkien word meaning "afraid to lose"). He always wants things to be better, to get more in life and to strive to be first. It is a burning ambition which has resulted in an intensive paper chase, a rat race endemic in Singapore. The phenomenon may explain why some Singaporeans appear materialistic, discourteous, ungracious, impatient or arrogant. But while this undesirable social behaviour must be condemned, the relentless endeavour to be better than the next man is a positive quality. It is the right attitude to adopt. It embodies the Singaporean spirit, a key factor that keeps the nation on the ladder of success. It is a product of Lee's constant exhortations to "dare to excel" and to be "the best one can be".

What do Singaporeans think about all these uncomplimentary remarks levelled at them? By and large, they are not apologetic or defensive. They admit their faults and plead guilty to them. Perhaps this is a sign of maturity. The findings of the *Straits Times Interactive* published in the newspaper on 24 November 2003 seemed to confirm their forbearing attitude. Of a total vote count of 6,985, over 6,500 Singaporeans agreed that they acted with a superior air when abroad. As to what could be done to correct their obnoxious attitude, over 5,330 out of a total vote count of 6,957 replied that "the problem will resolve itself when other countries catch up and overtake us" while over 1,000 suggested that "we should just be humble and sensitive".

Another aberration that mars the new Singaporean character is the antisocial habit of littering and spitting in public places. Many still indulge in this unwholesome social conduct, despite punitive measures and years of the "No Littering" and "No Spitting" campaigns. Lee was disappointed to see the unvarnished truth himself while taking a stroll along Marina Bay to inspect the state of the Singapore River on a Sunday in July 1990, a few months before he resigned as Prime Minister. The river had been the highlight of the Clean-the-Waterways project since 1987 with several million dollars spent on it. Lee was repulsed by what he saw. The water was clean, but the banks were littered with empty plastic bottles, cans and other odds-and-ends. He sighed:

> Ahh, what an untidy, uncivic-minded lot of people. But the human being, the Singaporean, when he is not seen, just tosses things in. Do something. This is now your generation's duty. I have done enough.

Anti-social behaviour aside, there seems to be another desirable quality missing from the new Singaporean. Dr Toh Chin Chye, former Deputy Prime Minister and Chairman of the PAP, told listeners what it was in a radio broadcast aired in early August 1997:

> To be smart like computers and robots is not that difficult. Robots, computers can be programmed, or if you like, can be trained. But the trouble, of course, is that computers lack soul and what we need in Singapore is soul. Because it is soul that makes society.

The remark was certainly food for thought. A soul would no doubt be an added boon to the Singaporean character and make him a citizen truly worthy of a First World nation. Judging by those who are courteous, gracious and helpful, a soul already exists in many Singaporeans. By what means can the spirit be infused into others who continue to display a lack of social responsibilities?

On their part, Lee Kuan Yew and the Old Guard had indeed played their role well in removing the glass partitions in the aquarium and equalising the salinity of the water, and in giving Singaporeans a face they can be proud of.

14

LEE'S SPECIAL BONDING WITH MALAYS

Singapore is a vibrant and cosmopolitan nation where Malays, Chinese, Indians, Eurasians and other races work and live in harmony. The history books have it that the Malays were the indigenous people. Then came other races from countries such as Indonesia, China, India and Sri Lanka centuries ago seeking their fortunes here. The Indonesians formed the major ethnic group of the early arrivals. They inter-married with the indigenous Malays. Their racial, religious and cultural affinity made such a union natural. It was the Malays who largely contributed to Singapore's early population growth.

According to *Singapore 1996*, a publication of the Ministry of Information and the Arts (now known as Ministry of Communications and Information), the Malay population continued to grow and by January 1824, they had formed 60 percent of the total population of over 10,600. The Chinese accounted for 31 percent and the Indians seven percent. But six years later, the Chinese had overtaken the Malays, their numbers rising to as high as 65 percent of the total population of over 55,000 by 1867, as mounting waves of Chinese immigrants rolled onto local shores. Today, the Chinese lead numerically with over 77 percent of the indigenous population of three million, followed by the Malays at about 14 percent, the Indians seven percent and the other ethnic groups one percent.

The Malays are endowed with admirable characteristics. They are a gentle people; friendly, kind, soft-spoken, helpful, easy to mix and talk with. The older generation of Singaporeans are puzzled by the need for a national campaign to get the other races to mingle with the Malays and vice versa. They prefer to call it re-integration rather than integration. In their time, the Malays, Chinese and the other races thought nothing about socialising or eating at the same table. It was the natural order of things. Most were not conscious of their differences in skin colour or language. But today's generation sense these differences and need a push to show understanding and tolerance.

Another worthy characteristic of the Malays is their Malayness. It remains intact despite Western cultures and influences. Unlike the other races, Malays are not deculturalised, as Lee Kuan Yew aptly described way back in 1959 when he was talking about the role of the English-educated in society. Every Malay speaks, reads and writes the language, even if he or she is English-educated, reads Western literature or listens to Western music. In contrast, many Chinese and Indians educated in English have lost their own mother tongues and cultures. They speak, read and write only in English. They prefer Western cultures. They even dream in English. Many have adopted Christianity. That is why the government often exhorts Singaporeans to keep their ethnic roots.

Unfortunately, while the Malays form an integral part of Singapore's cosmopolitan society, they received the short end of the stick during the British colonial era. They were a marginalised people, the poorest among the ethnic groups and occupied the lowest rung in the socio-economic ladder. With a few exceptions, it was a hand-to-mouth existence for them. The British regarded them useful only as chauffeurs, gardeners, cooks, maids, office boys, messenger boys, postmen and the like. No attempt was made to offer them better education and other opportunities, or incentives to be ambitious and improve themselves. The Malay schools available lacked the type of syllabus and facilities that would train and produce students for better and higher paid jobs in the civil service and the commercial firms. That was why they remained sidelined from the mainstream of life.

It was not until the PAP formed the government in 1959 that their fortunes started to change for the better. Lee, as the Prime Minister, recognised the Malay community as an essential building block in the nation-building process and in the striving for a cohesive, multi-racial, multi-religious and multi-cultural state. Lee wanted the Malays to be equal citizens. He encouraged them to get better education and to be ambitious. He knew they could realise their full potential if given the chance and that they could make valuable contributions towards Singapore's progress. Improving their lives became one of the government's priorities. This can be seen in the action plan for the Malay community formulated in the early years. Among other programmes, the government formed a Malay Education Advisory Committee, started Malay secondary school education (not available under British rule), and provided free education for all Malay children up to tertiary level. (The last-named has since been discontinued.) Over the years, other types of projects were launched, such as a self-help group called Mendaki in 1981 and the Group Representative Constituency (GRC) scheme in 1988 to ensure appropriate representation of the minority groups, including the Malay community, in Parliament.

The special assistance schemes for Malays underscored Lee's unwavering policy of multi-racialism. But for Lee, helping the Malays was more than a vital national service. He had a personal interest in the undertaking. This was because of his special bonding with them. The bonding was forged in his childhood days when he had Malay friends and played with them. At Telok Kurau English School, which he attended at the age of six, many of his classmates were Malays. Lee revealed his experiences at a tea session with Malay community leaders on 27 September 2003. He recalled:

> So I grew up completely at ease with Malays: quite a few of my Malay fellow students went on with me to Raffles Institution. One bright Malay later became a senior customs officer. When I went to Raffles College, I met, for the first time, the Malayan Malay elite. They had come mostly on Federal government or state government scholarships. They were more race-conscious and mixed more among themselves

> than with Chinese, Indian and other students. It did not strike me strongly until after we joined Malaysia that they are different: a deep-seated feeling that the country, Malaya, Tanah Melayu, was for Malays.

After becoming a lawyer in the early 1950s and before entering politics, Lee's first court case involved defending four Malays who had been charged with the murder of an RAF serviceman, his wife and child while they were travelling in a bus along Geylang Serai during the 1950 Maria Hertogh riots. Lee got three of his clients acquitted. In February 1952, he had his "first big public exposure" when he was asked to negotiate with the British administration for pay increases for the Postal and Telecommunications Uniformed Staff Union. Nearly all the members were Malays.

When he entered politics in 1955 to fight in his first general election, Lee deliberately chose Tanjong Pagar as his constituency not only because it was a poor neighbourhood but also because it was the home of the postmen whom he had helped in their negotiations for better pay and working conditions in the early 1950s. In addition, the constituency housed a large number of Malay workers of the Singapore Harbour Board (now PSA International). As it happened, his confidence of their support for him in the election was not misplaced.

Lee said Singapore Malays were different from Malaysian Malays. He found more differences when trouble started after merger in 1963. Some Malaysian Malays created communal problems in Singapore. They did not accept him as a fellow citizen to share the country with them. Instead, they labelled him a lodger, whereas the Singapore Malays accepted him. He related two "traumatic experiences" where the Malay members of the PAP supported him to whom he was grateful.

The first trauma befell him in 1961 when the PAP's pro-communist assemblymen defected to form the Barisan Sosialis. All the Malay PAP assemblymen stood firm and prevented the communists from overthrowing the government. The second crisis surfaced during the riots in 1964, instigated by UMNO ultra-extremists. The Malay PAP assemblymen again backed the PAP. A bonding developed between Lee and his Malay team members whom he remembered fondly as "my lifelong friends and colleagues".

> When we became independent in 1965, I made a firm commitment not to let our Malay community down. That commitment was shared by all my colleagues of that original team [the Old Guard]. It has been our policy ever since. When we had to rebuild the city, we made sure that as the *suraus* or prayer rooms were demolished, new mosques were built in the new towns, better and bigger. We made sure that our Malays were free to practise their customs and religion. We made sure that there was as much inter-mingling as possible with the other races in housing, schools, markets, shopping centres and community centres. We have made progress.

Lee admitted of the difficulties he faced during the demolition of old Malay settlements and the re-housing of the people. There were concerns of their ability to adapt to rapid urbanisation and industrialisation. Nonetheless, they took the changes in their stride and found out for themselves that life in the new housing estates was indeed better. The education policy opened the door to higher academic qualifications leading to better-paying jobs and enabling them to pay for their new homes. Their confidence rose.

He expressed his satisfaction that since his retirement as Prime Minister in 1990, the second-generation team in charge had also established personal ties with the Malay community of this generation. They had worked together to uplift the educational performance of the community and to help them achieve their aspirations and goals. He said:

> Today, there are far more better-educated Malays than ever in the history of Singapore. The group of tertiary-educated Malays in institutes of higher education is growing. Social attitudes and values of Singaporeans, including Malay Singaporeans, have changed over the last 38 years. They have also changed in Malaysia, but in different ways. This is because the two countries have different education systems and different social structures that have made for different social relations between the races. However, despite these differences, the ties of kinship and common basic cultures remain. This is what makes us closer to Malaysians than our other neighbours.

But he warned of the growing Islamisation and the distinctiveness of Muslim practices. Singaporeans had to watch this trend carefully and prevent it from dividing their society. He found it reassuring that the 11 September 2001 attacks on the United States and the arrests of Jemaah Islamiyah (JI) conspirators in Singapore recently had not adversely affected relations among the races. He elaborated:

> The leaders of the Malay community have been solidly with the government to ensure no divergent religious teachings take place, and people are vigilant against possible terrorist groups. These issues will not go away soon. Developments abroad, in the Middle East, in Iraq and Palestine, in Indonesia and Malaysia, will influence the thinking and feeling of Muslim Malays in Singapore.
>
> But we must always remember that we share one island and a common destiny, that we have to protect this island and each other's interests. We should always be able to make whatever accommodation is needed and overcome our difficulties as one nation. We are in a period of stress and change in the Arab world of the Middle East that will have unpredictable repercussions on Muslims everywhere, including Singapore. This will require careful and skilful management. But whatever the developments, I am confident Singapore Malays will be able to find their place in our society as equal citizens.

Lee then spoke of the transition to the third-generation leadership to be led by his son, then Deputy Prime Minister Lee Hsien Loong. He was confident that the present Prime Minister would be able to enjoy "an easy relationship with our Malay community". His son is well-versed in Malay. Hsien Loong studied the language up to '0' level. His teacher enrolled him in a wolf cub troop in Kampong Jagoh Primary School at Telok Blangah so that he could socialise with Malay boys and make Malay a living language. Hsien Loong "now reads *Berita Harian* daily and should not have any problems in interacting with our Malay community". But he pointed out this difference between him and his son:

> I grew up studying and playing with Malays during a period in pre-war Singapore when the British were in charge and racial communities lived in quiet harmony. Loong grew up in a period when political differences between the races were deliberately sharpened during our years in Malaysia, 1963–65. He is therefore very conscious of the dangers of antagonistic race relations and understands that the sensitivities of race and religion have to be managed tactfully.
>
> I am confident that you will be able to get access to him and to other top PAP leaders, including Yaacob Ibrahim [then Minister of Community Development and Sports and Minister of Muslim Affairs], and that the PAP's fundamental policies of promoting racial harmony and equal opportunities for all, regardless of race, language or religion, will continue under the third-generation leadership.

Indeed, there are signs that the process of racial integration, or re-integration as the older folks prefer it, is making good headway.

It is significant to note that the Singapore Malays had rejected communal politics long ago. They forcefully demonstrated their stand during the 1963 general election, when the battle centred on the PAP and the Barisan Sosialis. The Singapore Malays rejected all the UMNO ultra-extremist candidates contesting in the Malay-dominated constituencies of Geylang Serai, Kampong Kembangan, Pasir Panjang and the southern islands. Instead, they elected the PAP Malay candidates. They saw UMNO as a communal political party and the PAP as multi-racial and concerned with their welfare. The ultras' insinuation that the PAP was anti-Malay ran counter to the fact that the PAP government was improving their lives.

Othman Wok, former Minister of Social Affairs, recounted in a talk to Tampines Junior College students on Racial Harmony Day on 21 July 1997 that the rejection sparked the ultras' attempt to cause disunity among Singapore's population. They made inflammatory speeches as their main weapons of hate. These were published not only in Malay vernacular newspapers but the script was also in Jawi so that the other races could not read it. Othman told the students that the ultras' speeches contained a pack of lies to rouse suspicion among the Malays that their religion, language and culture were being threatened.

In recent times, Singapore Malays demonstrated their desire for peace and harmony by their non-interference not only in the arrests of JI conspirators but also in the delicate *tudung* (Islamic headscarf) issue in 2003. Four primary schoolgirls were suspended for wearing the *tudung* to national schools because it was not part of the school uniform. Their parents insisted that the girls were practising their religion and customs. The government rejected the idea, explaining that in schools, all students must wear a unified code of dress. Uniformity was part of the policy to teach the young the meaning of unity. Malay girls and women could wear the *tudung* anywhere else, since there was no ban on the wearing of the headscarf in their everyday lives in the country. The government stood firm on its stance.

It was cause for comfort for all Singaporeans that there was no serious backlash from Muslim countries about the sensitive issue. On the contrary, there was a positive reaction from none other than the Middle East, the centre of Islam. An online portal, *Islamic Online*, reported in February 2004 that the Grand Sheikh Mohammed Said Tantawi, leader of Sunni Islam, agreed with Singapore's right to ban the *tudung* in schools. Senior Minister Goh Chok Tong (then Prime Minister) met him when he was in Egypt during his Middle East visit that month. Goh praised Sheikh Tantawi, of the prestigious Cairo University, for being "a wise and practical person who looks at problems from the point of the larger interests". He described Dr Tantawi as "one of the scholars" but stated that for Singapore, "we would of course look towards the Mufti". He reasoned:

> The Mufti must be the spiritual leader for Singapore so we would expect Muslims to take guidance from the Mufti. And I expect our Mufti, in turn, to be studying the work of other scholars elsewhere and apply it to the Singapore context.

Certainly, Singapore Malays are not without problems and challenges as they continue their ascent on the economic ladder. Of particular concern are the many undesirable practices creeping into the lives of Malay teenagers—drug abuse, casual sex, youth delinquency etc. These social problems are also plaguing teenagers of other ethnic communities. The issue of moral values among the young often ranks high on the agenda at public dialogue sessions organised for the Malay community. At one such session held by the Feedback Unit on 26 January 2004, several parents voiced their concerns about "the rebellious nature and sexual permissiveness" of some teenagers. The problem was serious enough to warrant the publication of a book designed to help Malay youths and parents address these "pressing issues" besetting the Malay community. The 118-page hard-hitting book in Malay was published by three organisations—the Registry of Muslim Marriages, a branch of the Thye Hua Kwan Moral Society, and the Malay-language daily *Berita Harian*. The Thye Hua Kwan Moral Society is a welfare body promoting good morals regardless of race and religion.

The Malay community must be commended for taking concerted remedial measures to curb immoral practices among their children. By their action, they are discharging their duties as responsible parents and citizens of Singapore, as well as demonstrating their value in the nation's cosmopolitan fabric. Indeed, the status of today's Singapore Malays is infinitely better than that of yesteryear, owing to Lee Kuan Yew's special assistance programmes that paved the way towards their rapid socio-economic advancement.

They are creating a "New Malay Singaporean", one who is self-reliant, independent of mind, and able to respond to and stay ahead of the changing environment.

15

END OF AN ERA

It was 31 years since Lee Kuan Yew first occupied the driver's seat. The road towards nation-building had been long, tortuous and dangerous. Lee could look back with immense satisfaction at Singapore, a tiny island he had transformed from a state of poverty, illiteracy and ignorance into an affluent and world-class metropolitan nation, from a Third World to a First World nation, as he described it in his memoirs. And there was a successor able to lead Singaporeans safely into the future. Lee had announced his impending resignation months before. Now he was ready to let his co-driver take over the wheel.

The great moment in history took place in the Drawing Room of the Istana at 2.40 pm on Monday, 26 November 1990 as Lee gave President Wee Kim Wee his letter of resignation as Prime Minister.

The letter, dated 26 November, read:

> You are aware of my long-standing plan to resign as Prime Minister to enable Mr Goh Chok Tong to take over.
>
> As this is the first change of Prime Ministers in 31years, I have tried to ensure a smooth transfer of authority. Goh Chok Tong and I have worked together to achieve this. From Cabinet papers and minutes, you will know that since 1985, I have taken all Cabinet decisions in close consultation with Goh Chok Tong and his team, and that since 1989, he and his team have taken all Cabinet decisions.
>
> I hereby tender my resignation and that of my government. The resignation is to take effect from the time the new Prime Minister is sworn in on Wednesday, 28 November 1990.
>
> I now formally advise you to call upon Mr Goh Chok Tong, as the person who is able to command a majority in Parliament, to form the new government.

In the same venue the next day, 27 November, President Wee formally appointed Goh as Singapore's new Prime Minister in a five-minute ceremony. At City Hall the following evening, Goh took his oath of office, telecast live on television. The changing of the guard was a simple and quiet affair. Goh's pledge was:

> My mission is clear: to ensure that Singapore thrives and grows after Mr Lee Kuan Yew, to find a new group of men and women to help me carry on where

> he and his colleagues left off, and to build a nation of character and grace where people live lives of dignity and fulfilment, and care for one another.

The Lee Kuan Yew era had ended and the Goh Chok Tong era had begun. After the swearing-in ceremony, the new Prime Minister, Goh Chok Tong, led his Cabinet to the steps of City Hall to meet the people. The new team members were all dressed in full suits. On the Padang across the street, the well-wishers clapped, cheered, sang "Oh My Goh Chok Tong, We Love You" to the tune of Clementine, and chanted "Chok Tong Cheer" to the beat of Singapura Cheer. Some flourished poms-poms. They were a happy, well-fed, well-dressed and orderly crowd. It was a peaceful scene. Goh beamed and waved in acknowledgement.

This was in stark contrast with 3 June 1959, when Lee had faced a mammoth, boisterous sea of faces on the Padang after forming the government. The throng comprised a mixture of delighted PAP supporters and angry anti-PAP activists. They cheered and jeered respectively. It was a wild scene. As Old Guard S Rajaratnam later recalled, the anti-PAP followers filled half the field, yelling anti-Lee Kuan Yew slogans.

Singapore had, indeed, come a long way in 31 years.

Lee was appointed Senior Minister to give Prime Minister Goh the benefit of his political experience if needed. As he told Japan's leading economic newspaper *Nihon Keizei Shimbun* on 16 July 1990 before leaving the driver's seat, his role as Senior Minister was to help package and present policies in order to win the next elections. He explained:

> I have been doing this job for 31 years and I have won eight general elections. So I have some experience on how to present a policy in a way that will win the next elections.

Earlier, in May 1990, Lee told a French journalist during his visit to Paris to address the Institute of International Relations of France:

> I will be very unhappy if I felt that all that I have done has been a waste of time. Therefore I would like to spend the rest of my life making sure that what I have done has not been a waste of time. I think the best way I can do that is to make sure that the new team is successful in carrying Singapore forward. Not doing it my way, because that may no longer be relevant or the best way, but a younger generation, more in spirit a part of the new generation that has grown up in Singapore in the last 20–30 years of growth and general well-being. It has to be raised to a new level of accomplishment, of achievement. If I can help in some way to get them to jack standards up, I would have occupied my life usefully.

Lee said he did not aspire to be President of Singapore because being one "is irrelevant to the job". He explained: "The new elected President would have a custodian role, to prevent the reserves from being expended, but that can be done by anybody. It doesn't have to be me."

At the PAP Ordinary Party Conference on 18 November, Lee spoke more of his duties and those of the new Prime Minister. He told the party delegates:

> What they cannot expect of Goh Chok Tong is the capacity to mobilise and galvanise people behind policies as effectively as I have done. That is not his forte. Of course my older colleagues helped me. They were great players in an orchestra. However, I was the soloist and played the cadenzas. Chok Tong will be the conductor who has to get other players to play the cadenzas. He will decide on the right policies. He has the courage to take tough decisions, like reversing the two-child family policies. But he will need help in mobilising and galvanising ground support.
>
> After 30 years, we have created our own political culture out of our experiences to meet our needs. Visitors to Singapore know we are different. The difference is in the political culture, represented by the attitudes of mind and values which govern the conduct of people who run Singapore. In many countries, people want power because power means money, and money can buy everything.
>
> A key feature of our political culture is that leaders cannot be selfish or self-centred people. Every cadre member in the PAP must have that dash of altruism, that willingness to do something for his fellow man. How do we transmit and preserve this political culture? We embarked on an unusual, but fortunately,

> successful method of inducting like-minded people, those with similar motivations. When we recruited from the party branches, we could not find enough people of ability and talent. So we went out to induct them. Then by close interaction on the job, they learned and understood why the highest standards are required of those who hold power in Singapore.

Goh was one of those inducted. He was Managing Director of Neptune Orient Lines after serving as a senior civil servant before entering politics in 1976. Goh had been designated as Lee's successor as early as after the 1984 general election. After that election, Goh was named First Deputy Prime Minister. It was he who decided on the new Cabinet and Lee had approved of it. Goh said at a press conference at the Istana on 31 December 1984 to announce the Cabinet:

> We have discussed this with [Prime Minister Lee]. He's very happy that we are going to play a leadership role. The exercise of self-renewal is irreversible. He has planned for this and he is delighted that we are prepared to take the challenge to play a more dominant role in the Cabinet in running the country's affairs. My colleagues and I will play a prominent role. The Prime Minister will take a backseat but he will not play the role of the back-seat driver. He will play the role of goalkeeper.

Lee had accepted this role. At the oath-taking ceremony of the Goh Chok Tong Cabinet in the State Room of the Istana on

2 January 1985, Lee said as he addressed President of Singapore C V Devan Nair:

> Mr President, you will have noted that the centre of gravity in the Cabinet has shifted. This is as it should be in the final phase before a post-Independence generation takes complete charge of the government. Meanwhile, they will have to fill up several Cabinet positions left vacant, and held by several ministers doubling and trebling responsibilities.
>
> I played centre-forward or striker from 1959 to 1980. I moved and played half-back or mid-fielder from 1981 to 1984, leaving the position of striker for younger men. At the beginning, four, later three, men tested themselves out in this role as they went around the constituencies. They have had the time and opportunities to take the measure of each other, and add up the pluses and minuses for each. The team has settled for a new striker. I shall now play goalkeeper.

To Lee, however, being goalkeeper did not mean being inactive in the political scene. He alluded to this at the traditional Lunar New Year function at the Tanjong Pagar Community Centre on 24 February 1985: "But the goalkeeper should not wait till the ball gets into the penalty area. That's dangerous. Keep it outside the penalty area."

Lee held a high opinion of successor Goh Chok Tong. He revealed some of his thoughts at the National University of Singapore's Political Association on 23 July 1990:

> He has still to set his style, but my guess is he will be more like President Suharto [of Indonesia] than Dr Mahathir [Malaysia's Prime Minister from 1981–2003]. He may speak softly, but he is no softie. Otherwise, he would not have been Defence Minister for so many years [eight years] and nobody doubts that Mindef is a tightly run outfit. Nor would he have won the support of the other members of his team, which includes several who I know are dexterous in the use of the stick. The largest single difference in style between Goh Chok Tong and me will not be because of differences in temperament or character, but because of his commitment to team leadership. He consults all relevant ministers and other key parties affected before he takes major decisions.

Lee told members of the Political Association that Goh had made tough decisions on sensitive issues ranging from economics, politics, manpower and defence, to racial and religious harmony. These included wage restraint and reforms in 1985, arrests of Marxist conspirators in 1987, restricting the circulation of foreign publications for biased reporting in 1986–87, the new population policy in 1987, immigration policy in 1989, preventing racial enclaves in Housing and Development Board estates in 1989, the vehicle quota scheme in 1990 and the Maintenance of Religious Harmony Bill in 1990.

On Sunday, 26 August 1990, Lee addressed his final National Day Rally where he delivered his parting message as Prime Minister.

He reviewed the past and made suggestions for the future. On the past, Lee mentioned the rise and fall of fascism and the rise and fall of communism as two great events in his life. Both ideologies failed because they could not create their superior world and keep their communist bloc. The Communist Party of Malaya (CPM) gave up their armed struggle and they should not be given a second chance. Lee warned of problems, such as racial extremists and now, religious extremists or fundamentalists. These people would not disappear. However, because they lacked that organisational capacity to build up a system that could take over the government, they were not quite the same threat as the communists. He said:

> Therefore, I feel sanguine enough to say that there has never been a better set of conditions for open democratic politics because there is no need for united front politics. There is no need for manipulation behind the scenes of committees, of non-political organisations and getting them to go political, joining the fray. It's what [the communists] did. They worked on old boys' associations, chambers of commerce, musical associations, and they got them to issue all kinds of innocent statements on the surface, but actually designed to foster a particular issue and to agitate. So when an English-educated group tried the same technique and moved into Christian students' union or Catholic students' union and got them to go political and moved into the Law Society to take the government on, I think that was just stupidity.

Turning to the future, Lee said Goh would face different problems because the situation was changing very radically. This needed fast, flexible responses. Policies must be changed, though it did not necessarily mean a change in directions or objectives.

As an example, he cited the change in the "very unpopular and very objectionable" policy of giving graduate mothers preference in school for their children. But the principle of getting more educated mothers to have more children had not changed. Another example was reversing the population policy which now urged people to produce more children, instead of telling them to stop at two before.

Singapore should consolidate and deepen ties with Malaysia and Indonesia, and establish common economic projects where these neighbours would see the value of continuing cooperation. Equally necessary was a common ground. With Malaysia, for example, the Old Guard had no problems because they had some common reference points. The younger Singapore leaders did not have this common experience as they grew up in separate entities and languages were different. He explained:

> When I was a young boy, Malay was the *lingua franca* of Singapore. It is bazaar Malay. It is what I relapse into when making a Malay speech and I am tired and I can't put the prefixes and suffixes. I just go back to the root word. But Goh Chok Tong's generation can't even speak the root word. Maybe that's an advantage. So they just speak English and there is no misunderstanding. But they make use, and I tell them to make use, of the time that Dr Mahathir will give Singapore to broaden and deepen these ties, build up

> a relationship which is naturally cooperative.
>
> Both sides gain from it. Just talking cooperation without tangible benefits in dollars and cents either in increasing tourism or increasing investments and trade does not help. Better still, give them investments in Singapore so that when Singapore develops, property prices go up, they gain. Find some such nexus and reach out to the next generation of leaders. I am sanguine about Malaysia because they have had three leadership changes—from the Tunku [Abdul Rahman, Malaysia's first Prime Minister] to Razak [Abdul Razak] to Tun Hussein Onn to Dr Mahathir. So the next one will be a fourth change. It is more or less within a certain framework. [Malaysia's fourth Prime Minister was Datuk Seri Abdullah Badaw and the current one is Najib Razak.] But remember in all new countries, the character and personality of the leaders count for a great deal in deciding bilateral relations.

In addition, Singapore must remain competitive, by having more and better technicians, engineers, better management and higher productivity, because Malaysia and other countries in the region were catching up with the nation. Being competitive also meant anticipating changes. Inevitably, Lee touched on emigration which he had often decried. He said this remained a problem. Quoting figures from the Population Unit, he revealed that Singapore had a net loss of 70 in 1986, but the number had increased to 2,500 the following year. The largest number of net loss was in 1988, at 2,900, meaning that 11,700 Singaporeans (about 4,000 families) left the country. In 1989, there was a net gain of 5,000 and in the first six months of 1990, 11,000 came in and 2,800 went out. Although there was a net gain of 8,500 over that period, it did not mean all was well. He wanted to know why Singaporeans left in large numbers in 1988. The Population Unit gave the recession as the reason.

This fact worried him because it meant that the younger generation wanted things better every year or they would go elsewhere. But he found it significant that most of those who left retained their Singapore passports. Women who married foreigners kept their Singapore passports and also their children's, in case their husbands' countries did not give them a passport, or if they were divorced. Lee said:

> We have to solve this. We can't leave it as things are because the number of our own graduates marrying graduates is stagnating. It was going up by 4 percent each year now, it's regressed this year. I think we have got to deliver another shock. And I can. I have figures which will shock them. But it'll shock a lot of other people, too. Our graduate women are marrying mostly Caucasians or whites, highly qualified professionals whom they've met either here or abroad.
>
> This is a different kind of family. I think we should change the rules. And Goh Chok Tong has asked George Yeo [then Minister of Information and the Arts] to chair a committee to see what changes are

> necessary. We cannot leave it as it is. We are going to lose a trained woman graduate and we also lose the husband who's going to be a plus. And many of them would like to come and work here. So if they are highly trained, I say give them the PR after two or three years, they can adjust, they want to take citizenship, let them. Then the children will become citizens. Then even if they are divorced, the wife can stay with the children in Singapore.
>
> The Singapore woman is not so stupid. She knows that white men marry you freely, they also divorce you freely. And I believe the children will also be a plus because they are going to be highly competent and well-trained persons. Of course, you know there are innate prejudices. And I do not pretend that I don't share those prejudices. I do. If one of my sons had come back and said: "I've got this American lady whom I met in America," my first question is, what colour is she?

Lee said Singapore also needed a bold and prudent government. It must be bold to tackle "difficult, sensitive, almost insoluble ones", and for this, the ablest and best people must be inducted into politics. They must be well-paid because with "a government on the cheap, you end up with a cheap government". Paying them the market value, or near it, was necessary because this was a different world. The 1959 generation could not be reproduced. They were a product of the Japanese Occupation. He and the Old Guard, like Dr Toh Chin Chye, Dr Goh Keng Swee, Ong Pang Boon and S Rajaratnam, were determined to topple the British and change the system. They were not looking for a career. Singapore was now a steady state and it should look for steady state leaders and carefully select them.

Prudence was crucial to prevent Singapore from mortgaging the future, like other advanced, developed countries were doing by giving free health, unemployment benefits and pensions. Their national debt was growing. Singapore avoided going down the same path. Because the nation had bold but prudent government, it had not mortgaged its future. Every Singaporean was really an owner of assets, reserves. He foresaw that in the next 20 years, they would at least be worth twice as much.

Lee described life as a marathon, a figure of speech of the late Kohei Goshi, former Chairman of the Japan Productivity Centre. Goshi said productivity was like a marathon. A person finished the race and started another one immediately. Likewise, Singapore must move on and finish the race. The prize was an increase in assets. If Singaporeans had that will, they would make it work. What made the difference in Singapore was that a group of men in 1963, 1964 and 1965 decided when Singapore was in Malaysia that they were going to live only one life. If they had to die, they would die for a cause worthy of their lives. He believed Singapore had a group of men similarly determined. Although he was not sure whether in a crisis they had the same tempered steel, he thought quite a few would measure up.

> So the final message I give to Singaporeans is: your future really depends on what you make of it. The

> government can give you the framework, can give expression to the will of a people, but the people must have the will. If you do not have it, there is nothing a government can do.

On 24 November, just four days before passing the baton to Goh, Lee made his last visit to Malaysia as Prime Minister. Naturally, reporters asked him what last advice he had for Goh. Lee replied:

> I have no last advice. All that I wanted to tell him, I've told him in the last 14 years, and he's not interested in listening to any more advice from me. He has got to get on with his job and he has got his mind full of the things that he wants to do.

Asked about his greatest success and failure, he said:

> I would count as my greatest achievement a successor government in Singapore that is able to carry on as well as if not better than we did; that would be the most prized achievement.
>
> My greatest regret is that our major or basic objective, political objective, namely, merger with Malaya to form Malaysia, failed. I don't think there was a bigger disappointment in my life, politically.

Lee would like to forget that unhappy episode. However, there was the bright side to it. Singapore gained its independence through merger, so in a way that objective was achieved. Furthermore, the two years in Malaysia "taught Singaporeans the lessons of life, they understood then what it was like to be trapped in a communal situation", as Lee said in a televised documentary on 31 July 1990, produced by then Television Corporation of Singapore (now MediaCorp TV).

The experience gave Singaporeans the resolve to chart their own future and "to try very hard, no matter how tough it got. Without that spirit, we couldn't have made it. If we took independence as a matter of course, and continued behaving as we used to—strikes, go-slows, taking liberties with the employers, taking liberties with ourselves—we would have failed".

One might add there were other failures. Notable was the bilingual policy which had been the bane of students and parents for some four decades. Long ago, Lee had told parents that "your child has a brain bigger than the biggest computer man has ever built". He later realised that not everyone could be effectively bilingual in, for example, English and Chinese. He admitted his mistake at a meeting of the Chinese Language Curriculum and Pedagogy Review Committee on 11 Oct 2004. As a result, he said: "We have turned off one generation, which is a great pity for us—they are forced by parents and schools [to learn Chinese]—they hate it, they want nothing more to do with it."

In Parliament on 25 November 2004, Lee explained why the bilingual policy must undergo a radical change.

> I used to believe that you can learn two languages at the same time, whatever your IQ. I was wrong. You have to master one language enough to read and absorb knowledge for all the other subjects. Had I known all the difficulties of bilingualism in 1965 as I

> know today, would I have done it differently? Yes—in its implementation, not in its policy.
>
> What I am saying to all parents is: "You make up your mind just how much English you want for your child and how much Chinese. But remember, the more English, the less Chinese; the more Chinese, the less English. There is no such thing as 100 percent English, 100 percent Chinese... The choice is yours. If you make the wrong decision over your child's capability, don't blame the government."

At a Citibank Legacies of Leadership forum on 15 April 2005, Lee revealed three more mistakes he had made when he was the Prime Minister. One was preventing some international institutes from locating in Singapore in the 1970s because he was worried that local academics would be tempted to join them, resulting in the loss of local talent. He said: "But now the world is their oyster anyway, so we might as well have them here. But it's too late now."

Another "stupid decision" was banning motor-racing in the 1970s which used to thrill Singaporeans and tourists. He later realised that this is a spectacle that generates huge revenues for the host countries. He admitted: "I think we made a mistake in not building a Formula One course. Monaco has a Grand Prix. I think I was dim-witted then."

The third mistake was forgetting pop culture in the 1950s in his striving to make Singapore a First World city in a Third World region, a cultured place with libraries, theatres and museums. He conceded that pop culture "attracts millions of young viewers around the world, and there is big money in this". He went on to say: "So from a business point of view, whether I like it or not, I should be—the government should be—interested in this...I learnt a lesson and I'm telling my younger chaps, look, pay attention to all this, this is what will make Singapore buzz."

After his retirement after 31 years in the driver's seat, the impact of Lee Kuan Yew's personality remained strong. He involved himself in national affairs up to his final days, but as a goalkeeper, not a striker. He attended political, business and social functions where necessary, and gave his views and suggestions on important matters. Singaporeans appreciate that he had kept his word to deliver them from want, servitude and danger. Everywhere he went, the reception was rapturous, bordering on awe and adulation. One function he attended on 7 December 1990, just nine days after passing the baton to Goh, serves to illustrate the point. It is also an interesting comparison with the types of reception he used to get in the heyday of the social revolution.

The occasion was the opening of Yokogawa Electric's new factory in Tampines. The event was officiated by then Senior Minister of State for Education Dr Tay Eng Soon. Lee attended as a special guest and came after the ceremony was over, obviously to avoid stealing the thunder from Dr Tay. Company Chairman Shozo Yokogawa had invited Lee to join in the celebration, for the former Prime Minister had been instrumental in encouraging the company to set up its operation in Singapore in 1985. The day was gloomy, worsened by a persistent drizzle. At the main entrance, Chairman Yokogawa and his senior executives waited. A group of the company's workers lined both sides of the steps leading to the administration office. When Lee arrived at 11.30 am, they gave him a rousing cheer and thunderous applause. They shook his hand. Lee always dressed simply but tastefully. That morning, he wore a light pink long-sleeved shirt, a red tie, light brown trousers and dark brown shoes. He smiled and seemed relaxed, the heavy burden of office now no longer on his shoulders.

Company officials led him on a 30-minute conducted tour of the new factory, with Lee asking many questions about the intricacies of the company's operation. A long queue of company officials and guests followed. After refreshments and before leaving, Lee, Dr Tay, Chairman Shozo Yokogawa and Managing Director H Hara each planted a jacaranda sapling in the compound under the cover of umbrellas. The send-off was equally grand. They were honoured by his attendance at their function.

I was present and I was amused by what I witnessed. I cast my mind back to the early days of the social revolution when Lee used to get hostile receptions. He was even verbally and physical abused at some functions by disgruntled and angry trade unionists and workers. The communists and communalists were determined to destroy him. The English-educated and business circles feared and scorned him, some suspecting him to be a communist. They would keep their distance for as Lee had admitted long ago, "to be associated with me was to invite Special Branch attention".

But times have changed considerably. The current generation of Singaporeans esteems Lee. At the Yokogawa factory, company officials and staff welcomed him with open arms. They and their guests jostled to get near to him. This occasion reminded me sharply of the remarkable transformation that has taken place through the years. Of course, most of the company employees and the guests were too young (or not born yet) to know of Lee's traumatic early political life. All they knew was that he was a symbol of Singapore's success. That is how Singaporeans perceive Lee Kuan Yew today.

As Singaporeans enjoy the sweet smell of success, it is appropriate to mention the fate of Chin Peng of the CPM, Lee's arch enemy, to complete the picture. Born Ong Boon Hua in 1924 in Sitiawan, Perak, Chin Peng had been banned from entering Singapore. But the Home Affairs Ministry temporarily lifted the ban between 6 and 8 October 2004 to allow him to attend and speak at the seminar of the Institute of Southeast Asian Studies (ISEAS). It was a closed-door event and his first visit to Singapore since he went underground.

He was a spent force. The end of his era came when he signed a peace agreement with Malaysia and Thailand on 2 December 1989 at Haadyai, after five rounds of negotiations that began in early 1987. At the signing ceremony, Chin Peng promised:

> As Malaysian citizens, we pledge our loyalty to His Majesty the Yang di-Pertuan Agong and the country. We will disband our armed units and destroy all weapons to show our sincerity in terminating the armed struggle.

True to his word, all CPM activities ceased in early 1992. The erstwhile No. 1 Malayan communist died of cancer in a Bangkok private hospital on 16 September 2013, aged 88. By a strange coincidence, that was Lee Kuan Yew's 90th birthday.

16
REMEMBERING GALLANT COMRADES

During his long years in politics, including 31 years as Prime Minister, Lee Kuan Yew had men of high calibre in his team. The most essential qualities found in these men were not academic achievements but raw courage and total dedication and commitment to the cause of freedom from British colonial rule and of fighting the communists and the communalists in the 1950s and 1960s. Of such stalwarts, Lee once said: "You will find out whether a person has it only when a real crisis puts him to the test. I know several MPs who never went to university, never got a school certificate, or a primary school leaving certificate. But they will stand up to fire without withering."

They were made of sterner stuff. Without stout-hearted comrades like them bolstering the PAP, the course of Singapore history would have been different. Lee was grateful to them and rewarded them appropriately.

In March 1982, for example, Lee hosted a valedictory dinner for 11 of these gallant Old Guard to show his gratitude. Among them were four former ministers, two ministers of state and five MPs. They had stepped down or retired in 1980 under the PAP's self-renewal programme. The four ministers were Dr Toh Chin Chye, Lim Kim San, Jek Yeun Thong and Othman Wok. Their departure marked the first dispersal of the original core of the PAP leadership whom Lee described as "men of great moral strength and conviction, or they would not have survived".

Lee recalled that many young Singapore students in London talked about revolution, but few lived up to their convictions when they returned home. He singled out Dr Toh as one of those who pursued their conviction and they fought together in the past 26 years in close tandem. He said Dr Toh was a man who remained calm in the midst of adversities and he thought positively. The former Deputy Prime Minister demonstrated these qualities in the crucial year of 1961 when the fight between the PAP leadership and the pro-communists had erupted. Lee himself was down in spirits. But Dr Toh was a tower of strength. He advised Lee and the other crestfallen leaders that instead of wringing their hands and staring at the ceiling, they should start thinking about their next move. "It made sense," said Lee at the valedictory dinner.

Of Lim Kim San's major achievements, Lee told the guests:

> He got the Bukit Ho Swee fire victims re-housed before 1963. [The fire was one of Singapore's worst. It razed an entire squatter colony in Chinatown on

> 25 May 1961, leaving four people dead and about 16,000 others homeless.] He got the skeleton of Cantonment Road flats up by September 1963. I was a special target of the communists controlling the Chinese middle school students' associations and Nantah [Nanyang University] students' union. That block of flats, a quarter completed, was demonstration that we could get things done.

Jek Yeun Thong, former Minister of Culture, was a life-saver when Lee faltered in his Chinese during one of his earliest election campaigns as he tried to seek support from the Chinese population. Lee was so grateful that he kept a record that reminded him of Jek's assistance. He said:

> Among my documents, I treasure one sheet of paper in simple Chinese, the first and simplest speech I have ever made in Mandarin for the general election in April 1955 at Bandar Street. It was before the biggest crowd Singapore had ever seen, around 60,000. With Jek's one sheet of paper, I tried to prove I was Chinese and Jek kept on writing speeches and pamphlets. Now, it does not matter much. Then, when I could not speak Chinese, it was crucial.

About Othman Wok:

> Othman Wok fought the election in 1959 and lost. He fought again in 1963 and won. I remember discussing his joining the government. It was at

> Temasek, KL [Kuala Lumpur, Malaysia]. *Utusan Melayu* for whom he worked had moved to KL. He had openly identified himself with the PAP and exposed himself to the risks. He never expected to be a minister.

Lee said he was sad to see them go: "I lament the loss of an era when people did great deeds with a casualness that belied the great peril to themselves, and with no thought of personal gain. Like Toh Chin Chye, I do not enjoy asking old comrades to step down. It is unpleasant. It is a nasty business. It makes me unhappy."

Finally, he thanked them all for services rendered to the country.

Singapore's gratitude to the Old Guard could not have been better expressed than by the conferment of testimonials on 21 of them in the 1990 National Day Awards. They were the men who had helped shape the nation between 1959 and 1963 and contributed to the post-independence development.

The roll of honours included S Rajaratnam, E W Barker, Ong Pang Boon, Yong Nyuk Lin, Chua Sian Chin and, of course, Dr Toh Chin Chye, Jek Yeun Thong and Othman Wok. The general citation read: "Without their sturdy, resolute and spirited stand, the Government of Singapore would not have been able to withstand the assaults of the communists from 1961 to 1963 and of the communalists from 1963 to 1965."

The highest award, the Order of Temasek (First Class), went to Rajaratnam. Dr Toh, Ong and Barker received the Order of Nila Utama (First Class), while Yong, Jek, Othman and Chua were bestowed with the Order of Nila Utama (Second Class). The others received the Distinguished Service Order, Meritorious Service Medal and Public Service Star and Public Service Star, Bar.

Lee also used the occasion of his 75th birthday gala dinner celebration on 16 September 1998 to remember old comrades. Lee told his 1,200 guests:

> Those who took part in those tumultuous years from 1955 to 1965 are a special fraternity. We went through fire together and helped each other survive. Re-reading the records of our fights against the communists and then the Malay ultras, I recall vividly the parts you played in pulling off victory from the jaws of defeat. I was fortunate to have had such comrades in those battles.

Lee remembered fondly the vital support of the early Malay PAP strong men for his vision of a multi-racial country. He shed tears as he related it. One of these men he deemed worthy of mention again was Othman Wok, former Minister of Social Affairs. He reminisced:

> I have known Othman Wok since 1952 when I acted for the postmen in their strike and had to get publicity for their cause through Othman, then a journalist in *Utusan Melayu*. I persuaded him to stand for election in September 1963 and he became a minister soon after that, and remained one until 1981.

Addressing Othman Wok directly, he said:

> Othman, I remember your staunch support and loyalty during those troubled days when we were in Malaysia

> and tensions were most severe immediately before and following the bloody racial riots in July 1964. At that time, the greatest pressures were mounted by UMNO Malay extremists who denounced the PAP Malay leaders, especially you, as infidels and traitors to the Malay race. Because of the courage and leadership you showed, not a single PAP Malay leader wavered.

Othman said that he had joined the PAP in 1954 because he had been attracted by Lee's vision of a multi-racial political party to represent all workers, irrespective of their race, language or religion. He recounted: "We closed ranks. We supported him fully because we believed in him, we believed in multi-racialism."

In his tribute to Lee, Othman said:

> Singapore went through the blackest period when we were in Malaysia. The pressure from Kuala Lumpur was tremendous. Led by SM Lee, we stood firm and fought for our rights despite threats. We would not have been what we are today without the leadership of SM Lee during the difficult period.

He mentioned Lee's contributions towards the advancement of the Malays. These included schemes such as the Mosque Building Fund which enabled mosques to be built in the new towns, and the provision of free education for the Malays which was implemented in 1959. Lee's idea was that better education would improve their abilities and raise their confidence to progress faster and eventually catch up with the other communities.

He remembered the day in 1970 when Lee told him:

> The time will come in the near future when we will see the difference between the Singapore Malays and the Malays in this region. They may have the same colour hair, the same colour skin and practise the same religion, but the difference will be in the way they think and behave.

Lee was right, Othman said. The Malays' attitude and thinking changed thereafter. They discarded their communal stand and they could compete and mix with the others. There are now more highly qualified Malays, and they are holding good jobs and enjoying better income over those 20 years before.

Another PAP pillar Lee singled out was Dr Goh Keng Swee, former Deputy Prime Minister and the architect of the Singapore economy when he was Finance Minister. In an interview with Television Corporation of Singapore (now MediaCorp TV) telecast two days before the gala dinner, he described Dr Goh as his alter ego and the strongest among his Cabinet colleagues, saying:

> He is a very important player. Without him, we would have had a different Singapore. He is a very robust man, very stout-hearted in a crisis. He does not panic or take fright. He got this place going.

Dr Goh, congratulating Lee on his 75th birthday, said:

> Today you celebrate your 75th birthday; further you have a clear mind and a desire to get things done. May this attitude remain firm in the years ahead. Singapore

> has benefitted enormously under your care and, I hope, will continue to do so.

There was also nostalgia during Lee's 80th birthday party on 16 September 2003 attended by about 1,000 guests. He described his life as a great adventure, exciting, unpredictable and exhilarating. He thanked the "special fraternity" of men who went through "the crucible of fire" with him, and all the civil servants for bringing many of the plans to fruition. Most decisive was the support of the community leaders who came forward during the years from 1962 onwards, turned the tide against the communist united front and stood firm against the UMNO ultras. Those in Tanjong Pagar provided him with a solid base for his own political longevity.

He related his "unique experience," after resigning as PM in 1990, of being in the Cabinet with Prime Minister Goh Chok Tong as he built his new team, and of seeing them "grow in experience and confidence." Goh inducted three batches of new MPs in 1991, 1997 and 2001. Lee said their ability, education and knowledge of world affairs kept pace with that of the people. Each batch yielded a number who became Cabinet ministers. Several of them now formed the core of the new team. It had not been plain sailing for them, having to steer through several crises including the Asian financial meltdown and the SARS outbreak.

Despite the new challenges facing Singapore, Lee was optimistic about its future, saying:

> The present generation grew up in Singapore where life improved year after year. Unfortunately, no growth path is without reverses. The present pessimism of the

faint-hearted, reflected in the media, that Singapore has seen its best days, that the music has stopped and the party is over, is totally unfounded. That is not how I see the future of Singapore.

After 13 years which included several severe crises since 1997, there is no doubt that the present team has the capability, the grasp and the determination to lead Singapore safely through a very difficult period in its history. Singaporeans are proving Samuel Huntington wrong, when he wrote that the system I had built would disappear with me. A new generation is not only upholding the system, but is taking Singapore to its next level of development.

Describing his personal life in politics, he said:

I am grateful that I got where I am, happy that I have made a contribution to the lives of many people. I am glad to be alive, relatively healthy and active. When I look around at my contemporaries, I'm struck by how differently time and circumstances have treated us. Could I have lived my life differently? Maybe yes, probably not. At each stage I made what was then the best choice. Having taken that decision, I changed direction and there was no turning back. I cannot say that I planned my life. That's why I feel life is a great adventure, exciting, unpredictable and at times exhilarating. At the end of the day, what I cherish most are the human relationships.

Then he paid tribute to his wife and family:

> With the unfailing support of my wife and partner, I have lived my life to the fullest. It is the friendships I made and the close family ties I nurtured that have provided me with that sense of satisfaction at a life well lived, and have made me what I am.

Paying his compliments, Old Guard Lim Kim San, former National Development Minister, described Lee's nature and dedication to the nation:

> One characteristic that sets him apart from most men is that he is 24 hours on the job. His job is Singapore, and how to ensure the security and stability it needs. He thinks, talks and, no doubt, dreams about this. He is a workaholic, working sometimes till dawn. Senior Minister is a great mentor, able to coax your best out of you. Working for him was an experience not to be missed. He is not easily satisfied, but I think he must now be satisfied that his 80 years have been well spent.

Lim agreed that Lee's wife had been a pillar of strength. She stood by him through thick and thin, working in tandem with him for the good of Singapore. Lim said Lee had mellowed, was more sociable and friendlier as he moved around greeting old friends and colleagues to ask how they and their families were getting on. The caring side of his nature was now more evident.

The Old Guard fully deserved the accolades for their success in nation-building. They all had played good music and in perfect unison, with conductor Lee Kuan Yew orchestrating the movements. In their radio broadcasts in August 1997, Dr Toh Chin Chye, Dr Goh Keng Swee and Lim Kim San recounted their traumatic experiences and gave their thoughts for the future.

Dr Toh said the generation of the 1950s and 1960s took the plunge into politics "without ever calculating the costs or the risks and the benefits to be gained." They were driven by ideology, but today's generation had none to follow. They were schooled in business management culture and were averse to taking political risks. He said:

> But I cannot blame the present generation, because they see the heavy-handed response by the government to dissenting views, even though they know that these matters involve their daily lives. So the result is that we have produced a younger generation who are meek and therefore very calculating. They are less independent-thinking and lacking in initiative. It does not bode well for the emergence of future leaders in politics or business.

Dr Toh also spoke about Singapore-Malaysia relations. He did not believe the two countries could put their past behind them and have ties similar to those between the United States and Canada. It would not happen in his lifetime. There must be "a sort of *modus vivendi* between the people, because we are interlocked in many ways with trade". He doubted if this would lead to better political bonds as after 1965, there was, and still is, no assurance or guarantee that the political surface would be calm. It might take another generation for the younger generation "to smooth all things out". Although Malaysia had a new generation that had taken over, he would not say "that is equally true for Singapore".

Dr Goh Keng Swee recalled that during the anti-colonial campaign, the British had concluded that the PAP would lose in the fight against the communists and that there would be a communist government elected in Singapore. It was the British who drew up the scheme to absorb Singapore into Malaya and who sold the idea to Tunku Abdul Rahman. The plan was to include Brunei and the Borneo territories of Sarawak and Sabah to balance the racial composition. He said that one of the biggest bugbears about merger was that the Tunku was not interested in financial arrangements or a common market. Singapore struck a bargain. It asked for a common market to allow its goods duty-free entry, as well as autonomy in education and labour. In return for this, Singapore would reduce its representation in the Federal Parliament, below the number it was entitled to. Outside experts including a senior World Bank official, were asked to arbitrate and suggest a solution. They proposed a compromise that gave Malaysia the right to determine what products should go into the common market and the pace of the development of the common market. Although the terms were unsatisfactory to Singapore, there was no choice but to agree.

Dr Goh maintained that Malaysia "never had any serious intention of giving us the slightest advantage and the slightest access to the market". Instead, Malaysia warned investors that if they set up their factories in Singapore, their goods would be denied entry, but that if they opened in Malaysia, they would get whatever Singapore gave them. He said:

> They acted in utter bad faith. And that is why the longer we stayed in Malaysia, the more doubtful we became that we did the right thing. And things grew from bad to worse and eventually, we were reduced to a pretty desperate state.

Lim Kim San's experience was in building the much-needed public housing. The former National Development Minister said it began when, "out of the blue", Prime Minister Lee Kuan Yew told him to be chairman of the Housing and Development Board in the early 1960s.

Getting into his job, he found out for himself "the bad living conditions" in the slum areas in Chinatown. The residents were poor and the shops were selling second-hand goods. Some were so poor they shared communal facilities, bunks and even clothes. It was an eye-opener for him. Going round to inspect some of the flats being built, he was shocked to find shoddy workmanship. In fact, he saw with horror one block of flats at Margaret Drive to be crooked, literally. His technicians confirmed it. He got the contractor to rebuild the block. On another occasion, he found the wiring in a block under construction to be below specifications and had it replaced. He gave the contractors firm notice that "we didn't want any fooling around". They got the message. Lim said:

> Here again, when we discussed with the professionals, we made sure that we did not over-specify so that the contractors could fool around. So these are some of the things. And once the contractors understood what we wanted, where they stood and how we would treat

them, then we had no more problems with them. Standards of work improved.

Besides being dauntless, the Old Guard were men of financial and political integrity. This was the dominant key of their success as they played good music in concert. Lee Kuan Yew struck the note while addressing the PAP's dinner on 21 September 2003 organised to celebrate his 80th birthday. Lee said the party had institutionalised honesty and integrity into its governance and these had been the hallmark.

He reminded the gathering that the PAP started on a shoestring, with very little money. It had "to pass the hat around among the leaders each time we held a function". For the launch of the party at the Victoria Memorial Hall on 21 November 1954, their wives sewed the rosettes for the party officials to wear. During elections, all the party workers were volunteers. The only time the party had to pay election workers was in the general election for the Federal Parliament in 1964 as there was no time to build a party organisation. Because of that, the party "got into considerable debt".

Lee said the PAP stayed honest and had no obligations to return favours because it gave no hostages to fortune. The party did not ask for donations from trade unions or big businesses, unlike the Labour Party and the Conservative Party in Britain. And unlike the Liberal Democratic Party in Japan, the PAP had "no links with construction companies for kickbacks in party donations". Thus, the party was able to maintain its role as a balancer between the interests of capital and labour, between the owners, managers and workers.

Furthermore, the PAP had established a clean and open electoral system where not much money was needed to run for and win an election. This system worked, not just for the party as a governing party but also for the opposition. In most countries, politicians needed big money to participate in an election. Lee told the gathering:

> We have been able to maintain people's support since 1959 when we first formed the government, that is for 44 years. We have stayed clean and honest. We have never tried to be overpowering or oppressive. No big party headquarters, no party branches pestering small businesses for donations. We made it a virtue to be modest but effective in reaching out to people. That is the way we have to remain.

Giving an example of modesty, he said ministers and officials, for their ordinary business, had no special cars, no special number plates, no flags fluttering. Until recently, when security became a problem, ministers had no security escorts. All these practices had served them well. People had not found them dishonest or oppressive. The government leaders had been able to command respect and support. They were determined never to allow power to go to their heads. It was so easy to "slip into bad habits" after over 40 years in power since 1959, and lose their sense of proportion "as self-indulgence" became ever more pronounced. They would become "megalomaniacs, divorced from the people on whose behalf we exercise power".

Lee said the party had "studiously avoided the build-up of personality cults, like displays of painting, photos, statues of leaders" and that the only photos the government sponsored were those of the President and his wife. The PAP's volunteers were proud "in being associated with a good governing party, a hardworking MP, the idealism to serve the people and the satisfaction that comes with making people's lives better".

He believed that as long as the party kept these qualities of integrity, openness and effectiveness in looking after the lives of the people, "we will not be easy to challenge".

Lee led by example. He shunned the trappings of office. He lived in his own home at Oxley Road, instead of in the official residence at the Istana. He did not want to give his children "a wrong impression of life, with servants and cars and everything like that", as he told a journalist. It was his wife who decided it would be bad for the children "and I think it has worked out well".

He dressed simply but tastefully, saying he was quite casual because he was not out to impress anybody, but he disliked being slovenly as "it shows no respect for other people". Although he enjoyed drinking, he did so in moderation to avoid having a hangover. He used to smoke heavily until he lost his voice after the City Council election in 1957. Towards the end of his life, he was allergic to cigarette smoke, saying that it gave him "a runny nose and burning eyes".

Despite his sharp intellect, strong leadership qualities and great capabilities, Lee knew his limitations. He was self-deprecating when he was asked whether he would have liked to head a larger country than Singapore. Lee replied that he would, but he was realistic.

He said: "Supposing I'd been in China, conspiring with millions of others as bright, if not brighter and tougher. My chances of climbing to the top of the heap would have been 0.001 percent. I look at Deng [Xiaoping], for example, I wouldn't have beaten him. He's brighter, he's wilier, he's tougher."

Asked if he considered himself tough, he agreed he was tough when making hard decisions, but not for the sake of being tough. He liked to be "kind to people and not hurt anybody" unless he had to "because it's necessary to get them out of the way". He admitted to being fairly autocratic when something had got to be done. The most important single skill a leader must have, according to Lee, was the ability to judge people. In his own words, "that's one of the fortunate attributes that I have" and "I can judge people quickly".

In an interview with *The New Paper* in February 1995, Lee revealed that another secret of Singapore's success was the avoidance of populist policies. Such policies would destroy the nation's assets built up systematically over 30 years. The government had pursued consistent "sound, long-term policies of high expenditure on the key factors which determine a people's future—health, education, infrastructure, technology". These had enabled the country to gain a lead over its competitors.

Financial prudence had placed Singapore in the enviable position of having negligible external debt. Even its internal debt was small. The nation enjoyed high savings in an era of short money supply. This would not be so if the government subsidised public transport, utilities, unmarried mothers and their children and unemployment. The country would start borrowing, leading to the depreciation of the Singapore dollar, high interest rates, economic slowdown and budget deficit. Lee cautioned Singaporeans against wanting to have the things which many Western countries had.

The present government had the responsibility of sustaining the time-tested policies and of mobilising the people to stay on course. He foresaw a problem for the younger generation, as they were unaware of "how we got into this virtuous cycle" of "a strong Singapore dollar, low inflation, a growing economy getting stronger each year". He stressed:

> I want to see Singapore go further up the ladder which means effort—effort on the part of the government to get the people to understand, effort on the part of the people to do their best and to contribute to the industrialisation of our neighbours in East Asia.

Lee also stressed the need for mavericks, those who thought out of the box, as well as team players. He did not realise the importance of mavericks when he and his colleagues rolled up their sleeves to transform an island beset with strikes, arson and riots into "a leaner, trimmer place that works, a First World oasis in a Third World region." He confessed to his ignorance while addressing the Global Brand Forum in Singapore on 1 December 2003. He told the audience of about 700 business leaders:

> I know this now. Your workforce must have the cohesiveness, but to make the big leap forward, you need your mavericks, your geniuses, your people who can think outside the box and say: "I can do it better, simpler."

Giving the example of Japan and the United States, Lee thought that although the Japanese excelled in teamwork, they could not match the Americans "for sheer innovation". He said he had not set out to brand Singapore, only to make it different from other countries in the region. He was aware that his neighbours were catching up. The answer was that Singapore must differentiate itself from them by making "our system work better".

In his golden years, as he remembered his gallant comrades, Lee remained obsessed with ensuring that the system he had established continue to work for Singapore's survival. He wanted Singaporeans to continue to "dare to excel" and to be "the best one can be". Although the younger generation of Singaporeans has no ideology to follow, as Dr Toh Chin Chye had said, Lee wanted them to play good music in concert and to have an accomplished conductor to orchestrate the movements, as the Old Guard did. Lee's constant drumming of the note even after he had retired as Prime Minister reflected his undying love for the nation he built. He promised to remain in the government as long as he was fit, to see that the orchestration went well. To recall his statement that epitomised his total dedication to Singapore, delivered during the National Day Rally in August 1988:

> And even from my sick bed, even if you are going to lower me into the grave and I feel that something is going wrong, I'll get up. Those who believe that when I have left the government as Prime Minister, that I've gone into permanent retirement, really should have their heads examined.

17

WHAT THE WORLD THINKS OF LEE

"Is your Prime Minister well-educated?" our next-door neighbour asked my wife Teresa in her cockney accent one day.

"Oh, yes," replied my wife proudly and without hesitation. "He studied in Cambridge and got a double first in law."

"Oh, so he is well-educated then," said our neighbour whom we shall name Mrs Brown. A plump, kindly woman of about 40, Mrs Brown was the wife of a British army sergeant. She and my wife were engaging in one of their casual chats over the fence.

This was sometime in the early1960s when the PAP had just formed the government, and the British still had their military forces in Singapore. At that time, the lower-ranking officers and their families were housed in middle-class residential estates, such as mine, situated at Upper Thomson Road. Most of them, like the

Brown family, were genuinely friendly, with no superior airs. Their three young children, two girls and a boy, aged between six and 12, often dropped by to play with our three children who were of about the same age, and sometimes ate with us.

Our amiable Mrs Brown could be excused for her ignorance of Lee's academic qualifications. After all, how many Singaporeans knew about the educational background of Harold Wilson (the British Prime Minister at that time)? But Mrs Brown and others in Britain and many other countries in the world had heard about the Singapore Prime Minister. He was acquiring an international reputation for his nation-building efforts, enormous intellect, deep perception of world affairs and great vision, even in this early stage of his political career. His light was already shining far and wide. Britain, Singapore's former colonial master, would be an appropriate place to start with the listing of some of the global accolades accorded to Lee.

In January 1968, Lee flew to London to ask Prime Minister Harold Wilson of the Labour Party government to delay the British military withdrawal, explaining the reasons for the request. The British had announced the accelerated withdrawal in 1968 to take effect in early 1971. Lee succeeded in getting nine months' grace, to 31 December 1971. While in Britain, he gave interviews on television and made speeches. He was an instant success with the British public. It seemed that they had been frustrated with their own government. Several vented their anger in the press. They recommended an exchange of prime ministers.

The London Evening Standard published an interesting and amusing sampling of their comments. One reader wrote:

"Footballers are transferred. Why not politicians? The men we want are Lee Kuan Yew as Prime Minister and Abba Eban [Israel's Foreign Minister] as Foreign Secretary. With them in charge, we should really get somewhere."

Another reader asked: "Put Singapore's Prime Minister and our own Prime Minister side by side and which one must any rational person follow and respect? How this country needs its own Lee Kuan Yew, with his patriotism and keen intelligent outlook without a taint of egotism, to steer it from the wreck of Labour misrule."

A third reader offered this suggestion: "The swap idea is attractive. But it would have to be on a player-plus-cash basis. Our economy could hardly afford the enormous cash payment Singapore would require."

But one resident objected to the exchange proposal. A Mrs Elizabeth Pitman of Modern, Surrey, who claimed she was a Singapore citizen, retorted: "What have the people of Singapore ever done to the people of England that you should want to wish Mr Wilson on us? You have Mr Wilson, so keep him. We are very happy with Mr Lee and hold him in very high esteem, and we would like to keep him for ourselves."

Several British journalists also went out in praise of Lee. For example, Hazel Hoad of the *Evening News*, commented:

> The good humour, clarity and charm with which he answered questions on television must have gained him thousands of admirers. Long after this dynamic man has returned home he will be remembered here with respect and affection. He would win hands down in any vote on the personality of the last few weeks.

Acclamations from other countries followed. In October 1968, Lee Kuan Yew stopped over in Hong Kong on his way to Japan. *The Hong Kong Standard* published a glowing full-page article headlined: "Here Comes Mr Singapore." The article threw into light what the world thought of Lee. It read:

> Into Hong Kong today comes the man who is making Singaporeans into what they are and what they will be. But what kind of man is the leader of a government which is recognised as one of unusual ability and is probably the most honest in Asia? Mr Lee, like the stainless steel of frightening competence in his Cabinet, is in a hurry. Mr Lee's politics is aggressive. So aggressive, his opponents abhor his methods and call him a dictator, but Mr Lee is not Sukarno. He has his feet on the ground. He knows where he is going. By nature combative, assertive and abrasive, Mr Lee can also be charming and persuasive. He lives simply with no pretensions of pomp and grandeur. He walks among his people with the ease of one who knows them as a friend. And they love him simply because he is like one of them.

Noting Singapore's big looming problems caused by the proposed accelerated British military withdrawal, the article said: "The problems have to be solved. And if you know Mr Lee, they will be solved."

Another foreign media assessment of Lee's character was made by a Filipino newspaper columnist, Maximo Soliven, in December that year. Writing in the *Manila Times*, the oldest existing English language newspaper in the Philippines, Soliven observed: "Lee Kuan Yew may not be a lovable type, but you have to give him his due. We have already heard too much talk about revamps and reshuffles in this country [the Philippines]. Lee doesn't talk about revamping his government. He just goes ahead and does it. He runs a clean shop in his microscopic city state of 1.9 million people, a population smaller than that of Manila."

Once, recognition of his enormous intellect came from no less than Harvard University which invited him to be Visiting Fellow of the John Fitzgerald Kennedy School of Government in 1967. Lee accepted the invitation in 1968. Prof Richard E Neustadt, Associate Dean of the School, remarked: "We regard the Prime Minister as an ideal choice to further the scope of our programme. We think of the Fellows we choose as natural intermediaries between the academic world and the world of government."

Lee, who stayed in Harvard for about three months, addressed a number of seminars and impressed his audience with his views and analyses of global affairs. In one seminar, he spoke about the future of Southeast Asia. He predicted a more stable region because the next generation of Asian leaders would not make the mistakes of their predecessors. The mistakes he enumerated included alienating the minorities, particularly the small businessmen who were often not indigenous to their countries, such as the Chinese and Indians. The younger generation realised that free enterprise was the cornerstone of progress. What they needed was area-wide cooperation on different problems facing the region. Lee's panacea for success was peace and security.

Many of his former Cambridge classmates also remembered Lee Kuan Yew. One of them was Percy Cradock. He had become the British Charge d'Affairs in Beijing. Cradock said: "You know, it didn't surprise me that Mr Lee became Prime Minister of Singapore. He was an outstanding student, so much so, it would have been difficult to miss him. We were both in the Cambridge Union and the Cambridge Labour Club. Once, I remember, Mr Lee gave the Labour Club a talk on foreign policy and possibly also on China. He made quite an impression."

Lee received numerous international awards for his accomplishments. One of the highest was the Honorary Companion of Honour bestowed on him by Britain's Queen Elizabeth in her New Year Honours List in January 1970. The exclusive order is conferred on those who have done conspicuous national service, but carries no title. The badge, a gold medallion, is inscribed with "In action faithful and in honour clear".

Liverpool, the city where he had first landed in Britain in 1946 to pursue his law study, not only remembered him but also honoured him. In 1971, the University of Liverpool conferred on him the honorary degree of Doctor of Law. Lee's wife, Geok Choo, and his daughter, Wei Ling, witnessed the ceremony. Lee wore a red gown and mortar board as befitted the occasion. The Vice-Chancellor, T C Thomas, officiated at the function before a distinguished gathering of about 500.

Thomas, who was once Lee's law teacher, described his former student as "a statesman whose courage and idealism have become a byword among those people who continue to show affection for the Commonwealth".

In his address, the Public Orator of the university, Prof L Rosenhead, lauded Lee: "Mr Lee is a man who possesses elements of that elusive mystery called greatness. He is an unusual combination of politician statesman and intellectual, a man strong in leadership, a pragmatist and an idealist. His passion is Singapore and for its welfare and future. He is fiercely ambitious.... Mr Lee is no stranger to Liverpool. Exactly 25 years ago, he descended from the troopship into grey, war-torn and weary Liverpool. He took one long look at us and fled to the south by the first available train."

In the 1970s, Lee often touched on the controversial Vietnam War issue and his comments were taken seriously by world leaders. He held the view that United States intervention in the conflict was not useless. His reason was that this involvement gave smaller nations the choice to go their own way. The continued US presence in Asia was desirable while the United States, mainland China, the Soviet Union and Japan worked out new arrangements.

In April 1973, Lee visited then US President Richard Nixon to discuss international affairs. One American newspaper, the mass circulation *New York Sunday News,* took the opportunity to suggest that Nixon, as well as past presidents John F Kennedy and Lyndon Johnson, should have consulted Lee on how to explain the Vietnam war to the rest of the world. The newspaper's Washington columnist, Jerry Greene, interviewed Lee and commented afterwards:

> He is an impressive politician, fierce in his determination that the small nations of the world be left alone by the big powers. He sees a sharp distinction between the open, non-communist free world and the closed society and economy of the communist

> states. His example has in a dozen years shown the way for the little countries. He sees spots of success in neighbouring lands.

Former US President Nixon did not overlook Lee in his memoir, *Leaders*, published in 1982. Nixon described the Lee as one of the two ablest leaders he had ever met. The other leader Nixon mentioned was Robert Menzies of Australia. However, Nixon also described Lee as "opportunistic". Lee was unhappy with that.

In July 1982, Lee received another high British tribute when he was conferred the Honorary Freedom of the City of London. The Chamberlain, John Percival Criggs, waxed lyrical in his commendation. Borrowing words first uttered by the late American President Theodore Roosevelt, Criggs eulogised: "He was one of those leaders of men with inspired idealism and great vision who dream greatly and can kindle the people with the fire from their burning soul. He was the prime architect of a modern city state which attracts the admiration of the world."

When Alexander Haig was US Secretary of State, he was asked in January 1981 to name Third World leaders he would be comfortable with and whom he would call upon for advice. Haig gave a few names, and one of them was Lee Kuan Yew. His reasons: "I have known him in the past and have discussed the Asian situation with him."

Another American admirer of Lee was Dan Quayle. When Quayle was US Vice-President, he visited Singapore in 1989 after a 12-day tour of the Asia Pacific region and spent five hours with Lee. He described him as "one of those rare individuals who see the world from a historic and strategic perspective". He said he was struck by Lee's "emphasis on the necessity of a powerful American presence in the Pacific as a counter-balance to other less benign forces, and as a guarantor of the peace".

Former British Prime Minister Margaret Thatcher summed up her respect of Lee in these words in November 1990 at the time of Lee's resignation:

> I have always valued his advice, experience and friendship and greatly appreciate the perceptive analysis which he has brought to our discussions at Commonwealth and other international conferences. It is a tribute to Mr Lee's extraordinary leadership and vision that a small island state has been transformed into one of the world's most dynamic trading and financial centres.

Even after he had left office, Lee continued to be sought for his views and assessments of world affairs. In January 1991, for example, then US President George Bush asked Lee to break his journey in Washington while he was on his way to accept an invitation to visit Mexico. This was during the height of the Gulf War. The two leaders met for one hour not at the Oval Office but at the White House Family Quarters which are out of bounds to the public and journalists.

What did they talk about? They had known each other since 1982 when Bush visited Singapore as Vice-President. Lee's reply was non-committal: "We have kept in touch and although I'm no longer Prime Minister, he has asked me to call on him whenever

I'm in the Washington area, to have a chat." He said that Bush wanted to inform him about the reactions of Third World leaders to events in the Gulf. During that brief stopover, Lee also met Dan Quayle, Defence Secretary Dick Cheney and other top US government officials.

Recognising Lee's status as a world leader and a great strategic thinker, the Advisory Council of Stanford University's Institute for International Studies invited him to be a member. The august body was headed by former US Secretary of State George Schultz and comprised present and past heads of state such as Gerald Ford, Valery Giscard d'Estaing and Helmut Schmidt, as well as international corporate chiefs and eminent academics.

From Asia, former Japanese Prime Minister Noboru Takeshita paid this tribute on the eve of Lee's resignation in November 1990: "I was prejudiced by the knowledge that Prime Minister Lee Kuan Yew is one of the most talented men to have graduated from Cambridge University. But from the very sociable, smiling face with which he received me when I met him, I was made to feel his humility more so than his sharp intellect."

Another Japanese statesman, former Finance Minister Kiichi Miyazawa, also paid a glowing tribute in 1990: "I think his contribution to the world is that he showed that by good leadership and hard work, a small island can be a first-rate nation in the community of the world. I think there is no contribution greater than that in the free world. Singapore really stands up. In Mr Lee Kuan Yew, there is a beautiful mixing or combination of East and West, which makes him a man with a strong sense of mission, courage, integrity and decency."

Even many of his old foes, like the Plen (Fang Chuang Pi) and Dominic Puthucheary, had a good word for Lee, never mind the clash of ideologies in the past. In an interview with *Shin Min Daily News* in 1990, the Plen thanked Lee for an act of kindness towards his sister, Fang Yin Ching, whose face had been badly scarred following a pressure lamp explosion in 1958. Lee helped to arrange skin grafts for her and his wife visited her in hospital. "It is something I've remembered over the last few decades. We communists have feelings, too, you know," he told the interviewer.

Puthucheary, a lawyer in Kuala Lumpur, said during an interview with *The Sunday Times* published on 30 November 2003: "I had great affection and admiration for Mr Lee. He was a capable, competent leader and espoused many of the ideals that I felt for. I believed we were talking the same language."

Puthucheary was a staunch friend of Lee. But he was upset when Lee weeded out his close friends in the PAP, including Lim Chin Siong, as communists. Although he believed his friends had a separate agenda, he did not see the sinister aspect of it. He kept their company and could not tum around and fight them. In the end, he decided to stand by them. He accepted that they had "a moral impulse to create a just society". That was how he and Lee parted company. Puthucheary maintained that he and his older brother James were not communists. "If the communists had come to power, the likelihood is that James and I would be one of the earliest to be shot dead," he said in the interview.

Lee was described as a worrier. In fact, his late mother used to tell relatives and friends that her son would spend sleepless nights when problems surfaced, worrying and looking for the solutions.

He admitted this tendency to worry in the May 1978 issue of *Leaders*, an American quarterly:

> Yes. I make a habit of looking out for the troubles and dangers ahead. This has often helped me to avoid or overcome them.
>
> However, there have been problems which could not be avoided or overcome. I have had to live with the consequences. Worrying after the event does not help. I do not think I am an intellectual. What has helped me to get along with other people in government is practical common sense. Analysis and abstraction of principles I afford myself in my spare time, reading and ruminating.

One of Lee's other qualities that the world admires is that he was not power-hungry, which put paid to the constant allegations that he was a dictator. The general opinion is that in a world where heads of government rarely give up their jobs voluntarily, Lee must be one of the rare exceptions. He stepped aside from a job he had held with distinction for 31 years and when he was still at the height of his powers and under no pressure to relinquish his post.

Lorn Priantit, a columnist of *Thai Rath*, Thailand's largest circulating daily newspaper, and a bitter critic, put it succinctly: "Lee's resignation was a good show of democracy."

Indeed, it will be remembered that Lee began grooming the next generation of leaders as far back as 1966, after the Old Guard had ruled for only seven years. He considered self-renewal necessary for ensuring continuity.

True to form, Lee produced seven new faces to contest the by-elections of 1966 and 1967 to fill the seats left vacant by the resignations of the Barisan Sosialis MPs following their boycott of Parliament. The process of self-renewal continued with more new blood fielded in subsequent by-elections and general elections. They comprised men who were to play leading roles. In 1976, it was Goh Chok Tong and in 1984, it was Lee Hsien Loong, Lee Kuan Yew's eldest son. Being the Prime Minister's son, Hsien Loong's entry into politics caused a tremendous stir. Lee denied that he had anything to do with his son's decision to take up politics, or that he was creating a Lee Dynasty. He said Hsien Loong had to compete for his place like everyone else. His son has proved himself, rising to become Deputy Prime Minister and now Prime Minister.

One by one, the Old Guard made way for the New Guard. Lee took the opportunity to explain again the need for leadership rejuvenation when he addressed his Tanjong Pagar constituency on 26 July 1997:

> Without people willing to step aside and let others carry on the job, we will have a break and a break is disastrous. I have stood down [as Prime Minister] for seven years. I could have carried on for at least five more years but that would have been risky. That would have been a grave disservice if anything went wrong.
>
> Now you have a government of young people, fully conversant in all aspects. I am just the 12th man in the team. Maybe from time to time, they can draw on my experience. I can say: "Watch out, this is dangerous, be careful." But otherwise, there is no problem. A

> new generation has taken over. That is the single most important job that Singapore must achieve at every level. We must keep on having a flow of people to look after the rest of the community.

In 1984, Lee also introduced the concept of an elected president. One of the president's vital functions is to prevent future governments from spending the nation's foreign reserves indiscriminately. He explained that even a government as honest as the PAP could well be pressured into handing out subsidies to win votes. The leaders might not have the resolve to resist the temptation. He warned that depletion of the reserves would reduce the value of the Singapore dollar and with it, the value of the people's hard earned savings kept in the Central Provident Fund and that of their homes.

Lee always upheld his nation-building principle that what works is a good government, meaning "a government that considers itself a trustee of the people, and not the people in charge who built a nest-egg or settled an annuity for themselves". As he told his audience in Hong Kong on 14 December 1992 after delivering the inaugural Li Ka Shing Distinguished Lecture:

> I have never believed that democracy brings progress. The British never governed these countries by one-man-one-vote policies. It was one British Governor, one British Resident and his word was law. My thoughts on decolonisation, I think, they are grim because Western political scientists have not lived in these societies, have not understood that what is

> required is economic progress, development and the final blossoming of a large educated middle-class which can sustain democracy.

At a dinner talk he gave to the Singapore Press Club and the Foreign Correspondents' Association on 7 June 1996, Lee provided more insight into his style of government. An American journalist had asked him why he was against the US liberal democratic philosophy while he welcomed the US military presence in the Asia-Pacific region. Lee replied that he had to alert English-educated Singaporeans to the dangers of going down the road propagated by the Americans.

He told the journalist:

> The more you want to sell this idea of a free-for-all society, each individual for himself, the more you are threatening the survival of Singapore. I don't run you down for the sake of running you down. I need you here. But I have to tell my people to counter your propaganda that if we follow you, we'll be as happy as you are, I don't think that will be the result.
>
> The Golden Triangle is just two hours by air, where there are the drug addicts who will kill or murder to get money to buy more drugs to satisfy their cravings. I cannot run this country. We have got it under control because we've got very tough laws which in your system is unconstitutional.
>
> I've never governed by the polls. I've governed by my gut instincts and often, against the face of opinion,

> but I've always swung it around in the end. And I've not the slightest doubt that what I did or what my wife did was right. And I'll prove it anywhere, any place and I will swing Singapore around.

Asked about the loyalty of Singapore's national servicemen, he expressed confidence that they were willing to fight for the country and were not shirkers, saying:

> I've no poll to prove this, but I go by my gut feel and one of my indicators has always been whether our young men take their national service seriously. I've seen no reports from Mindef [Ministry of Defence] that they are shirking. Everything said and done, in the seriousness of the quieter moments, they know deep down, that they are going to fight for this place. I don't see that will lacking. So I think there's hope.

Lee upheld loyalty to country dearly and his passion for Singapore was total. To recall his inspiring statement delivered at his traditional National Day Rally in August 1989:

> To build a country, you need passion. When we fought in 1961–63, against the communists, when we went through hell in 1963–65, many people thought we were crazy. We could lead peaceful quiet lives. Why were we doing this? It was an act of conviction. This is my country. This is my life. This is my people. You will trample over us, over our dead bodies. We dug our toes in, we built a nation.

Indeed, as Professor Diane K Mauzy, a University of British Columbia political scientist and co-author of *Singapore—The Legacy of Lee Kuan Yew*, commented in November 1990:

> Leaders do make a difference to the history of a state. Singapore has been very fortunate for a variety of reasons to have a long-serving leader like Lee Kuan Yew. If I had to choose one thing to emphasise as a tribute to the Prime Minister, it would be that he gave Singapore a financially responsible and non-corrupt government. That is a rare legacy in the Third World, and, indeed, uncommon in any part of the world.

Not least was the tribute paid by *Time* magazine in its 18 April 2005 issue which hailed Lee Kuan Yew as one of the 100 most influential people in the world, and one of the 12 Asians, in the annual ranking. Author Ian Buruma said:

> Although he can still fine-tune Singapore's efficiency and development, when all the tinkering is done, one feels that Lee would have liked to have had a larger, grander stage on which to project his vision of perfection.
>
> Since Singapore is too small to shape the future of the world, Lee's mark on history would have to be as a great thinker, a kind of Asian philosopher king.

But what do Singaporeans think of Lee Kuan Yew?

18

WHAT SINGAPOREANS THINK OF LEE

Going around Singapore, one is struck by the conspicuous absence of monuments or other symbols of Lee Kuan Yew. He shunned all such displays of adulation. He wanted no monuments of himself. He once remarked that he was not a model of anything. He just wanted to make Singapore work.

Lee was not a megalomaniac. Old Guard S Rajaratnam once explained: "I think that his statue is Singapore—what he created and left behind. And after he's not here, this statue must not perish."

Even his monumental memoirs had been written only because of strong persuasion by former Old Guard colleague Lim Kim San. Besides the memoirs, the only projects bearing Lee Kuan Yew's name one can think of are those connected with intellectual and educational development. A good case in point is the Lee Kuan

Yew School of Public Policy which then Prime Minister Goh Chok Tong announced in September 2003 to mark Lee's 80th birthday. The institution is a training ground for Asia's future policy makers. The Dean is Kishore Mahbubani, a veteran diplomat who was once Singapore's Permanent Representative at the United Nations.

But there are Singaporeans who strongly feel that the former Prime Minister richly deserved a visible and lasting form of remembrance. They suggested in the local newspapers that the time had come for the nation to think seriously about honouring him in a concrete manner.

One letter-writer proposed renaming Changi Airport as Lee Kuan Yew International Airport. Another insisted that Lee might not want monuments built, "but I think that in this instance we have a right to disagree with him." He proposed a statue be erected at the City Hall steps for all to see, and postage stamps and currency notes produced with Lee's image. He concluded: "This will be a fitting tribute not only to him but also to old-timers who responded positively to his call, when he was prime minister."

Indeed, a statue would seem to be the most appropriate expression of Singapore's gratitude and tribute as it would be most visible to all, Singaporeans and visitors alike, and City Hall would be the ideal location since it was the venue of Singapore's historic events such as the Japanese surrender, the assumption of power by the PAP in 1959, the Declaration of Independence in August 1965 and the changing of the guard in November 1990.

But another letter-writer thought that the statue should be erected at Empress Place to replace the one of Stamford Raffles which had stood there for umpteen years, glowering down at passers-by. His reason: "I have always wondered why Raffles' statue is still there at all. He was not the only one who helped Singapore's economy grow in the early days. There were other pioneers from Malaya, Indonesia, China, India and elsewhere who did as much if not more."

The proposal drew an angry rejoinder the next day from an outraged Singaporean. He argued that Raffles contributed greatly to Singapore's economic development and removing his statue was erasing an important chapter of Singapore history.

Both points are valid but on deep reflection, Lee did have an edge over Raffles. The latter stayed in Singapore for only nine months. What could he possibly have achieved during that short time? Why single him out as a national icon? On the other hand, Lee led the country for 31 years and accomplished much more than what Raffles did. Lee was the founding father of modern Singapore and therefore deserved the eulogy more.

So, what do Singaporeans think of Lee Kuan Yew? To find out, I asked several friends and relatives for their views. Here is a sampling of their accolades:

> Lee Kuan Yew was a giant among men who deserved the highest pedestal of history. He was a formidable leader. He was not intimidated by anybody. Leaders of superpowers held him in high esteem and valued his advice on international politics.
>
> He was completely incorruptible. Woe betide anyone who pulled the wool over his eyes. He was an astute politician, a world-renowned statesman, a super intellect with a degree of intellectual arrogance.

He would suffer no fools. Although a tough man, he did not forget loyal and faithful friends and rewarded those who rendered excellent service.

For Singapore, he did what had to be done, beholden to no one. He gained world respect for the tiny nation, a vital asset we treasure.

Mr Lee was a strong, courageous and forceful leader. He had strong convictions, was passionate and determined in achieving his dreams and goals. He had very good foresight and planned long-term: 5, 10 years. He wanted and strove to be the best in his chosen fields of endeavour. At the peak of his golf game, he had one of the lowest handicaps among prime ministers in the region. Above all, he was a family man with strong traditional Asian values.

Lee Kuan Yew planned well. He was respected by world leaders which was important for Singapore to thrive as a business hub. He made foreign investors confident to do business in Singapore. He established a sound infrastructure, built public housing or else we would be living in slumps. He helped Singaporeans save through the Central Provident Fund and cared for the welfare of the needy. He gave the Malays free education that improved their well-being.

Mr Lee was able to make Singapore into a financial and industrial powerhouse despite the lack of natural resources. He strengthened the island's defences by introducing conscription and purchasing modern

> weaponry. He managed to unite the various races into one nation through the various policies.
>
> If not for Lee Kuan Yew, Singapore might still be a colony. It would not have made a name for itself on the international scene. Even the petrol pump attendant in Hungary where I worked for two years was aware of the performance of the Singapore government, especially the corruption-free governing style.
>
> He was intelligent, sharp, bright and articulate, and set clear goals. He was a good judge of character, able to recognise a leader in others. He was generous and had a strong sense of service to the country.
>
> One of the greatest things he had ever done was to step aside gracefully unlike other foreign leaders who stay on and struggle to keep holding on to power.
>
> We are fortunate to have such a strong and brilliant leader. He was the best prime minister in the world, one of the greatest strategic thinkers with a satellite view of things.
>
> If he was tough, he was also human with a soft heart, as we have seen in the number of occasions when he shed tears in public over events that had saddened him.

Old political foes spoke their minds, too. David Marshall, Singapore's first Chief Minister, had this to say: "I am so grateful for a government of quite outstanding ability. I do not believe that I could have done as well." Marshall wondered why Singaporeans were afraid to criticise the government if they disagreed with policies such as the chewing gum ban. Marshall died of lung cancer in 1995.

Dr Lee Siew Choh, a former PAP man who defected and formed the Barisan Sosialis in the early 1960s, admitted: "Without doubt, he has achieved a lot for Singapore. But he is still autocratic, arrogant. He still wants to fight people head-on." The veteran opposition politician died of cancer in 2002.

Fong Swee Suan, a former top-notch communist trade unionist and Barisan Sosialis supporter, said that he realised how much Lee and his PAP team had transformed the country. Fong, who was also a member of the PAP Central Executive Committee in the 1950s, described Lee as a man of vision and a model leader in Asia and the rest of the world.

Fang Chuang Pi (the Plen), a long-time communist leader, singled out Lee, Dr Goh Keng Swee and S Rajaratnam as those who had made major contributions to Singapore's stability and progress. The Plen died of cancer on 6 February 2004 in Thailand at 79.

Opposition MP Chiam See Tong of Potong Pasir regarded Lee as the best teacher available. Chiam gave him top marks for Singapore's economic success, although he had been upset when Lee had compared publicly his academic qualifications with those of the PAP's Mah Bow Tan during a political rally for the 1984 general election.

On the occasion of Lee's 75th birthday in September 1998, S R Nathan, then Ambassador-at-Large, believed that one of Lee's greatest contributions was his multi-racialism policy. Nathan, who became the President of Singapore in 1999, said that Lee's commitment to multi-racialism was not just lip service: "Both in word and deed, he has upheld that promise". Examples were his keen interest in the school performance of the children of the various ethnic groups, and the setting up of self-help organisations such as SINDA where the better-off Indians could help improve the performance of weaker Indian students.

Nathan worked closely with Lee through many battles from the early 1960s. He recalled that to Lee, each problem affecting Singapore was deserving of his personal attention. Nothing was too small to be worthy of his concern. His "steadfast commitment" to multi-racialism had stood the test of time and enabled Singaporeans to stand on the same ground, while "keeping alive their respective heritage and religion".

As Nathan related it, Lee was steadfast even when faced with a diplomatic dilemma. This happened during his first visit to China in 1976. Then Chinese Prime Minister Hua Guo Feng presented him with a paperback, declaring that it was a "correct version" of the China-India war. The obvious political significance was that China wanted to make Singapore an adherent state, Nathan said. After a cursory look at the book and despite protocol, Lee returned the book, deciding that it was China's version of the war and that India had another.

He told Hua: "Singapore is in Southeast Asia. We have people of Chinese, Malay and Indian origins. Singapore has no direct interest in such wars."

This stance, said Nathan, tallied with Lee's pledge made during a news conference held after separation from Malaysia: "I make this promise. This is not a Chinese country, nor a Malay country, nor an Indian country."

While accolades on Lee were aplenty, there were some unfavourable comments about him:

> Lee Kuan Yew lacked emotional intelligence when he ruled and he ruled with an iron fist. People were afraid of him. He wasn't a people's person. His education policies were too stringent, like streaming students into "normal" and "express" classes. Kids at a young age, the impressionable years, relegated to the normal sessions were labelled stupid and stigmatised. The family planning policy of "Stop at Two" was against some religions.
>
> Mr Lee ruled with ultimate authority. He introduced too much competition in schools such as streaming.
>
> He introduced controversial policies such as encouraging graduate mothers to give birth to more than two children. He also proposed giving those with children more than one vote. He instituted the "Stop at Two" family planning policy which led to the rapid ageing of society.
>
> Lee Kuan Yew was shrewd but inflexible. He had a stern face and did not smile enough. He did not forget easily. He seemed to have a problem of letting go. He did not play and relax enough.
>
> The former Prime Minister created a paternalistic environment that earned Singapore the unflattering title of a nanny state. The government watches everything people do and takes care of everything.

> Most people feared to speak and just obeyed. We have become docile and over-dependent on the government.
>
> Lee Kuan Yew was always telling us what to do and often scolded us. Almost every speech he and his ministers made sounded like an order.

The image of Singapore as a nanny state and that it is over-regulated is real. Many Singaporeans were unhappy with Lee's father-knows-best attitude. They were conditioned to believe that without the PAP, they could do nothing, foreign capital and technologies would bypass Singapore and that Singapore would be ruined. They were even made to believe that if Stamford Raffles' statue at Empress Place were removed, Singapore would lose its attraction as a business base.

It is possible that Singaporeans are not entirely blameless for the existence of the nanny state. They do not speak up and criticise. They assume a defeatist attitude, always saying resignedly: "What can we do?" But then, there is the fear of reprisals. It is a vicious cycle. Yeo Lay Hwee, Senior Research Fellow at the Singapore Institute of International Affairs, wrote a thought-provoking commentary on the subject in *Today*, 1 January 2004, titled "Singapore Formula Starts to Fray". Yeo asked:

> Are there genuine grounds for fear or is it just an excuse for our sheer laziness and/or lack of passion and idealism? The reality is that many of us lack the passion and the imagination to pursue anything beyond material rewards and self-aggrandisement.

> Are we a nation of pragmatists and materialists simply because of government's policies or are there some cultural underpinnings to our "national" character?
>
> Fear, in itself, is not a bad thing. Sometimes, fear is necessary to galvanise people into action. Poverty, deprivation and insecurity—in actual or ever-present potential form—dynamise civil society. So how do we "fire up" a generation that has never experienced poverty, deprivation and insecurity and perhaps also unable to imagine them? How can we capitalise on the "fear factor" and tum it into a driving force, rather than allow it to become a "psychological drag" that immobilises us?

She suggested: "Let's not be too quick to condemn and chide the younger generation and blame the government. Let's do our part to encourage, support and egg each other on to do our best even if it is only to change a small portion of events or a small part of our lives."

Lee was aware of the rumblings on the ground over his stringent style of governance and his unpopular policies. As always, he frequently defended his tough stand by saying that he was not in government to be popular but to make Singapore a success. He preferred the robust approach when tackling tough problems. Long ago, at a PAP rally in August 1988, he had pointed out that his style had taken the first-generation leaders through crises from which they had emerged tough, battle-hardened and not intimidated. He argued:

> You can have a velvet glove, you can even soft-pad the velvet glove. But if you have a spongy hand, you can put it in a steel glove, that is no use. There won't be the capacity to use that steel.

That was the nature of Singapore's first Prime Minister. The question often asked is whether he could have governed Singapore less severely as Singaporeans wished he had and still made the nation a success. One will never know. What is known is that successor Goh Chok Tong had opened the door for a more consultative, softer style of administration.

As Lee himself admitted on the eve of his resignation: "I think Singapore has seen and heard enough of me for 31 years. A break will be good for Singapore."

On another occasion after leaving office, he said:

> My greatest contribution now is to do as little as possible. It is up to the younger team to decide how they are going to mobilise the people behind them.

But in a BBC interview in May 1990, he had also said:

> From time to time, if it is necessary and if I disagree with what is happening, even if I'm no longer associated with the government, if I were to express my view on a serious matter which troubles the public and where the government is not completely in agreement as to what course to pursue, I'm bound to have an influence.

However, he added: "If I misuse that influence, after two, three or four times, my impact would be minimal."

Dr Toh Chin Chye, former Deputy Prime Minister and Chairman of the PAP, welcomed the new era of government in Singapore. He expressed the belief that the government should now be able to take dissent in its stride, instead of coming down heavily on those who chose to differ. He described the new political environment succinctly in an interview with *Petir*, the PAP's official organ, published in August 1990:

> Thesis and anti-thesis lead to synthesis. It is not a Marxist aphorism, but that is really how management decisions are arrived at to reach a consensus. In the absence of an opposition of influence, the government is its own enemy. It was so in the early 1980s. The sense of power can be overwhelming because not even a worm was in sight.

Dr Toh recalled how the PAP set up the Central Complaints Bureau after the split with the Barisan Sosialis in 1961. The more consensual style of government, adopted after the 1984 general election when the party's stranglehold was loosened with the victory of two opposition parties, was a similar response to the new situation.

So was the Feedback Unit formed in 1985. Judging by the results of the 1988 general election when the PAP collected 63.1 percent of the popular vote, the Feedback Unit must have been an effective vehicle. Dr Toh said consensual politics deserved commendation because it meant the government was prepared to modify or even scrap a policy without feeling that it had lost the people's confidence.

Lee expressed his full confidence in Singapore's future at the Tanjong Pagar GRC Chinese New Year celebration dinner on 30 January 2004:

> Friends tell me many young Singaporeans believe Singapore's best years are behind us. Because we made it from Third World to First World in one generation, they believe that there will be no further dramatic transformations in their lifetime, that the best pickings of cheap stand-alone houses that their elders got are no longer available.
>
> They are pessimists and wrong. Singapore is like an aircraft flying at 30,000 ft. We have another 6,000 ft to rise to 36,000 ft, the height that top US and EU airlines are flying at. Furthermore, we have not reached First World standards in the finer things in life—music, culture and the arts, the graces of a civilised society. The generation now in their 30s and 50s can take Singapore there in the next 15 to 20 years. The best is yet to be.

There is no gainsaying that Lee left behind a solid foundation in the form of a clean and efficient government, world-class infrastructure and a business-friendly economy, which he termed "gold standards". The results of his efforts speak for themselves. Singaporeans enjoy a high standard of living. They are better educated, more productive, confident and world-wise. They live in good homes and 80 percent of them are homeowners. Their assets have risen in value over the years. Their per capita GDP income of US$71,300 is about 60 times higher than the figure before 1959. The Singapore dollar is strong and the foreign reserves are healthy, at over US$350 billion.

The education, health, recreation, transport and other facilities are world-class. Everything works efficiently. Singapore is a global centre for manufacturing, trade, finance, banking and other high value-added economic activities. Singaporeans work and sleep in peace and security as industrial strikes, student unrests and other civil commotions are history. They are a cohesive and loyal community, living in a First World nation, even if some still indulge in anti-social habits. Under the present government, the political atmosphere is freer. The list of benefits goes on.

Today, Singapore remains on course. What else does the new Singaporean really want? Opinions differ, as reflected in the letters to the newspapers. One male letter-writer maintained that "if one stops striving to achieve more, to be better than one is now, to set a higher target once the target is reached, one has stopped progressing". In the opposite camp, a female letter-writer argued that there was "more to life than chasing money". She and her family were happy living in a HDB flat and with the public transport system and that "there are flowers to pick, open fields to run in, birds to chase". A third letter-writer, a male, struck the middle ground. He thought there was "nothing wrong with aspiring to better oneself and aspiring to higher goals", although "that target does not necessarily have to be money". He suggested that "one can yearn to achieve more by spending greater quality time with the family, volunteering one's time and money to charity causes, learning to play a musical instrument, upgrading oneself through study courses, taking a higher degree".

This middle position echoed what Lee Kuan Yew had suggested years ago: "Life should be more than just existence, the business of making a living. This is the new way of life."

Lee was not perfect, although he performed his duties to perfection. There were successes as well as failures. However, his achievements far outweighed his failures. There are Singaporeans who are happy and unhappy with the house that Lee built, who will continue to debate the wisdom and foolishness of his style of government, credit and discredit him, love him and hate him. The debate will rage on. But as Singaporeans grapple with their thoughts, some questions to be asked are:

What if there had been no Lee Kuan Yew? What if a 19th century Hakka from China named Lee Bok Boon had not migrated to Singapore? What if the marriage of Lee Kuan Yew's parents had not been match-made? What if he had died at the hands of the Japanese military, or when his car overturned at Thomson Road? What if he had lost the battle with the communists? What if, instead of him, there had been a communist of his calibre? What if he himself had been a communist?

19
THE REIGN OF GOH CHOK TONG

Lee Kuan Yew left a large imprint in Singapore politics. When Goh Chok Tong succeeded him on 28 November 1990, he said he would not be able to fit into his shoes. Nevertheless, he was equal to the task of Prime Minister. He kept Singapore strong and successful through wise leadership and a host of bold, innovative socio-economic reforms. He built on the "gold standards" Lee had set. Goh was a product of the planned and orderly self-renewal process which his predecessor had initiated and entrenched in the political system as early as in the 1960s. Goh preserved it.

Goh had not been Lee's first choice as his successor. He was the choice of the second-generation ministers and Lee had agreed. The process of political succession began after the 1984 general election when Lee decided it was time to groom a younger team to take over the helm. Goh's Cabinet colleagues chose him as First Deputy Prime Minister who would be the striker with Lee as goalkeeper. So Goh had had good training and experience by the time he stepped into office.

Lee and Goh were entirely different in character and style of governance. While Lee's rule was harsh and he was stern and aloof, Goh's method was consultative and he was amiable and approachable, earning himself the title of "the people's prime minister". He was the type of man you would impulsively go up to and shake his hand when you saw him in the street. Singaporeans welcomed his gentle touch and his smiling face. With his tall and lean frame, he cut an imposing figure, too, during his reign of 14 years.

Veteran Singapore diplomat Professor Tommy Koh gave a good description of Goh Chok Tong in his tribute published in *The Straits Times* on 11 August 2004. He said: "He is intelligent and knowledgeable without being arrogant or dogmatic. He is shrewd, but not cynical. He is sincere, but not naïve. He is an original thinker and a fountain of ideas. He is warm and personal and has a gift for winning friends."

Lee and Goh also had different goals because the generations they served were different. Lee catered for a pre-independence generation who wanted to fill their stomachs, and his days were turbulent. Goh worked for a post-independence generation who wanted to fill their pockets, while not neglecting the older generation, and his days were relatively peaceful. The young generation, who formed the majority of the population, was more sophisticated and world-wise, and therefore more demanding and critical. Goh obliged by introducing plans to build a new Singapore order and allowing greater freedom of expression. Prime Minister Goh's platform for a new Singapore order was called "The Next Lap", launched in 1991. This covered the broad directions for long-term national development. In subsequent years, he introduced other programmes such as "Singapore 21" in 1999 which set the direction for Singapore in the 21st century, and "Remaking Singapore" in 2002 to make the nation lean and agile by determining what sacred cows to keep and what to slaughter.

He shared the fruits of Singapore's prosperity with the people with schemes such as Edusave for children aged 6 to 16, Medifund to boost the people's Medisave savings, top-ups of their Central Provident Fund savings to enable them to buy discounted SingTel shares, New Singapore Shares, Economic Restructuring Shares and upgrading of the Housing & Development flats, where 80 percent of the people lived, to increase the value of their assets.

In the social arena, Goh established community development councils to promote bonding among the different races, improved the education system and facilities, liberalised the arts scene (like allowing bar-top dancing), showed understanding and tolerance towards the gay community, and allowed the possibility of a casino which Lee Kuan Yew had frowned upon when he was in charge.

For the business sector, Goh called for more innovation in manufacturing and services to move Singapore to the knowledge-based economy. He termed the new way of doing business "technopreneurship". He urged businessmen to plug into the regional and international stage which he dubbed the "second wing" of the Singapore economy. He urged them to take risks. He removed the long-ingrained stigma of failure. He encouraged those who had failed to rise up and begin again, declaring that failure was not shameful and that everyone deserved a second chance. During the recent recession, he offered a package of cost-cutting measures like rental rebates on state industrial facilities to lessen their plight.

Then there was the greater freedom of expression allowed. The most tangible evidence of this was the provision of a Speakers' Corner where Singaporeans could voice their views on any subject under the sun, except race and religion. It was the ideal political platform for the young who constantly cried out to be heard. But so far, their response had been poor. Even members of the so-called civic and civil society kept away. In fact, the few speakers who had taken advantage of the Corner had been the older folk. It could be because the climate of fear of offending the establishment still prevailed, a hangover of the Lee Kuan Yew era. Or perhaps it was just that most had no axe to grind after all.

Nonetheless, it was certainly a sign of the times when a former top civil servant recently openly pointed out the misses in public policy-making. Ngiam Tong Dow, an economist who had served as permanent secretary in the finance and several other ministries for 40 years, told a luncheon meeting of the Economics Society of Singapore on 15 January 2004 that many policies had gone wrong, such as those relating to public finance, the Singapore dollar peg, transport and land. There was no backlash from the government.

Despite his mild and warm nature, Goh was not soft. He never flinched from taking tough decisions, even before becoming Prime Minister. To name some, these were wage restraint and reforms in 1985, arrests of Marxist conspirators in 1987, restricting the circulation of foreign publications in 1986–87 for biased reporting, new population policy in 1987, the immigration policy in 1989, preventing racial enclaves in Housing and Development Board estates, and the Maintenance of Religious Harmony Bill in 1990.

Understandably, the wage and immigration policies were unpopular among wage earners as these meant less take-home pay and greater competition for jobs. True, wages had to be cut during the economic recession of the past few years to make companies stay competitive, and that foreign talent was needed to enlarge the pool of manpower vital for bolstering economic growth. But disgruntled wage earners complained about the rising cost of living and about foreigners taking away jobs they could do themselves. To aggravate their plight, there was a spate of retrenchments in 2003, even among government-linked companies. Those with empty stomachs and families to feed found all these hard to swallow.

Bonding seemed to be such an essential item on the national agenda that Goh took the subject to a new level by producing the concept of shared values, similar to Indonesia's *pancasila* (five principles), when he was First Deputy Prime Minister. After becoming Prime Minister, Goh and his team published a White Paper that was passed in Parliament in January 1991. The Paper spelt out the values as: nation before community and society above self; family as the basic unit of society; community support and respect for the individual; consensus not conflict; and racial and religious harmony.

Goh revived the controversial topic of emigration in his National Day Rally in August 2002 and caused a public furore. He raised the mercury in the barometer when he portrayed those who left as "quitters" and those who remained as "stayers". The word "quitters" stung. The general public opinion was that the word was offensive; it was wrong to denounce those who left for greener pastures abroad as "quitters." There were dozens of reasons for emigrating, such as unhappiness with the paternalistic attitude, the fears of repercussions if they criticised the establishment, the bilingual policy, the inability to get the right jobs or to get places in the local universities for their children, and the limited physical space. Was not the government encouraging its citizens to be internationally minded, to be citizens of the world, in tune with regionalisation and globalisation?

Goh should not have been unduly worried about the mobility of people. It was the reality of today's life. There were benefits to be accrued from the movements of people, just as there were benefits from the mobility of capital. As a global village and an open society, Singapore, with its economic opportunities, was a beacon which was attracting growing numbers of foreign professionals. These foreign talents were somewhat compensating for the loss of indigenous talent.

One of the best rejoinders came from Associate Law Professor Eleanor Wong, a former high-profile deputy public prosecutor who had spent four years in New York. Wong, who is also a playwright, said in an interview with *The Straits Times,* 13 September:

> Trust yourself [PM Goh], trust the people, give people credit, and focus on the things that really matter to ensure that this is a place with sufficient character and attraction. Not everyone will find it their cup of tea but enough people will. In this way, the critical mass will always be passionate about the country and more than willing to cycle back in.

Goh could be angry, too. A Singapore journalist once related the time she saw him, during one of his walkabouts, "turn near purple in the face" when a mother carrying her sick toddler complained that she had been turned away from a hospital because "she could not afford the fees." It turned out that the woman had misunderstood the doctors. On another occasion, the journalist heard a middle-aged woman ask him for a favour or she would not vote for him. Goh wagged a finger at her and warned: "Don't ever threaten me with the vote."

And woe betide those who tried to smear his character. Like Lee Kuan Yew, he jealously guarded his integrity and would take those who slandered and libelled him to court to clear his name.

Domestic issues aside, Prime Minister Goh put Singapore more prominently on the world map by strengthening its international relations. He mooted new ideas for better ties between Singapore and Asean and other countries, among the members of Asean, between Asean and other Asian nations, and between Asean and Europe and the United States.

Indonesia was a good example. Goh initiated the move to develop Batam and Bintan into industrial and tourist hubs. During the 1997 Asian financial crisis, he offered then President Suharto a loan of US$5 billion to be used after the loans from the IMF and the World Bank had been consumed. He originated the Growth Triangle concept for the joint economic development of Singapore, Indonesia and Malaysia's southern-most state of Johor. With Malaysia, which Singapore had long-standing problems still unresolved during his tenure, Goh did his best to keep relations as warm as he could.

Farther up north, he worked closely with his Thai counterpart to launch the Singapore-Thailand Enhanced Partnership, the Singapore-Thailand Enhanced Economic Relationship, the Asean Free Trade Area (AFTA), the Asean Regional Forum and the Asia Europe Meeting (ASEM). For the four new Asean members of Cambodia, Laos, Myanmar and Vietnam, he introduced the Initiative for Asean Integration to help these countries integrate into the grouping quickly. In addition, he spearheaded the establishment of the Singapore-Vietnam Industrial Park.

Outside Asean, Prime Minister Goh forged stronger economic links between Singapore and China, Japan, Korea, India, Pakistan and Sri Lanka through free trade agreements (FTAs) and other business-boosting programmes, like the Suzhou Industrial Park in China and the Bangalore IT Park in India. Negotiations on FTAs with these countries are on the cards.

Singapore already has FTAs with many countries, including New Zealand, Australia, Canada, Jordan and the United States. Singapore became the first Asian country to have such an agreement with the US which Prime Minister Goh and President George W Bush signed in Washington in May 2003. The new trade accord with the world's strongest economic power was a coup for Singapore.

Goh also promoted closer ties between Asean and China, Japan and South Korea, naming the grouping Asean+3. Since 1997, Asean+3 has had an annual summit to discuss and resolve issues of common interests. Following this, he moved for an Asean-India summit which similarly has become an annual event. Goh's dream was to integrate Southeast Asia, Northeast Asia and South Asia to form an Asian economic power to challenge the European Union. If realised, it would be the world's largest regional economy.

With Europe, links were cemented through, for example, the Asia Europe Meeting (ASEM) which Goh initiated in 1996. ASEM brings together the European Union, Asean, China, Japan and Korea. The grouping meets once every two years, alternating between Asia and Europe. On top of this is the Asia-Europe Foundation which since 1997 has organised over 200 projects involving more than 5,000 people from Asia and Europe.

Beyond Asia, Europe and the United States, Goh sought to deepen Singapore-Middle East relations. He made personal visits to many Middle East countries to explore new business opportunities for mutual benefit. Besides the FTA with Jordan, he proposed similar agreements with Bahrain, Qatar, Egypt, Iran, Kuwait and South Africa. He also wanted the whole of Asia to have closer ties with the Middle East and initiated a channel of communication called Asia-Middle East Dialogue to start the ball rolling.

Goh also extended his hand of friendship to Africa and South America. In Botswana, Singapore helped to build a very successful productivity centre. For South America, which he wanted to connect with East Asia including Australia and New Zealand, his initiative was the Forum for East Asia-Latin America Cooperation which he launched during a visit to Chile in 1998. Although it will take some time to close the knowledge gap and identity areas of mutual interests, the Forum was a good beginning.

Other than promoting business, Goh contributed much to the United Nations Security Council. During his tenure, Singapore became a member of the Council for the first time, holding the post from 2000 to 2002. Goh was actively engaged and helped Singapore to resolve several difficult issues the Council had to deal with. Under his leadership, Singapore expanded its role in peacekeeping and humanitarian relief programmes. He co-launched a Global Initiative on Sustainable Development with Germany, Brazil and South Africa.

On the whole, Singaporeans were happy with the 14-year reign of Goh Chok Tong. This was best demonstrated through the ballot box, although the electorate appeared cautious at first. When Goh stood for his first general election as Prime Minister in 1991, the PAP got only 61 percent of the vote, against 63.1 percent in the 1988 polls, much to his chagrin. He took the drop to mean rejection of his style and his policies. But the people soon accepted him, as shown by the results of the 1997 and 2001 general elections when the percentage grew to 65 percent and to a massive 75.3 percent respectively.

On 12 August 2004, he closed his chapter when he passed the baton to his successor, Lee Hsien Loong. Lee had been Deputy Prime Minister and Finance Minister, and chairman of the Monetary Authority of Singapore. His appointment as Prime Minister opened not only a new chapter in Singapore history, but also a historic one as he is Lee Kuan Yew's son. The political transition process began at 10 am on 10 August when Goh submitted his letter of resignation and those of his ministers to President S R Nathan at the Istana. Half-an-hour later, Lee Hsien Loong arrived and the President asked him to form the next government. The process was completed with the swearing-in ceremony on 12 August. All went peacefully and smoothly, as in the first transfer of power from Lee Kuan Yew to Goh in 1990.

For Goh, leading Singapore had been a satisfying experience.

He was happy that he could leave office at the time of his own choosing, and that the economy was recovering strongly from the recession, and expecting to grow between 8 percent and 9 percent in 2004. As he told the media on 18 July 2004: "I am very happy that I'm coming to the end of—I would say—14 glorious years."

In fact, the "glorious years" were lashed with storms along the way. In his final National Day Message delivered on 8 August 2004, he described the first seven years of his stewardship as a period which "produced bountiful harvests. We distributed the fruits and helped lower-income Singaporeans".

The next seven years "became lean years" caused by the Asian financial crisis, September 11, terrorism, SARS (severe acute respiratory syndrome) and economic recession. SARS, which caused many deaths and crippled businesses, was "a frightening time".

Goh commented:

> A good number of our loved ones died. This was my saddest moment in government. But we did not throw up our hands in despair. We rallied and fought back. We worked and grew our economy again. We went through fire together; the steel in us strengthened. This is what I am most proud of, my fellow Singaporeans, this fighting spirit, the character of our people, our strong bond and social cohesion.

Of his successor, he said:

> I am confident about Hsien Loong and his team. They are ready to take our nation to a new level. But they cannot do this on their own. They will need your

full support and active participation to fly Singapore to greater heights.

At the National Stadium the next day, 9 August, Singaporeans enjoying the extravaganza in celebration of National Day gave Goh a rousing standing ovation, in tribute to his accomplishments.

In the new Prime Minister's Cabinet, Goh Chok Tong was named Senior Minister, while Lee Kuan Yew became Minister Mentor whose job would be to provide advice. Goh was also appointed chairman of the Monetary Authority of Singapore.

As Goh put it on 11 August, after chairing his final Cabinet meeting: "I'm still in the same boat. So now there's a new captain, but I'm still a member of the crew. I've still got to mend the rigs, I've got to help steer the boat if necessary. So I don't miss anything."

He revealed at a National Day dinner in his Marine Parade constituency on 27 August 2004 that the work "to help steer the boat" includes continuing strengthening ties with countries important to Singapore such as the United States, China, India, Japan, Australia, Britain, France and Germany, as well as the Middle East.

Goh Chok Tong had never intended to be a politician. His dream had been to become a professor. The eldest of five children born on 20 May 1941, he attended Pasir Panjang Primary School and Raffles Institution, before going to the then University of Singapore. He graduated in 1964 with a Bachelor of Arts in Economics (First Class Honours) and enrolled as a research scholar. But because his university education had been financed through a government bursary, he had to serve his bond. He became an administrative officer in the Economics Planning Unit of the Ministry of Finance.

His boss, Deputy Secretary J Y Pillay, recognised his potential and sent him to Williams College in the United States in 1966 for his Master of Arts in Development Economics. An interesting episode unfolded here. On his return, then Prime Minister Lee Kuan Yew wanted him as his private secretary. Pillay objected, saying he had not sent Goh to Williams College to be a private secretary. He won the day, earning the admiration of Lee himself for his bravery.

Goh proved his worth as a civil servant. Then his career path changed twice. First, in 1969, he was seconded to the national shipping company, Neptune Orient Lines. He rose to be the Managing Director in 1973. Second, in 1976, the late Finance Minister Hon Sui Sen invited him to enter politics. Goh accepted because he felt it was his duty and privilege to serve the country, to pay back what he owed society. His family had been poor and he had been able to get a university education because of a government bursary. He also appreciated the meritocracy system.

He stood in the 1976 general election held on 23 December in the newly created constituency of Marine Parade and was an immediate success. He trounced his opponent, Mansor Rahman of the United Front, by 14,418 votes to 3,922 votes. Goh became a Member of Parliament for a year. Thereafter, his promotion up the political ladder was rapid: Senior Minister of State (Finance), Minister for Trade and Industry, Minister for Health, Second Minister for Defence, Minister for Defence, Second Minister for Health, First Deputy Prime Minister and Minister for Defence, and Prime Minister—all within the space of 13 years.

Despite his heavy burden of office, Goh did his best to spend time with his family. He and his wife, Tan Choo Leng, a former classmate at Raffles Institution and now a lawyer, have twins, a boy Jin Hian and a girl Jin Theng, born in 1968, and five grandchildren, all girls, three from Jin Hian and the other two from his sister. Jin Hian is a medical graduate of the National University of Singapore, while his sister is a graduate of a British university who lives in Britain with her own family.

"My parents are very humorous and they love to joke. So we were influenced by them, growing up in this environment," Jin Hian, a medical doctor, said in an interview with *Lianhe Zaobao* in August 2004. He described his father's parenting style as being very much like his political leadership style—open and consultative. "My father will not force you to do what he wants you to do."

He added: "Actually, my dad is not very different from other dads. When there's time, he will play with the children and take us out for walks." He was happy to see his father retire, saying: "He has aged a lot these few years, his hair has turned white. Hopefully, he can now spend more time with his grandchildren."

Indeed, Goh Chok Tong gave much back to Singapore. He had not been Lee Kuan Yew's first choice. However, when he stepped down, Lee was moved to say, in a statement published in the media on 12 August 2004:

> He has added to what my generation built and created more opportunities for our people in so many fields. He has done well for all of us. I am proud and happy that I was a member of his team. We worked well together.

In return, Goh paid Lee this compliment in Parliament on 2 September 2004:

> He was an invaluable member of my team. When he stepped down as PM, he made it his mission to ensure that the second-generation leaders succeeded. He was honest in his critique and generous with his advice. He had a large databank of wisdom and experience and an international network of contacts built up over 31 years...from which we drew and benefitted.
>
> I found SM Lee an immensely useful, wise and trusted counsel. That was why I advised Prime Minister Lee Hsien Loong to retain Mr Lee Kuan Yew in Cabinet as Minister Mentor. MM is a national resource and too valuable an asset for Singapore to lose.
>
> I can tell you that fears that PM Lee will find it difficult to be himself because of his father's presence in Cabinet are unwarranted. I have worked with both MM Lee and Prime Minister Lee for more than 20 years now. I know that PM Lee is his own man and that his father will not cramp his style or stifle his ideas.

How has Lee Hsien Loong performed as Prime Minister?

20

LIFE WITH LEE HSIEN LOONG

Lee Kuan Yew set the stage for Singapore's current peace and prosperity. Successor Goh Chok Tong kept the nation marching forward. How has current Prime Minister Lee Hsien Loong performed? Singaporeans expect him to do well not because he is Lee Kuan Yew's son (although that is a natural expectation) but because their livelihood is in his hands.

Chinese Singaporeans believe that his appointment is very auspicious because his given name in Chinese means "illustrious dragon". As every Chinese knows, the dragon symbolises kingly power. With the adjective "illustrious" added, we have not only a dragon but a distinguished one.

But Lee Hsien Loong should be judged by what he can do, not by what his name portends, since whether the constellations really shape people's character and influence their lives is debatable. As Cassius succinctly pointed out in *Julius Caesar*: "The fault, dear Brutus, is not in our stars but in ourselves that we are underlings." There are several realities of Lee that have emerged.

One, Singapore's third Prime Minister is a man of the people, as Goh Chok Tong was. His constituents in Teck Ghee will vouch for that. He genuinely cares for people. He is open, warm, spontaneous and compassionate. He mixes freely with them, reaching out, seeking to solve their problems, and always with a smile on his face and a twinkle in his eye. He infuses a sense of *joie de vivre*. He has no airs, although he is the son of a famous man. Certainly, in character, he is unlike his father.

His subordinates and others who know him have been quoted in the media as having said that he is firm and fair, a man of vision, a skilful problem-solver and has a helicopter view of events. With his tall, lean frame, he cuts an imposing figure, too. His desire to be with the people was abundantly manifested at the swearing-in ceremony on 12 August 2004.

The milestone event took place on the Istana grounds, instead of at City Hall, the historic venue of the oath-takings of Lee Kuan Yew in 1959 and Goh Chok Tong in 1990. Lee Hsien Loong had wanted Singaporeans from all walks of life, including the disabled, to join him to celebrate his climb to the peak in his political career. In all, the guests numbered some 1,400. City Hall, with a capacity for only about 200 people, could not have accommodated the massive attendance.

In his inauguration speech, Lee Hsien Loong sent out the message that he wanted Singapore to be an inclusive society for all

Singaporeans, taking everybody in, regardless of their stations in life. He said:

> I will strive to be Prime Minister for all Singaporeans. Work with me to make Singapore a home we love, a community we belong to, and a country we are proud to call our own. Our people should feel free to express diverse views, pursue unconventional ideas, or simply be different. We must also have a place in our hearts and our lives for the disabled, who are our brothers and sisters too. Join me to write this next chapter of the Singapore story.

After the ceremony, he mingled with the guests. Then, accompanied by wife Ho Ching, he made a bee-line for his constituency of Teck Ghee to celebrate this momentous moment with his people. A glittering reception awaited him. They were proud that their MP had become the Prime Minister of Singapore, just as the electorate of Marine Parade had been with Goh Chok Tong back in 1990. Lee spent some time with his constituents whom he had represented for 20 years, talking and joking with them, thanking them for their support through the years, asking them for their continued support to propel Singapore forward, and repeating his invitation to all to come to tea and help build the nation together.

Two, Lee Hsien Loong is a man with his own mind and is bold, like the dragon. He is prepared to undertake radical socio-economic reforms where necessary and to slaughter sacred cows in the bureaucracy that have become an albatross, to make Singapore lean and agile. This was patently evident by the host of ground-breaking proposals he announced in his maiden speech as Prime Minister at the National Day Rally on 22 August. The initiatives cover the family, the Civil Service, medical benefits, education, older Singaporeans and free speech. Many of the changes had been "taboo" to both Lee Kuan Yew and Goh Chok Tong.

For the family, in order to encourage them to have more children, mothers get 12 weeks of maternity leave instead of eight, an infant care subsidy, a baby bonus not only for the second and third child, but also for the first and fourth child, two days per year child-care leave, and lower maid levy. Those where grandparents help with child-care get tax reliefs. These incentives are expected to reverse the falling birth rate which stands at about 1.26, about half the replacement rate of 2.1 a year needed to renew the population.

In the Civil Service, schools and army camps, it is now a five-day work week, although officers still have to work a 44-hour week and the two days off will not necessarily be Saturdays and Sundays since essential public services must remain available on Saturdays. The move means more time for officers to spend with their families. On top of this are new medical schemes where male and female officers enjoy equal benefits. For moribund older schemes, the benefits are extended to children below 18 of women officers.

In schools, the Chinese language, long the bane of many students forced to take the subject under the bilingual policy, will be taught as a living language and not an academic subject, with the focus on spoken communications and reading. The change applies to the teaching of Tamil and Malay languages too. Following the announcement, the Chinese Language Curriculum and Pedagogy

Review Committee met on 11 October 2004 to disclose its proposals. The meeting was chaired by Minister Mentor Lee Kuan Yew who had begun the bilingual policy some 40 years ago. Among the changes, the teaching of Chinese will be made more flexible by allowing schools to take into account students' home language backgrounds and aptitude.

Among other changes announced by Lee Hsien Loong at the National Day Rally, older Singaporeans will now get more financial assistance. The government will review their medical costs, financial security and living environment matters, and give them something extra especially from Medisave when there are surpluses to distribute.

The purpose of the Speakers' Corner, opened on 1 September 2000, has been broadened. Now, Singaporeans can vent their frustrations there on any issue except race and religion, as well as hold exhibitions and performances, and without a Public Entertainment Licence, too. One of the few drawbacks is that the "opening hours" remain at between 7 am and 7 pm. Activists want the hours extended. No entertainment licence is required for indoor talks, unless they touch on race and religion. The question is whether Singaporeans will take advantage of the greater space given. During Goh Chok Tong's time, the Speakers' Corner was always under-utilised.

Three, Lee Hsien Loong is a man of his word. When he was Deputy Prime Minister and his appointment as Prime Minister more or less confirmed, he pledged to adopt his predecessor's consultative style and to give Singaporeans greater leeway to speak up. Addressing the Harvard Club's 35th anniversary dinner on 6 January 2004, he acknowledged that the government had no monopoly on knowledge and ideas and that Singaporeans wanted more involvement. The government would do its best to continue to build a civic society and would retreat from being all things to all citizens. It would provide the guidelines to engender civic participation, debate issues rigorously and robustly, go beyond words to action in civic participation and get the media to adopt a national perspective on issues. The government would continue to lead the way.

Lee is certainly in tune with the times. As he put it at his National Day Rally speech:

> It's a new generation and it's got to take Singapore another step forward, another level higher. To do that, we need fresh and bold approaches. We've been successful, wildly successful, otherwise we wouldn't be sitting here today. But we can't stand still because the world is changing, our people are changing and so must Singapore and so must the way we govern Singapore.

Four, Lee is a man of principles, standing firmly to preserve Singapore's sovereignty and integrity. He demonstrated this quality during the controversy over his visit to Taiwan in July 2004 when he was Deputy Prime Minister. It was an unofficial and private visit to meet friends and study the situation there. But China was unhappy, saying that "no matter what excuse he uses to visit Taiwan, it will be a serious violation of the Singapore Government's commitment to the One-China policy and will harm the political foundation of Sino-Singapore relations." China went so far as to cancel the scheduled talk in Singapore by Bank of China chief Zhou Niaochuan, and to threaten to shelve negotiations on a free trade agreement (FTA).

Lee reassured China that despite the visit, Singapore upheld its One-China policy. His reply to China's complaint absolutely defined Singapore's position in international affairs:

> Singapore's relations with China are based on equality and mutual respect. Singapore is a good friend of China. But to call off the trip at China's request would have undermined our right to make independent decisions, and damaged our international standing. As a small country, this is a vital consideration in our dealings with all countries.

At that National Day Rally on 22 August, Lee not only reiterated Singapore's commitment to the One-China policy but also confirmed the nation's stand on the contentious China-Taiwan issue. He declared:

> If a war breaks out across the straits, we will be forced to choose between the two sides. As a friend of both, any decision will be painful. But if the conflict is provoked by Taiwan, then Singapore cannot support Taiwan.

China seemed satisfied with that pledge. In a statement on 25 August, Foreign Ministry spokesman Kong Quan said:

> We have noted that Singapore's new leader reiterated in his speech that Singapore holds firmly to the One-China policy and is resolutely opposed to

> Taiwan independence. This position is in line with Singapore's interests and the common view of the international community, and will benefit peace and stability in the region.

However, he also warned: "We are resolutely opposed to leaders of countries with diplomatic ties with China visiting Taiwan in any capacity and sending any wrong signals to Taiwan independence forces."

Five, Lee Hsien Loong had 20 years of political experience before becoming prime minister. He acquitted himself well in the portfolios of Deputy Prime Minister and Finance Minister, chairman of the Monetary Authority of Singapore and other appointments, and as the MP for Teck Ghee. His accomplishments in all these positions are well-known here and across the oceans.

Six, Lee is passionate about Singapore. This was discernible at an early age. Perhaps the best evidence of his passion emerged at Trinity College, Cambridge, where in 1972 he graduated with first class honours in mathematics in two years instead of three. The university was so impressed with his scholastic achievement that it offered him an academic career in mathematics.

Lee, then 20, refused. He told his tutor, Dr Denis Marrian, that a mathematician had little say in matters of the world. It did not matter to large developed countries but it mattered a great deal to him in Singapore. He wanted to participate in Singapore affairs, if not in politics, then either in the Civil Service or the Armed Forces. On his return, he joined the latter, rising through the ranks to become a brigadier-general. That was why when Goh Chok Tong invited him to enter politics in 1984 Lee Hsien Loong accepted it, although it was a big change from the army. Relating the crossroads in his career at his inauguration speech, he gave two reasons. One was this: "I had gone to university on government scholarships (he was a President's Scholar), and benefitted from the Singapore system." The other reason was:

> As a boy, I had watched Singapore become independent. Then, as a young man I saw it grow against tremendous odds, and strengthen year by year. Those were my formative years, and it left a deep impression on me. I wanted to contribute to the Singapore story. Entering politics was a way to do this, and to repay the obligations which I felt. And since then, I have served in the government with Mr Goh for 20 years.

Lee Kuan Yew, who of course knew his son best, talked more about his son's passion during a television interview in Beijing in June 2004, which was broadcast in Singapore on 20 June and published in the local media two days later: "It so happened that he was of that frame of mind and in his generation, he was committed, more passionate about the future of the country than other people." He added that it was "a stroke of destiny" that his elder son would become prime minister of Singapore.

More changes to the system and more national development programmes can be expected. His predecessor, Senior Minister Goh Chok Tong, hinted at this at the National Day dinner in his Marine Parade constituency on 27 August 2004. He said:

> PM Lee will be bold in making changes to meet the new global and domestic environments. He genuinely welcomes a robust debate. He will accept good arguments which are in the interests of Singapore. But he will not change just to please some Western-influenced liberals who apply their notion of democracy, pluralistic policy and freedom of the press unthinkingly to Singapore. He will take a practical approach of what works for Singapore.

This was most evident over the very controversial casino issue. Lee Hsien Loong made the bold decision to give the green light to the project by announcing in Parliament on 18 April 2005 that casinos would be included in two mega integrated resorts which the government will develop to boost tourism. This is a big gamble to take. Singaporeans and the Cabinet had been sharply divided over the contentious subject. Proponents see the integrated projects with casinos as a great catalyst to higher economic growth. PM Lee is convinced that it is a good bet for the longer-term. Opponents warn of the social ills befalling Singaporeans.

Lee Kuan Yew had been dead set against having a casino in Singapore when he was the prime minister, so his son's decision was a radical departure from the norm. And Lee Kuan Yew was prepared to go with the new tide. He explained in Parliament on 19 April: "I have not changed my basic mind or my basic values. But I have had to change my attitude of casinos in Singapore, when it is part of an integrated resort...The price may be high, but the price of not doing so is even higher."

However, those concerned with the welfare of the people did not accept this argument. The well-known social costs, such as bankruptcies and broken families, should not be negated in the bid for more business. They wished the integrated resorts could proceed without a casino. It is a tendentious topic.

Goh gave further insight into Lee Hsien Loong's character when he said in Parliament on 2 September 2004:

> As my deputy, he was like my badminton doubles partner. He could smash and retrieve, which complemented my strength in drop-shots and net play.
>
> He was not only a most supportive and valuable deputy but also a key minister handling many jobs at any one time. He dealt with difficult issues like pulling Singapore out of recession and restructuring of the economy and financial sector.
>
> Just look at the holes he has left behind now that he has become Prime Minister. He has to retain the Finance portfolio and I have to cover the Monetary Authority of Singapore because the younger ministers are not ready.

Can Lee Hsien Loong deliver the goods? He has a heavy burden to shoulder and his own set of vexing problems to resolve. One of the most difficult is fulfilling the aspirations of the better-educated, better-informed and more demanding post-independence generation, those born in 1965 and after, who form about 55 percent of the population. The older generation also have their own peculiar needs and problems deserving attention.

Not to be overlooked is the crucial need to maintain good relations with Malaysia and other Asian countries, as well as with the rest of the world. His predecessor did much to enhance Singapore's status in the international theatre during his 14-year reign. He will continue to help strengthen the regional and global links in his capacity of Senior Minister.

Lee Kuan Yew gave some good advice on how his son should govern Singapore, during a TV interview in Beijing in June 2004:

> At the end of the day, he has to decide, he has to feel this generation because to be a leader, you must not only be logical, you must not only be right, you must be able to persuade and to mobilise your people, get them to follow you because this is the best way.

On his son's capability, he said:

> I think his intellectual power is considerable. He picked up from me a certain way of thinking, certain logic, certain cut of mind. He has got from his mother a facility with words, and a certain intuition. I hope he will be able to do better than me. My worry is for him because the people's expectations are high and they will always (compare) subconsciously.

Beyond political acumen and intellectual powers, Lee Kuan Yew, who was then Minister Mentor, strongly stressed the need for the third-generation leaders to protect the "gold standards" he and his pioneer team had established from Day 1, that is, a clean and efficient government, world-class infrastructure and a business-friendly economy. These make up the Singapore brand name, he said in his address to the Global Brand Forum in Singapore on 16 August 2004. He told the participants, who comprised world business leaders, that his role is to tell the new team: "Look, these are gold standards, you jeopardise them at risk to yourselves."

When all is said and done, Singaporeans' top priority is feeding their families. The past few years had been hard times for many of them. There were wage cuts, reduced contributions to their savings in the Central Provident Fund, large-scale retrenchments and other cost-cutting measures adopted by companies, even government-linked companies, as well as steep drops in the values of their homes.

Second on the list of priorities is lower cost of living so that Singaporeans can stretch their dollar farther. Among others, they complain about expensive medical services, high bus fares, water and electricity costs.

Third on the list is internal security. In his father's time, during the restive social revolution, the threat to security came from the communists and the communalists. Today's threat is from terrorists with similar intentions. It is no less grave. There have been attempts by Al-Qaeda, Jemaah Islamiyah (JI) and, most recently, Islamic State in Iraq and Syria (ISIS) to blow up some installations in Singapore, including Changi Airport. Several suspects were arrested and detained.

The latest suspects locked up were two teenage boys. One of them, aged 19, was detained under the Internal Security Act (ISA) in April 2015 for trying to join ISIS. If he failed to do so, he planned to attack key facilities in Singapore, assassinate President Tony Tan and Prime Minister Lee, and carry out violent attacks in public places to strike fear among the populace. The other teenager, aged 17, was arrested in May the same year for further investigation into the extent of his radicalisation.

Deputy Prime Minister and Home Affairs Minister Teo Chee Hean warned that terrorism remains a global threat and the arrests showed that young people in Singapore are also vulnerable to being radicalised. He said: "It is not just a problem that is 'over there' in some other countries. It is over a problem that is 'over here': in our region and here in Singapore as well." The need to remain vigilant 24/7 cannot be overstated.

The demands on Lee Hsien Loong will be extremely great. Without denying his ability and political acumen, he is fortunate to have had Senior Minister Goh and Minister Mentor Lee, who between them brought more than half a century of political experience, to give him the benefit of their advice. In his present Cabinet are also "experienced ministers who will provide the ballast, while the newer ones the entrepreneurial spirit", as Goh described it in his Marine Parade speech on 27 August 2004.

Singaporeans are impressed with Lee Hsien Loong's performance so far. One of the best demonstrations of his leadership skills occurred during the Indian Ocean tsunami tragedy of 26 December 2004. Lee took the initiative by convening a summit of world leaders to draw up a plan of action for the victims of the killer waves. The meeting, held in Jakarta on 6 January 2005, drew leaders of 20 countries, including United Nations Secretary-General Kofi Annan, and six international organisations. He organised a large-scale Singapore relief effort for the devastated countries. As he put it: "Even as we mourn the dead, our greater responsibility is to deliver to the survivors the help they desperately need."

Lee Hsien Loong made his political debut in the 1984 general election held on 22 December. One of the PAP's bright sparks fielded under the self-renewal process, he overwhelmed his opponent, an unknown woman candidate named Giam Lai Cheng of the United People's Front, by 12,794 votes to 3,123 votes, a majority of 60.76 percent. The young MP (he was then 32) was popular from the beginning, especially among the young. What struck his electorate most was his friendly, informal disposition. In his first meeting with his grassroots leaders, he was reported to have told them not to be tense. They should relax and engage in small talk before starting discussions on the serious business of looking after the constituency.

Born on 10 February 1952, Lee Hsien Loong is the eldest of three children. He was entirely educated in Chinese, first attending Nanyang Kindergarten and then Nanyang Primary School and Catholic High School. He excelled in his studies, winning many awards, the most prestigious being the President's Scholarship in 1970, and topping Trinity College in his examination year. He took a diploma in computer science in his final year, adding to his scholastic achievement.

Although entirely educated in Chinese, Lee, who is left-handed, is fluent in English which he learnt from his mother and at university. He learnt Malay and Russian, and reads Jawi. His younger sister, Wei Ling, and brother, Hsien Yang, were also Chinese-educated and President's scholars. Wei Ling is the Director of the National Neuroscience Institute, while Hsien Yang is the Chairman of the Civil Aviation Authority of Singapore. They, too, are fluent in English.

If Lee Hsien Loong and his immediate family are brilliant, so is his wife Ho Ching. The Chief Executive and Executive Director of government investment arm Temasek Holdings was ranked by Forbes in 2004 as the most powerful businesswoman in Asia, the sixth most powerful woman in Asia, and the 24th most powerful woman in the world. Fortune magazine ranked her the fifth most powerful woman in business outside the United States.

Lee knows what trials and tribulations mean, for his personal life has been marred by tragedy. His first wife died in 1982 after the birth of their second child. Her death pained him deeply. He recovered from that and went on with his life. He met Ho Ching whom he married in 1985 and who bore him two children. Then in 1992, he was diagnosed with lymphoma. Fortunately, after several months of suffering and chemotherapy, and an agonising time for his parents and other family members, he survived and was given a clean bill of health in 1997.

His greatest concern now is the future of Singapore. Success depends not only on his leadership but also on the people's support. In this respect, the new Prime Minister has been heartened by the response to his call for civic participation. He revealed at the National Day dinner in his Teck Ghee constituency on 28 August 2004 that many had volunteered their services. They were young men and women, some of them still in school. Others recommended good people whom they knew.

He said: "I am overwhelmed with the response of Singaporeans and the hundreds of feedback that I have received through e-mail, letters, the Feedback Unit, our journalists and also MPs. I am confident that together, we can build a future that is better for all citizens, and make Singapore a dream home for all of us."

Indeed, able leadership and ground support are vital. The

alternative is chaos and disaster. So far, Singapore remains on course in the choppy waters of politics. Lee Hsien Loong has demonstrated that he has steel in him and wants to be a good captain. The litmus test is when a big storm breaks.

So far, Lee Hsien Loong has acquitted himself well in his duties as Prime Minister and most Singaporeans have accepted him in that role. This was borne out by his solid victory in his first general election as Prime Minister in 2006 held two years after assuming office. The PAP reaped 82 out of the 84 seats in Parliament and 66.6 percent of the vote cast. It was a ringing endorsement of his premiership. The other two seats, Potong Pasir and Hougang, were retained by long-serving incumbent opposition MPs Chiam See Tong of the Singapore Democratic Alliance (SDA) and Low Thia Khiang of the Workers' Party (WP).

Lee also won the 2011 general election (GE2011), although the PAP's winning margin dropped to 60.14 percent. What was more, he got a rude shock when the WP snatched the five-member PAP-held Aljunied GRC anchored by Foreign Minister George Yeo. That was the first GRC, hitherto considered invincible, that the PAP had lost. The winning team was led by Low. He had left Hougang, his stronghold since 1991, to a party member to contest so that he could gun for the GRC. The party also retained Hougang, giving it six elected MPs in Parliament. Then, the PAP incumbent in Punggol East was sacked because of a sex scandal. The WP captured that in a by-election in January 2013. That brought its tally to seven MPs in Parliament, in addition to two Non-Constituency MPs (NCMPs).

However, for Chiam See Tong, GE2011 was his Waterloo. He left Potong Pasir, which he had held since 1984, to his wife

Lina to contest in order to fight for the five-member PAP-held Bishan-Toa Payoh GRC. Both he and his wife lost, although she got a seat in Parliament as an NCMP. But Chiam, who suffered a mild stroke in early 2008, vowed to continue with the struggle for a democratic Singapore.

Overall, despite the WP's success in grabbing a GRC, GE2011 was a setback for the opposition in their bid for more parties in Parliament. Whereas there were the SDA and WP before 2011, there is now only the WP.

GE2011 also marked a turning point in the political careers of Minister Mentor Lee Kuan Yew and Senior Minister Goh Chok Tong. Soon after the polls, they relinquished their portfolios, Lee becoming an ordinary MP and Goh becoming Emeritus Senior Minster. The reason was "to have a completely younger team of minsters to connect to and engage with the younger generation".

Lee Kuan Yew had served Tanjong Pagar since 1955 and won 14 successive general elections and one by-election. Apart from his MP's duties, he continued to keep a watchful eye on Singapore's well-being, as he had done as prime minister, senior minister, and minister mentor. He once summed up his work for Singapore in what could be the understatement of the century: "All I can say is, I did my best. This was the job I undertook, I did my best and I could not have done more in the circumstances."

But he suffered from ill health, worsened by the death of his wife of 62 years, Kwa Geok Choo, in October 2010. He was devastated. He gradually withdrew from the public eye. Fittingly, his last public appearance was at the PAP's 60th anniversary celebrations on 7 November 2014 at the Victoria Concert Hall, where he inaugurated the party 60 years ago. His comrades gave him a standing ovation.

The beginning of the end came on 5 February 2015 when he was admitted to Singapore General Hospital with severe pneumonia. He died at 3.18 am on Monday, 23 March. He was 91. So totally dedicated was he that he served the nation to his last breath. He left a shining Singapore as his legacy. He deserved the state funeral accorded to him, the 21-gun salute, the seven days of mourning, the state flag flown at half-mast, and the deluge of grief, tributes and gratitude from Singaporeans and world leaders. Thousands queued up for hours to pay their last respects at Parliament House where the body lay in state. It rained heavily on the day of the funeral, Sunday, 29 March. Thousands lined the route to the crematorium, waving the state flags and chanting his name as the gun carriage carrying the body drove past.

Local English daily *Today* carried the headline: "The heavens opened and cried for him".

His family and Singaporeans deeply felt the loss of the man who had made the little red dot such a spectacular economic success and who had dominated the local political scene for more than six decades. It was particularly sad because he died in the year when Singapore is celebrating its 50th anniversary of independence. This is a momentous milestone for the nation. It is a special year. It celebrates half a century of nationhood, progress and prosperity. The symbolic logo "SG50" is everywhere in the country. The Golden Jubilee is being commemorated with much fanfare to make it a year to savour and remember. The highlight of the calendar of events is the annual National Day Parade (NDP) on 9 August 2015 at the Padang where the first NDP took place in 1966.

It is a cruel twist of fate that the founding father who proclaimed the birth of the nation at City Hall 50 years ago would not be here to celebrate with his fellow citizens the historic golden day. He will be greatly missed. However, he will be remembered and honoured during the NDP ceremony through a tribute segment in the programme, a video montage of his life and an empty chair where he would have sat.

Singapore will march on and blaze new frontiers for a richer tomorrow in the next 50 years. The government will use its new initiative called the SkillsFuture Credit Account scheme launched in February 2015 as the driver to take the nation forward into continued prosperity, peace and security. Under the scheme, all Singaporeans aged 25 and above will get an initial grant of S$500 for training courses. The aim is to motivate them to adapt to new technologies and trends, seize new opportunities, create new value and equip themselves for the future. Prime Minister Lee Hsien Loong described the scheme in his annual May Day Rally on 1 May 2015 as "upgrading the whole workforce step by step, year by year."

Lee mentioned "outstanding leadership" and the need for all Singaporeans to be "exceptional" as other essential ingredients for success. Indeed, the next general election, which must be held by January 2017, will focus on leadership renewal. Able leaders are critical not only for ensuring Singapore's continued survival, but also to stave off the challenges of the opposition. There are more than 20 registered political parties here and the newest, People's Power Party, was being registered as this book went to print. Although most are weak and inactive, anyone of them could spring a surprise.

EPILOGUE

John Arbuthnot, an 18th century writer and physician, once said: "All political parties die at last of swallowing their own lies". However, there are political parties which are different from the rest and which have stood the test of time. In Singapore, it is the PAP.

On 21 November 1954, the PAP came with such an impact that it split the country's political era into pre-PAP and post-PAP periods. The party survived the turbulent 1950s and 1960s when it fought the British, the communists and the communalists, and other crises. The longest surviving political party in Singapore, the PAP remains as strong and cohesive as ever. Its membership stands at a mind-boggling 15,000 cadres. Key to its success is the quality of its leadership and the principles of financial and political integrity it religiously upholds. From Lee Kuan Yew to Goh Chok Tong, it has delivered the goods. Lee Hsien Loong is expected to perform as well, if not better. There has been no other like the PAP before, and none since, in Singapore.

Most Singaporeans are happy with the status quo and with making a living. When all is said and done, they still want the PAP to govern, their grouses and protest votes in the past few general elections notwithstanding. Why kill the goose that lays the golden eggs? Perhaps this apathetic attitude may change if Singapore is in danger of collapse if, for example, the goose stops laying golden eggs and abuses its power, or if the PAP is unable to tackle the many problems it faces, including the threat of terrorism. Then the spirit of nationalism will arise from among the populace, producing perhaps another Lee Kuan Yew to lead the country out of danger.

It is therefore safe to say that Singapore, although it is a two-party state, will have to depend on the PAP for a long time to come. But can the PAP regain its 100 percent control of the House it first lost in the 1981 Anson by-election (after holding the monopoly from 1968) when J B Jeyaretnam of the Workers' Party won the seat?

After the 1984 general election when Chiam See Tong first entered Parliament and J B retained his seat at Anson constituency, Chan Heng Chee, then an associate professor of political science at the National University of Singapore, made an interesting prediction on the possible political landscape. Writing in *The Sunday Times* of 30 December, Professor Chan, former Singapore Ambassador to the United States and now Chairman of the Lee Kuan Yew Centre for Innovative Cities, painted four likely scenarios.

First, regaining 100 percent control would be "exceedingly difficult...in view of the growing belief that parliamentary democracy is incomplete without an elected opposition".

Second, a Parliament still dominated by the PAP would develop but with "an institutionalised presence of opposition MPs—anything from one to a dozen of them. This is the most likely outcome in the middle term and even in the long term so long as the PAP still retains its political acumen".

Third, a serious alternative to the PAP might emerge in which case "elections become a true contest between the PAP and the second party for the right to govern. If this prospect comes about at all, it will be a long-term development".

Fourth, which Professor Chan described as the most disturbing for Singapore, "is a drifting in future elections towards support for a fragmented opposition, many more marginal seats and the PAP winning by smaller margins of votes and seats, immobilised in the interest of political survival". In this scenario, she included "as a corollary the possibility at some stage of a coalition government of other parties with the PAP in opposition".

It is food for thought. One can argue that a coalition government with the PAP in opposition may not necessarily be disastrous for Singapore, if the coalition comprises parties as competent and as honest as the PAP. So far, though, only the first and second scenarios predicted by Professor Chan have come true, with Chiam See Tong and Low Thia Khiang in Parliament, after four subsequent general elections since the 1984 polls. The third and fourth possible scenarios must remain a matter for speculation. The situation can be gauged from the results of the next general election.

The PAP, of course, is taking nothing for granted. The party constantly refreshes itself by bringing in new blood and grooming them into future leaders, as well as producing new programmes. The Young PAP (YPAP) youth wing, for example, plays an active role in this. The YPAP, which is 6,000-strong, wants more of its members to become MPs in the next general election, and is nurturing a generation of future activists to be involved in party work in the 87 constituencies. A Young PAP School has been opened to teach members the PAP's values, culture and history.

The PAP is now under a third-generation leadership with Lee Hsien Loong as Prime Minister. This is the second change in Premiership since independence. Can he maintain the strength and cohesiveness as well as the excellent track record of the PAP? Can he regain the party's monopoly in Parliament? Singaporeans may be brass-collars, but they are unlikely to continue supporting the party if at some stage it fails to deliver the goods.

Singapore needs the right leaders to serve the nation, and an electorate who are conscious of the vital necessity of voting such people in. This is the kind of responsibility which the Greek philosopher Plato advocated more than 2,000 years ago. He warned: "The penalty that good men pay for not being interested in politics is to be governed by men worse than themselves." For any political party which aspires to govern successfully, this Chinese proverb offers excellent advice: "If you are planning for one year, grow rice. If you are planning for 20 years, grow trees. If you are planning for centuries, grow men."

Up till now, the PAP is the only political party in Singapore which comes closest to observing this tenet.

It is the foundation that Lee Kuan Yew laid.

ACKNOWLEDGEMENTS

I thank the following for helping me, in one way or another, in the preparation of this book.

My wife, Teresa, for her unceasing encouragement.

John Chan Kok Choy, Ang Kwok Te, Michelle Oei Yu Min, Chua Chew Yong, Wong Meng Quang and Vivien Lee Looi Chng for their comments and inputs.

The National University of Singapore Library for allowing me access to its archives and whose staff showed the utmost courtesy and patience towards me.

The National Library whose staff were equally helpful in my search for supplementary information.

The Registrar of the Supreme Court for helping me trace the date of a court case that took place in 1963.

Last but not least, all those who wish me well.

ABOUT THE AUTHOR

Anthony Oei was a journalist with *The Straits Times* and *Radio & Television Singapura*, public relations manager of the Economic Development Board and a writer with several advertising agencies.

This is his fourth book, a revised edition of his previous work, *Days of Thunder: How Lee Kuan Yew Blazed the Freedom Trail* (2005). That was itself a revised edition of *What If There Had Been No Lee Kuan Yew?* (1992). Another of his earlier works is *Building A New Niche: The Story of Dr David B H Chew* (1991). The latter two books were published by Heinemann Asia.

A Catholic, Oei was born in the Indonesian capital of Jakarta but spent most of his childhood days in Bogor and Sukabumi. His mother tongue is Sundanese, an Indonesian dialect. He also knows Bahasa Indonesia besides English, but no Chinese. His family migrated to Singapore after World War II. So he lived under three different colonial rulers—the Dutch and the Japanese in Indonesia, and the British in Singapore. He was educated at St Anthony's Institute and St Joseph's Institution and became a Singapore citizen in 1957 with the passing of the Citizenship Bill that year.

His wife, Teresa, is a Singapore Peranakan whose maternal grandmother hailed from Semarang. A former convent school education officer, she knows Malay, Teochew and Hokkien, besides English. They have three daughters, all bilingual in English and Chinese and now living in their own homes, and four grand-daughters.